Object-Oriented Programming with C++

Object-Oriented Programming with C++

Second Edition

Poornachandra Sarang

ABCOM Information Systems Pvt. Ltd.
Mumbai

PHI Learning Private Limited

New Delhi-110001
2011

Rs. 250.00

OBJECT-ORIENTED PROGRAMMING WITH C++, 2nd ed.
Poornachandra Sarang

ISBN-978-81-203-3670-4

The export rights of this book are vested solely with the publisher.

Third Printing   ...   ...   **July, 2011**

Published by Asoke K. Ghosh, PHI Learning Private Limited, M-97, Connaught Circus, New Delhi-110001 and Printed by Sareen Printing Press, Delhi-110042.

Dedicated to our son
Sanket

Contents

Program Listing .... *xv*

Foreword .... *xix*

Preface .... *xxi*

Preface to the First Edition .... *xxiii*

Acknowledgements to the First Edition .... *xxv*

1   OBJECT-ORIENTED PROGRAMMING CONCEPTS 1–8

Software Evolution 2

Procedure-oriented Programming 2

     Drawbacks 3

Object-oriented Programming 4

     Features 4

     Benefits 6

Object-oriented Languages 7

Summary 7

Exercises 8

2   LANGUAGE CONSTRUCTS 9–47

Introduction 9

Hello World Program 10

     Analyzing the Program Code 10

C++ Program Structure 12
    Function Prototype 12
    Program Structure 12
    Comments 14
    Program Execution Sequence 14
Accepting User Input 15
Identifiers 16
Literals 16
    String and Character Constants 16
    Integer Constants 17
    Floating Point Constants 17
Keywords 18
Data Types 18
Operators in C++ 19
    Mathematical/Arithmetic Operators 19
    Increment and Decrement Operators 20
    Relational Operators 22
    Logical Operators 22
    Bitwise and Bitshift Operators 22
    Unary Operators 23
    Conditional or Ternary Operator (?:) 24
    Comma Operator (,) 24
    Cast Operator (()) 24
    The Size of Operator (sizeof()) 25
Program Statements 26
    Variable Declaration Statements 26
    Conditional Statements 26
    Loops 33
Summary *42*
Exercises *43*

3   ADVANCED CONSTRUCTS 48–89

Arrays 48
    Declaring Arrays 49
    Accessing and Modifying Array Values 49
    Initializing Arrays 50
Character String Arrays 54
    String Reversal 54
    String Word Count 56
    Concatenating Strings 57
    Palindromic Strings 59
Multidimensional Arrays 60
    Two-dimensional Arrays 60
    Initializing Two-dimensional Arrays 62

Matrix Addition Program 65
Matrix Multiplication Program 68
n-dimensional Arrays 70
Pointers 70
Declaring/Initializing Pointers 70
Assigning 71
Accessing Variables Using Pointers 72
Printing Pointer Value 75
Address of Pointer Variable 75
Pointer to Pointer 76
Structures 78
Accessing Structure Elements 80
Array of Structures 82
Structures Containing Other Structure Data Types 84
Summary *87*
Exercises *88*

4   CLASSES IN C++ 90–112

Introduction 91
Data Type—Class 91
Declaring and Using Classes 92
General Form of Class Declaration 92
Declaring Classes 93
Using Classes 94
Dynamic Objects 96
Creating Objects Using new 96
Deleting Dynamically Created Objects 97
Defining Member Functions 97
Methods Defined within Class Definition 98
Scope Resolution Operator 98
Inline Functions 99
Variable Scope—Public, Private 101
Static Data Members and Functions 105
Static Data Members 105
Static Member Functions 108
Summary *111*
Exercises *111*

5   MEMBER FUNCTIONS 113–130

Passing Parameters 113
Pass by Value 114
Pass by Reference 116
Constant Parameters 119

Default Parameters 120
    Default Parameter Order 121
Friend Functions 123
    Declaring a `Friend` Class 127
Summary 129
Exercises 130

6   OPERATOR OVERLOADING 131–149

Adding Meaning to Operators 131
Syntax for Operator Overloading 132
Overloading Arithmetic Operators 132
    Overloading Binary Operators 132
    Overloading Assignment Operators 137
Overloading Complex Operators 139
    Overloading Array Index Operator 140
    Overloading Function Call Operator 141
    Overloading `Typecast` Operator 144
What Cannot Be Overloaded? 148
Summary 148
Exercises 148

7   CONSTRUCTORS AND DESTRUCTORS 150–167

Defining Constructor 151
Multiple Constructors 153
Using Parameterized Constructors in Dynamic Objects 156
Constructors with Default Arguments 156
    Default Argument Ambiguities 158
    Ordering Default Parameter List 158
Default Constructor 159
Copy Constructor 160
Class Destructor 162
    Destructor Syntax 163
    Cleaning Up Resources 164
Summary 166
Exercises 166

8   INHERITANCE 168–197

What Is Inheritance? 168
Single Inheritance 169
Access Modifiers 174
    Protected Modifier 174
Multiple Level Inheritance 178
    Protected Access 179

Public/Non-public Derivations 183
    General Syntax of Class Inheritance 183
Types of Inheritance 183
    Public Inheritance 183
    Private Inheritance 184
    Protected Inheritance 187
Calling Sequence for Constructors and Destructors 189
    Parameter Passing to Superclass Constructors 193
Summary *195*
Exercises *196*

9   MULTIPLE INHERITANCE **198–223**

Multiple Inheritance—An Illustration 198
Constructor Calling Sequence 201
Destructor Calling Sequence 203
Parameter Passing to Base Class Constructors 205
Access Modifiers 207
Protected Inheritance 211
Virtual Classes 214
    Virtual Inheritance 218
Summary *221*
Exercises *222*

10   POLYMORPHISM **224–240**

The Meaning of Polymorphism 224
Types of Polymorphism 225
    Static Polymorphism 225
    Dynamic Polymorphism 230
    Using Pointers for Calling Overridden Methods 231
Virtual Functions 234
    Pure Virtual Functions 234
    Merits/Demerits of Dynamic Polymorphism 237
Abstract Classes 237
Summary *238*
Exercises *239*

11   HANDLING EXCEPTIONS **241–264**

Exceptional Conditions 241
The `try`/`catch`/`throw` Constructs 242
    Argument Types for `catch` Statement 243
    Multiple `catch` Blocks 245

Throwing Exceptions 248
Rethrowing Exceptions 251
User-defined Exception Classes 253
Deriving further from Exception Classes 255
Exception Processing Order 258
     Exception Class Hierarchy 259
Catching Uncaught Exceptions 259
Summary *263*
Exercises *263*

12 TEMPLATES **265–284**

Need for Templates 266
Types of Templates 266
     Function Templates 267
     Class Templates 274
User-defined Data Types as Parameters 278
Summary *283*
Exercises *284*

13 C++ I/O **285–316**

The C++ I/O Systems 285
Streams 286
     Pre-defined Streams 287
     Formatting Output 287
     The `ios` Class Formatting Flags 290
Manipulators 291
     The `endl` Manipulator 291
     The `hex/oct/dec/showbase` Manipulators 291
     The `uppercase` Manipulator 292
     Floating Point Number Manipulators 292
File I/O 293
     Opening Files 294
     Reading and Writing Files 294
     Character versus Binary Mode 302
     The `type/cat` Utility 303
     File `dump` Utility 304
     File `copy` Utility 306
Random Access Files 307
     The `seekp` Function 311
Summary *314*
Exercises *315*

14 STRINGS **317–327**

Creating String Objects 317
    User Input Strings 318
    Concatenating Strings 320
    Substring Replacement 321
    String Sorting 322
    Word Extraction 324
  Summary *326*
  Exercises *327*

APPENDIX A **329–336**

APPENDIX B **337–342**

INDEX **343–346**

Program Listing

Listing 2.1:   C++ program structure 12
Listing 2.2:   Accepting user input 15
Listing 2.3:   Use of arithmetic operators 19
Listing 2.4:   Use of increment, decrement operators 20
Listing 2.5:   Use of bitwise and bitshift operators 22
Listing 2.6:   Use of ternary operator 24
Listing 2.7:   Use of cast operator 25
Listing 2.8:   Use of `if` construct 26
Listing 2.9:   The `if` construct illustration program 27
Listing 2.10:   The `if-else` construct illustration program 28
Listing 2.11:   The `if-else-if` construct illustration program 29
Listing 2.12:   The switch construct illustration program 31
Listing 2.13:   The `while` construct illustration program 33
Listing 2.14:   The `do-while` construct illustration program 35
Listing 2.15:   The `break` construct illustration program 37
Listing 2.16:   The `for` construct illustration program.. 38
Listing 2.17:   The `continue` construct illustration program 40
Listing 2.18:   The `goto` construct illustration program 41

Listing 3.1:   Program to illustrate the use of Arrays 52
Listing 3.2:   Fibonnaci number generation program using arrays 54
Listing 3.3:   String reversal program 54

Listing 3.4:   Program to count the number of words in a string 56
Listing 3.5:   String concatenation program 57
Listing 3.6:   Determining palindromic strings 59
Listing 3.7:   Program to demonstrate use of two-dimensional arrays 63
Listing 3.8:   Matrix addition program 65
Listing 3.9:   Matrix multiplication program 68
Listing 3.10: Program to demonstrate use of pointers 73
Listing 3.11: Displaying pointer address 75
Listing 3.12: Using double pointers 77
Listing 3.13: Program to demonstrate use of structures 80
Listing 3.14: Array of structure element 83
Listing 3.15: Nested structures... 85

Listing 4.1:   Demonstration of class construct... 95
Listing 4.2:   Inline functions in classes 100
Listing 4.3:   Demonstration of private and public declarations in classes 101
Listing 4.4:   The static data members in classes 107
Listing 4.5:   The static methods in classes 110

Listing 5.1:   Passing method parameters by value 114
Listing 5.2:   Passing method parameters by reference 116
Listing 5.3:   Alternate syntax for passing by reference 118
Listing 5.4:   Program to illustrate use of default parameters 122
Listing 5.5:   Demonstration on the use of Friend function 125
Listing 5.6:   Demonstration on the use of Friend class 127

Listing 6.1:   Program to demonstrate overloading of addition operator 135
Listing 6.2:   Program to demonstrate overloading of assignment operators 138
Listing 6.3:   Program to demonstrate overloading of some advanced operators 142
Listing 6.4:   Program to demonstrate overloading of `typecast` operator 146

Listing 7.1:   Class constructors 151
Listing 7.2:   Multiple constructors in a class... 153
Listing 7.3:   Default argument constructors 156
Listing 7.4:   Copy constructor demonstration program 160
Listing 7.5:   Class destructors 163
Listing 7.6:   Freeing object resources.. 164

Listing 8.1:   Program to illustrate single inheritance 172
Listing 8.2:   Demonstration on the use of protected access modifier 176
Listing 8.3:   Further demonstration on protected access modifier.................................... 181
Listing 8.4:   Constructor and destructor calling sequence demonstration 191
Listing 8.5:   Passing parameters to superclass constructor 194

Listing 9.1:   Program to demonstrate multiple inheritance 200
Listing 9.2:   Constructor calling sequence in case of multiple inheritance 201

Listing 9.3:   Destructor calling sequence in case of multiple inheritance 203
Listing 9.4:   Parameter passing to superclass constructors 206
Listing 9.5:   The private, public inheritance 209
Listing 9.6:   Protected inheritance 212
Listing 9.7:   Program to illustrate diamond-shape problem in multiple inheritance 217
Listing 9.8:   Demonstration on the use of virtual keyword 220

Listing 10.1:   Program to demonstrate function overloading 228
Listing 10.2:   Calling overridden methods using pointers 232
Listing 10.3:   Using virtual functions 236

Listing 11.1:   Exception handling 243
Listing 11.2:   Defining multiple exception handlers 246
Listing 11.3:   Throwing exceptions 250
Listing 11.4:   Exception passing 251
Listing 11.5:   User defined exceptions 254
Listing 11.6:   Subclassing user-defined exceptions 257
Listing 11.7:   Uncaught exceptions 261

Listing 12.1:   Using templates 269
Listing 12.2:   Overriding default templates 270
Listing 12.3:   Multiple argument templates 273
Listing 12.4:   Class template 276
Listing 12.5:   Using user-defined data types in class template 280

Listing 13.1:   Formatting output to console 288
Listing 13.2:   Entering boolean data by specifying formatting flag 290
Listing 13.3:   Use of manipulators 292
Listing 13.4:   Reading, writing standard data types 295
Listing 13.5:   Reading, writing strings 297
Listing 13.6:   Reading, writing user-defined types 300
Listing 13.7:   Program to dump text file contents 303
Listing 13.8:   Program to dump binary file contents 305
Listing 13.9:   The file copy program 307
Listing 13.10:   File random access 309
Listing 13.11:   Formatting output 313

Listing 14.1:   Demonstration of string class 318
Listing 14.2:   Accepting strings from user 319
Listing 14.3:   String concatenation 320
Listing 14.4:   Replacing substrings in a given string 321
Listing 14.5:   String sorting 322
Listing 14.6:   Extracting words from a given string 324

Foreword

C is one of the languages most suitable for systems and application programming. Computing is constantly evolving and programmers have seen a series of changes and improvements since 1989 with the introduction of object-oriented programming languages. C++ has its own importance in the programming language scenario of object orientation. It is widely used in industry and is therefore a pragmatic choice of programming language for learning by the students. The most striking features of an object-oriented programming language are (i) Encapsulation, (ii) Inheritance, and (iii) Polymorphism.

Among many languages which support these important features of object-oriented programming languages, C++ is one of them. The author has presented the features of OOPL (Object Oriented Programming Language) through C++. The initial chapters of the book present the procedure-oriented programming language C. These chapters cover identifiers, literals, data types, control statements, arrays, strings, pointers and structures. These basic concepts of procedure-oriented programming language must be first learnt by any beginner. The author has presented these concepts in a simple manner with many illustrative examples. Several of the following chapters deal with numerous features of OOPL. But the power of OOPL is inheritance. Simple and multiple inheritance are explained in a lucid language in two separate chapters. The polymorphism, another important feature of OOPL, is covered with many examples in an exclusive chapter. The remainder of the book is devoted to file handling, both sequential and random, template and string processing.

The book is rich in pedagogic features which help students concentrate on mastering the skills of programming. It focuses on practical work of writing programs which is vital to becoming fluent and confident at programming. There are exercises for the students at the end of each chapter to enhance their ability to program. Most importantly, these exercises help students to check whether they have understood the text properly.

This book can be used to build a logical development of thoughts and prepare students to assimilate a strong base to convert algorithms into programs and this basis can be further used to understand the concepts in OOP. The book can be of immense help to the students of Computer Science and Engineering at the undergraduate level and for those pursuing MCA and other equivalent courses in universities. To understand the theoretical importance of OOPL and develop programming skills and to implement ideas in a practical environment, this book should serve the purpose of all those who are interested in learning OOPL.

I hope the readers will find this book useful. I wish them fun in doing object-oriented programming in C++.

Prof. Shriram B. Patil
Dean
Faculty of Science
Mumbai University

Preface

With the encouraging response to the first edition, and valuable suggestions received from the students, teachers and well-wishers, it was considered appropriate to bring out the second edition of this book. This new edition has been expanded up to about 100 solved programming examples. Each example includes a screen output to help the reader understand and grasp the program, more easily. Chapters 2 and 3 have been comprehensively revised, and also a new chapter on Strings has been added.

Finally, the second edition incorporates support for Visual C++ and Turbo C++, to help the reader run each given example in an environment of his or her choice.

The first edition of the book is already being used as a textbook in some reputed universities. It is hoped that the revised edition will also find its way in the course curriculum of more universities. Helpful comments and criticisms and suggestions for improvements to the book will be gratefully acknowledged. I would like to thank the staff at PHI Learning, especially Ms. Pushpita Ghosh (Managing Editor) and Mr. Darshan Kumar (Senior Editor), for their keen interest and efforts in bringing out this book.

Poornachandra Sarang

Preface to the First Edition

Today's market is flooded with books on C++ and object-oriented programming. So what justifies another book on the same topic? Most of the books that are available in the market are either too detailed or too condensed and also lack the practical approach that will equip the learner of a new language with the skills for applying the concepts learnt. The aim of this book is to impart both theoretical and practical knowledge of O-O programming in C++. This book is sized in between the extremes of being too concise for a substantial coverage and too voluminous for a thorough study in a reasonable time. Several code examples that vividly illustrate the theory and a variety of exercises have been incorporated in every chapter so that the reader gains practical knowledge of the subject.

The book starts with a chapter that provides an introduction to object-oriented programming. This chapter covers the main features of OOP. The second chapter introduces the reader to the first program in C++. The chapter discusses how to accept user input and covers various keywords and primitive data types of C++ and also the various types of operators, conditional statements and program loops. Chapter 3 explains advanced syntax starting with single and multi-dimensional arrays and provides an in-depth coverage of pointers and data structures. Up to this chapter, the language features covered overlap with those of C language. Readers familiar with C language may skim through these chapters just to refresh their knowledge of the C syntax.

Chapter 4 introduces the reader to the new data type 'Class' marking the beginning of object-oriented programming. This chapter covers class definitions and discusses the static and dynamic instantiation of classes. The reader is introduced to data members, functions and their scope. The public and private scope for the class members and the use of static data members are explained. Chapter 5 introduces the reader to the techniques for passing parameters to methods and discusses the definition and use of friend functions and friend classes. Chapter 6 is devoted to operator overloading and Chapter 7 to the concept of class constructors and destructors. Chapter 8 covers another important feature of OOP: inheritance. The chapter details multi-level inheritance and introduces the reader tó protected access modifier. Chapter 9 covers multiple inheritance and the use of virtual keyword. Polymorphism, another characteristic feature of OOP, is explained in Chapter 10. Here both static and dynamic polymorphism are dealt with in detail. Chapter 11 dwells on exception handling in C++ while Chapter 12 describes a newly introduced feature called template that was not included in the original language specifications. Chapter 13, which is the last chapter of the book, describes the Input/Output operations in C++.

This book should prove to be very useful to anybody who is interested in learning object-oriented programming using C++. As the first part of the book gives enough coverage of the common C language syntax, readers who do not possess knowledge of C language, which is the background for learning C++, will also find this book extremely helpful in learning C++. The book will be an ideal textbook for students of science and engineering who have to learn C++ as part of their course curriculum.

Poornachandra Sarang

Acknowledgements to the First Edition

I wish to acknowledge the help rendered by Mr. Chandan Parulkar and Mr. Kaustubh Prabhutendulkar in testing the programs and providing constructive feedback by going through the first draft of the book. I thank Mr. Vijay Jadhav for providing valuable assistance in formatting the manuscript several times that helped me organize the text flow so as to make it easily readable. I also appreciate the efforts and cooperation of the editorial and production teams of Prentice-Hall of India in bringing out this book. My special thanks to Mr. Srinivas Chaubey of Prentice-Hall of India, without whose consistent coaxing for a year to write this book, this book would not have become a reality.

Poornachandra Sarang

1

Object-Oriented Programming Concepts

In the software industry it is observed that technology changes every six months. The industry has seen many such changes in various software consistently throughout its existence over the last few decades. The major changes in both software and hardware technologies have occurred during the last three decades. With technology fast changing, application programmers always find it difficult to keep their application software up-to-date. More importantly, a radical change in technology causes software applications to be rewritten, resulting in a huge loss in investments. So how do the software engineers protect their investment in the code they develop? One of the major solutions to this problem is offered by *object-oriented programming*. In this chapter, the reader will be introduced to programming concepts and features of object-oriented (O-O) programming. During the course of discussion, we will understand the importance of object-oriented programming in protecting the investment made in the code development by allowing reuse of existing code in future applications.

We will learn the following in this chapter:

- Evolution of software over the last few decades.
- Procedure-oriented programming and its drawbacks.
- What is object-oriented programming and what its benefits are?
- Important features of object-oriented programming.
- Meanings of features such as *encapsulation*, *inheritance* and *polymorphism*.
- What are the available object-oriented languages and the importance of C++ as one of the major O-O languages?

1

SOFTWARE EVOLUTION

The computer software has steadily evolved over the years since its birth. The early 1960s and 1970s were the days of assembly language programming where a programmer was required to understand the hardware architecture of the machine for which he or she would be writing the application. In assembly language, the programmer would access the internal registers of the CPU, as also the memory directly and do all I/O operations on his own. This required in-depth knowledge of the entire system architecture and also made each application machine-specific. A program written for one machine would run only on a similar machine having the same architecture. In brief, the *applications were not portable*.

In the 1970s, we saw the introduction and use of high-level languages. These languages almost replaced assembly language in application development making the programmer's task much easier. High-level languages shield the programmer from the internal details of the machine and enable writing programs which with few modifications may be ported on another machine. The C language is a procedure-oriented language (and has its own merits and demerits). We will describe procedure-oriented programming in the next section.

The next phase of evolution in the software industry was the emergence of object-oriented programming, a programming technique that solved many problems inherent in traditional procedure-oriented programming. Many new languages were designed to support the concepts introduced by object-oriented programming. One of the languages that greatly succeeded in this area is C++. The C++ was designed at AT&T by Bjourne Stroustroup and is considered to be the most successful among all the object-oriented languages to date.

Over a period of time, new languages that support object-oriented concepts were developed. One such language that succeeded in competing with the well-established and popular C++ language is Java. Java was developed in 1995 by James Gosling of Sun Microsystems. Though, in recent days, Java has been widely accepted by the industry, the importance of C++ has not been affected. There are many C++ fans as of now and the trend would continue in the current decade and perhaps for a few more decades to go. C++ is so strong, well thought of and complete in most respects as it allows you to develop virtually any kind of application, right from a program that has a low-level access to machine architecture to one which could be a very high-level application program as the ones used by insurance agencies, airlines or space missions.

In this book, we will learn this most-widely used language of the world: C++.

Before we discuss object-oriented programming, we will first describe the traditional procedure-oriented programming, its features and drawbacks.

PROCEDURE-ORIENTED PROGRAMMING

C is a procedure-oriented language. In such languages, we group logically related functional code into individual functions. A function (also called a procedure in some languages) consists of a series of program statements. These program statements together achieve some logical function in an application program. For example, we may develop a calculator program that provides various operations such as addition, subtraction, multiplication and division on two real number operands. The implementation of each such operation may be done in an independent procedure such as `add` procedure, `subtract` procedure, and so forth. We will then write one more function, say, main, that calls these procedures on the need basis. Each procedure provides a certain logical operation for the application and contains a tightly related code to achieve the desired functionality. The structure of the calculator program that defines four different functions to implement the four arithmetic operations is shown in Figure 1.1.

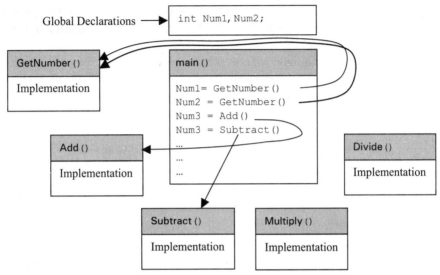

Figure 1.1   Calculator program for arithmetic operations.

In addition to the four functions used for arithmetic operations, the program also defines an additional function for accepting a number input from the user. The diagram also shows the pseudo code for main function. The program flow is controlled by the main function. The execution begins at the start of main function and ends with the last statement in the main function. During the execution of the main function, the program control is transferred to various functions as they are called by the main function.

It is possible for a function to call another function that, in turn, calls yet another function, and so on. Thus, the entire application may consist of several functions and the code becomes highly structured which eases its maintenance.

Drawbacks

If we carefully examine the pseudo code in Figure 1.1, you will notice that we have declared Num1 and Num2 variables globally. These variables are accessible to each of our arithmetic functions, viz. Add, Subtract, Multiply and Divide. Also, since these variables are declared globally, they are accessible to any program code within the application. This can result in inadvertent change in the data at times. The problem may be solved by declaring the variables within the main function and sending the variables as parameters to each of the functions during a call to it.

In general, the global declaration of data is considered the main drawback of function-oriented programming. The function that operates on the data does not hold the data to itself. Either such data is globally accessible or needs to be passed to another function as parameter. Ideally, the data on which the function operates should be tightly coupled to the function itself. This is where the idea of a new programming paradigm was born.

OBJECT-ORIENTED PROGRAMMING

We see several objects in our daily life, for example, birds, animals, plants, and many more. Each of them possesses some characteristics, which are unique to the object concerned. A bird can fly, an animal has four legs, and a plant cannot move (unless you help it move to another location). Every object in nature exhibits a unique behaviour. Every object has some data embedded in it and some functionality that operates on this data. So why should our programming style be different from what is exhibited in nature?

In object-oriented programming, we talk about objects, just the way nature defines various kinds of objects. Consider that we want to write a program for computing the monthly payroll for company employees. We can immediately think of employee as one of the objects in such a system. Each employee object will have a unique ID and some additional data such as basic salary, provident fund, leave travel allowance, etc. Naturally, we would not like this data to be globally accessible for every other person in the company. This is sensitive data and each employee's data should be protected from the eyes of other employees. Also, when we define the functionality such as computing the monthly salary of each employee, we consider that such functionality will be implemented in functions that operate on the data belonging to a particular employee under consideration.

Object-oriented programming provides both data hiding and data encapsulation. We will discuss these terms in detail in the next section. Currently, we will further our concept of objects. Every employee object in our payroll system will hold the data similar to every other employee object in the system and will also exhibit functionality that is exactly identical to the functionality exhibited by every other employee object in the system. Naturally, we will think of creating some template on which we will base our objects. In word processing, we create templates for various purposes; for example, there could be a template for resume writing. Every applicant uses the same template for submitting his/her resume to a prospective employer. In object-oriented programming, we create templates to define or to represent objects having common behaviour. Such templates are called *classes* in object-oriented programming. A class is really the heart of object-oriented programming, the base on which the entire system is built. The concept of classes is introduced in Chapter 4 and we will talk about classes in detail as we proceed through the book.

Let us now look at the important features of object-oriented programming.

Features

The three major features of object-oriented programming are:
  (a) Encapsulation
  (b) Inheritance
  (c) Polymorphism
We will now discuss each of these features in detail.

Encapsulation

As described in the previous section, it is a good practice to provide a tight coupling between the data and the methods (this is another word for function or a procedure, few languages such as Java prefer this word over others. All the three words will be used interchangeably throughout this book) that operate on this data. Such data should be hidden from the outside world; it means that it should be inaccessible to code outside the current context (to be more precise, the current object). This process of data hiding and combining data and methods in a single logical unit is called *encapsulation*. We say that the data and the methods that operate on this data are encapsulated in a single package called *class*. As already mentioned, we will introduce classes formally in Chapter 4.

A class consists of *data* and *methods*. These are called *members* of the class. The data members of the class are treated private to the members of the class; only the class methods have access to the data members. We can control the access to the data members. The data members may be made visible to the code outside the current class definition. We will talk more on this when we discuss classes in detail later in the book. It is sufficient to know at this stage, that we encapsulate the data and the related methods in a logical unit called *class*.

Inheritance

We already stated that a *class* contains the data and the methods that operate on this data. A class acts like a template on the basis of which different objects are created. Each such object possesses data which is unique to it; however, all the objects of the same class type possess the same characteristics. For example, when we create an *employee* class, each employee will contain the same data fields such as ID, basic salary, PF, LTA, etc. The values assigned to these fields will vary from employee to employee. Each *employee* object exhibits the same functionality defined by the methods of the *employee* class.

Over a period of time, we may wish to add more characteristics (functionality) to an existing class. We may do so by modifying the existing class definition and add the new function to its definition. This entails code modifications, debugging and testing. In the process of code modifications, we may introduce new bugs to the existing tested code. It is a good practice to create a new class that inherits the characteristics of an existing class.

We observe that children inherit some traits from their parents. We will find various families of classes in nature such as birds, animals, mammals, etc. Each family consists of several objects. All objects in a given family share some common functionality. The children in the family inherit from their parent objects. A child may also exhibit additional functionality than the one it has inherited from its parent.

In software engineering, when we develop software, we search for the presence of family of classes like what we observe in nature. For example, to represent different types of cars in a software application, we may design a parent class called *automobile*. The class *automobile* will define functionality that is common to all cars. We will further define classes based on this parent class (*automobile*). Such classes may be *car*, *truck*, etc. Each class will add some functionality to the functionality inherited from the *automobile* class. The added functionality will be unique to the defining class. It means that a *car* and *truck* will add some functionality to itself which is different than the functionality of the other classes in the same family of classes.

A *car* may be further classified under classes of *sportscar*, *sedan*, *limousine*, etc. We further define classes for this. A *sedan* will inherit from *car* class, which in turn inherits from *automobile* class. Thus, *sedan* will exhibit not only the functionality of the *car* class but also the functionality defined in the *automobile* class. The class hierarchy is depicted in Figure 1.2.

It is this inheritance that helps in preserving the investment in the existing code by allowing us to extend the functionality of existing classes. Inheritance is formally introduced in Chapter 8.

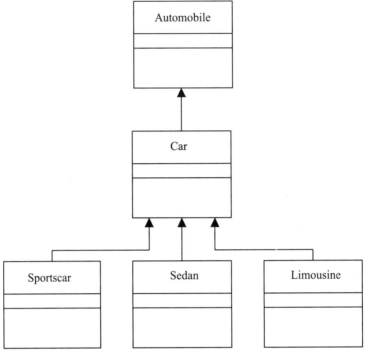

Figure 1.2 Class hierarchy.

Polymorphism

Classification of automobiles as described in the previous section, will generate different classes in class hierarchy for the car object. Each such car object will exhibit several common functionalities. For example, there could be an operation defined in each class such as *driving the vehicle* that is applicable to all the car objects. As this is a common functionality, we will define this in our parent class. The child class will also define a *drive* operation and may modify the inherited drive operation. Both operations may use the same name, viz. *drive*. For example, driving a truck would be different from driving a *sedan*. However, we may say "we drive the vehicle" with regard to both the vehicles. Thus, the functionality name remains the same, while the implementation varies across the objects. This feature is called *polymorphism* in object-oriented terminology. Polymorphism originates from the Greek word *polymorph*, meaning having different faces to the same object.

Polymorphism is an important feature of object-oriented languages and will be explained in detail in Chapter 9.

Benefits

We have examined the three main features of object-oriented programming. Object-oriented programming helps us in creating structured programs where the code developed once is easily re-usable. The programs can be extended easily with little effort allowing us to reuse the existing code (which is already tested), and thereby reducing the maintenance cost on the software.

OBJECT-ORIENTED LANGUAGES

With the invention of object-oriented programming, several languages were designed to support object-oriented concepts. Examples are ADA, C++, Java, C# (pronounced C-Sharp), just to name a few popular ones. Each of these languages defines its own grammar and syntax, and supports object-oriented features to a varied degree. For example, ADA though it supports object-orientation, does not support polymorphism. Most of these languages also support the earlier procedure-oriented coding style.

In this book, we will study C++ which is probably the most popular object-oriented language of the last decade and the current decade. C++, which is a superset of language C, supports the full syntax of procedure-oriented C language and additionally, the new features of object-oriented programming.

SUMMARY

This chapter began with a brief history of software evolution. The software techniques evolved over the last couple of decades, starting from the low-level machine language programming to the current techniques of object-oriented programming. In the 1980s, developers mainly used procedure-oriented languages. In the 1990s, object-oriented programming techniques caught wave.

The procedure-oriented programming style requires developers to write several procedures in their application. Each procedure consists of a logically related operation. Though the entire program is structured, it lacks an important feature, i.e. there is no tight coupling between the data and the procedures that operate on such data.

Object-oriented programming couples the data and the procedures that operate on such data under a logical unit called *class*. This feature of object-oriented programming is called *encapsulation*. Encapsulation helps in data hiding. The data defined in each class is considered private to the class and is not usually accessible to the code outside the class definition.

Object-oriented programming also introduced another major feature that helps in re-using the existing classes in our new applications. This is called *inheritance*. The inheritance feature allows us to inherit from existing classes and add more functionality to the newly defined classes. We create a family (an hierarchy) of classes starting with a single base class.

The classes belonging to the same family exhibit the same characteristics. To implement the behaviour, we write *methods*. A method may use the same name across several classes belonging to a single family; however, the actual implementation may vary across such classes. This feature of object-oriented programming is called *polymorphism*. Not all O-O (object-oriented) languages support polymorphism.

These days, several programming languages support object-oriented features. C++ is probably the most successful and the most widely used language in the world. C++ which has its roots in C language, supports both procedure-oriented coding style like C language and also supports full object-oriented programming style.

In the next two chapters, we will study the C++ language syntax that is common to the C language syntax. In Chapter 4, we will introduce object-oriented programming. The ensuing chapters will deal with the various features of object-oriented programming in detail.

EXERCISES

1. What is procedure-oriented programming? What are its drawbacks?
2. What is object-oriented programming? Describe its benefits in brief.
3. Describe the important features of object-oriented programming.
4. Explain each of the following features of the C++ language in about ten lines.
   (a) Encapsulation
   (b) Inheritance
   (c) Polymorphism

2

Language Constructs

In Chapter 1, we studied the general concepts of object-oriented programming. Object-oriented programming has three main features, namely encapsulation, inheritance and polymorphism. C++ is one of the popular languages that supports object orientation. We will begin our study of the C++ language in this chapter.

We will learn the following in this chapter:

- How to write a simple C++ program that accepts input from the user and outputs to the console
- C++ language constructs such as identifiers, literals, keywords, etc
- Writing conditional program statements
- Creating loops in a program

INTRODUCTION

C++ language is derived from C and supports the full C syntax. In this chapter, we will discuss the C language syntax and various constructs. C++ supports the traditional procedure-oriented programming as well as object-oriented programming. In this chapter, we will use the procedure-oriented programming style for the development of programs. In later chapters (Chapter 4 onwards), we will introduce object-oriented programming in C++ and then subsequently develop programs using the object-oriented programming techniques.

HELLO WORLD PROGRAM

It is rather traditional to begin learning a new language by writing a "Hello World" program. We will follow this tradition and write the first C++ program that prints a "Hello World" message on the user console.

The following program prints a message "Hello World" on the console.

```
#include "stdafx.h"
#include <iostream>
using namespace std;

int main()
{
    cout << "Hello World\n";
    return 0;
}
```

Before we analyze the program code, let us try to compile and run the program. The Microsoft Visual Studio has been used for the development of all the program examples in this book. The Visual Studio IDE (Integrated Development Editor) provides an excellent editor for entering and editing the source program. It also comes with an integrated debugger that helps in fixing the errors in your program code easily.

> **Note:** Appendix A describes how to compile and run the programs presented in this book in Microsoft Visual Studio, and Appendix B describes the Turbo ++ environment for compiling and running the programs.

If we decide to use any other IDE or the compiler, we need to follow the instructions provided therein for compiling, linking and running the program code.

When we run the program using the Visual Studio environment, we will see the output as shown in Figure 2.1.

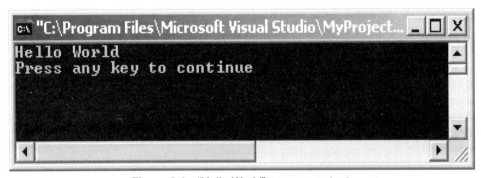

Figure 2.1   "Hello World" program output.

Analyzing the Program Code

Let us analyze the above program line by line. The first statement contains a directive to the preprocessor. Like C, the preprocessor processes the source file before it is compiled. The #include directive to the preprocessor tells it to include the contents of the file `stdafx.h` during compilation.

```
#include "stdafx.h"
```

The `stdafx.h` file is generated by Visual Studio IDE during the project creation. This is specific to Microsoft IDE and if you use some other environment such as Borland C++ or Unix C++ compiler, this file will not be required. As mentioned earlier, you will need to follow the compilation instructions provided with the specific compiler that you are using.

The header files contain function prototypes, constant and global declarations. Like C programming, you will be including several header files in your program code. The header files are included with the help of `#include` directive and this should be done at the beginning of the program source code.

The next statement includes the `iostream` file in your program code.

```
#include <iostream>
```

This includes the prototypes for the input/output classes that allow you to do I/O operations through your program code. In our program, we output a message to the console and thus the inclusion of this file becomes mandatory.

The next line declares that the program will use the standard namespace called `std`.

```
using namespace std;
```

All names other than operator `delete` and operator `new` in the C++ library headers are defined in the `std` namespace, or in a namespace nested within the `std` namespace. You refer to the name `cin`, for example, as `std::cin`.

The next line declares a function called `main`.

```
int main()
```

Every C++ executable program must contain a `main` function. The program execution begins at this function. The `main` function in the current program does not take any arguments as indicated by a pair of parentheses in front of its name. The function returns an `int` type. Every function must have a body. The function body starts with an open brace (`{`) and ends with a closing brace (`}`).

Within the body of the function, we write one or more program statements to accomplish our task. The current `main` program contains a program statement:

```
cout << "Hello World\n";
```

Each program statement in C++ is terminated with a semicolon. The above statement sends a stream of characters defined in the string constant `"Hello World\n"` to the output stream declared by `cout`. The output stream `cout` is attached to the screen (the streams are discussed in Chapter 13). Thus, when you execute this program, the string `"Hello World"` is printed on the screen. Note that `'\n'` is an escape sequence similar to the one in C programming language that defines a new line character. This sequence advances the cursor to the beginning of the next line.

After outputting to the screen, the program terminates by executing a `return` statement. The parameter `0` on the `return` statement indicates its successful completion to the operating system.

The first program has demonstrated the structure of a C++ program, and also how to compile, link and execute a program. It is strongly recommended to run the above code before proceeding with the rest of the book to ensure that our development environment is correctly set for the various code examples discussed in the book.

We will now discuss the general structure of a C++ program.

C++ PROGRAM STRUCTURE

Every C++ program consists of several function definitions. In the procedural-style of coding, there is a main function in a program that in turn calls other functions defined elsewhere in the program. Each function may call other functions. The program execution begins with the first statement in the `main` function. Each function is defined using a pre-defined style, also called a function prototype.

Function Prototype

The general prototype for a function is shown below:

```
return-type functionName (argument-list)
{
    // program statements;
}
```

The `functionName` specifies the name of the function. Each function has a name that is unique within the entire application. A function may take zero or more arguments specified in the `argument-list`. For each argument, we specify the variable name for the argument and the data type for the argument. A function may return a value to the caller. The data type for the return value is specified by `return-type`. If a function does not return any value to the caller, the `return-type` should be `void`. The word `void` is a reserved word that indicates to the compiler that the function does not return any value. The word `void` may be used in `argument-list` indicating that the function does not take any arguments. The function name declaration is followed by the function body enclosed in braces. Within the braces, we write the function implementation code. This may consist of several program statements. Each program statement is terminated with a semicolon.

Program Structure

The general structure of a C++ program is given in Listing 2.1.

Listing 2.1:   C++ program structure

```
// header files
// function prototypes
void function1();
void function2();
void function3();

// main function definition where program execution begins
int main (int argc, char *argv[])
```

```
{
    function1();
    function2();
    ...
    return 0;
}

// other function definitions
void function1 ()
{
    function3();
    ...
}

void function2()
{
    // some implementation
}
void function3()
{
    // some implementation
}
```

At the top of the listing, we list the header files that contain the prototypes of functions required within our program. The header files contain the various class definitions, function declarations, global and constant declarations. This is followed by the prototypes of the various functions used in our application code. Like C programming, we need to provide a forward reference to all the functions called in our program code.

We may specify the prototype of a function by listing all the arguments that the function takes along with its return type or simply listing the function return type. The compiler just needs to know the return type of each called function.

Following the function prototypes, we write the various function definitions. The first function, which we have written in the above program structure, is the main function. It is not necessary to include main at the top of the program listing. The function definitions may be put in any order in our source program. The only restriction is that the function prototype should be known to the compiler before the function is called.

The main function, in Listing 2.1, returns an integer value to the operating system indicating the success or error in the execution. Like in C programs, the main function may receive two parameters. The first parameter indicates the number of command line arguments passed to the executable at the time of invocation and the second parameter is a pointer to an array of character arrays. Each character array element contains a command line argument following the name of the executable. We list these parameters as follows while invoking the program:

```
exeName argument1, argument2, ...
```

We will discuss the use of command line arguments in Chapter 12.

The main function calls other functions in our application in whatever sequence as decided by the application developer. At the end, it returns a value zero (0) to the operating system indicating the application's success. It may return a 1 or some other value to the operating system to indicate an error. The value of the return code depends on our operating system.

After the `main` function definition, we define several functions such as `function1`, `function2`, etc. Each function may or may not return a value to the caller. In the above case, none of our functions return a value to the caller and thus they are declared as returning `void` (indicating that no value is returned to the caller). Each function may or may not receive the parameters. In Listing 2.1, none of our functions receive a parameter. This may be explicitly stated by using the `void` keyword in the parameter list as shown below:

```
void function1 (void)
```

Now, as we have seen the general program structure, let us study how to add comments in our program listing.

Comments

We may add several comments to our program to document the code. C++ allows us to add two types of comments:

- Single-line comments
- Multi-line comments

A single-line comment starts with the character sequence (`"//"`), i.e. the two forward slashes and ends with a newline character.

A multi-line comment starts with the character sequence (`"/*"`), i.e. a forward slash followed by an asterisk and ends with the character sequence (`"*/"`), i.e. an asterisk followed by a forward slash. As the name suggests, a multi-line comment may span multiple lines, that is, it may contain multiple newline characters.

Program Execution Sequence

The general syntax illustrated above also clarifies the program execution sequence. The execution begins at the first line of `main` function. The `main` function calls `function1`. The execution control is now transferred to the body of `function1`. Within the body of `function1`, we call `function3`. The control is now transferred to `function3`. After successfully executing the code in `function3`, the control is transferred back to `function1`; to the statement that follows the call to `function3`. The program now executes the rest of the code defined in `function1`. After completing the code in `function1`, the control returns to the `main` function. The `main` function now calls `function2`. The program control now transfers to the beginning of `function2`. After execution of the code defined in `function2`, the control is transferred once again to the `main` function. The `main` function now executes the rest of the code defined in it calling the various functions as encountered on its way towards the end. At the end, the `main` function executes the `return` statement and transfers the control back to the operating system with the appropriate return code.

As we can see from the above description, the program is procedure-oriented and the calling sequence of various procedures (functions) is determined by the code in the `main` function.

Having seen the general structure of a C++ program, we will now learn to input data in our program code using keyboard.

ACCEPTING USER INPUT

The program Listing 2.2 accepts the user name and prints a greeting message on the console.

Listing 2.2:   Accepting user input

```
#include "stdafx.h"
#include <iostream>
using namespace std;

int main()
{
    char    name[15];
    cout << "Enter your name: ";

    cin >> name;

    cout << "Hello " << name << "!\n";

    return 0;
}
```

The first three program statements include the necessary header files and the namespace as in the case of the previous program.

The main function declares a character array for storing the input received from the user.

```
    char name[15];
```

The following statement prints a message on the console requesting the user to input his/her name.

```
    cout << "Enter your name\n";
```

The next statement waits for the user input:

```
    cin >> name;
```

The cin represents an input stream that accepts input from the keyboard. The execution of this program statement waits for the user input. The statement terminates after the user presses the ENTER key on the keyboard. The string value input by the user is stored in the variable name. Note that the name variable is our char (character) array. Arrays are discussed later in Chapter 3. Thus, the user input string will be stored in our character array referred by the variable name.

The following statement prints the greeting message along with the user input name on the console.

```
    cout << "Hello" << name;
```

After printing the greeting message, the program terminates by returning a value of zero to the operating system.

When we run the program, we will see the following output in our command window.

```
    Enter your name: Raj
    Hello Raj!
```

Before going into further program examples, we will study the identifiers in C++.

IDENTIFIERS

We use identifiers to create variables, functions, classes, etc. For example, in the program code discussed in the previous section, `name` is an identifier.

Here are rules for defining identifiers in C++:

- Identifiers in C++ can contain characters, digits and underscore.
- An identifier cannot start with a digit.
- Unlike C, in C++ we can create identifiers of any length.
- C++ reserves a few words as keywords. We cannot declare an identifier having the same name as a keyword.

Examples of valid identifiers are:

```
intVariable            // an identifier containing the combination of upper
                       // and lower case characters

_myVariable            // an identifier can begin with an underscore

_YourVariable          // an identifier can contain underscore;
                       // note the second underscore in the example
B4U                    // an identifier can contain a digit

DoubleVariable, doubleVariable
                       // the two identifiers shown here are distinct,
                       // as C++ is case sensitive.
```

Examples of invalid identifiers are:

```
4uonly                 // identifier cannot start with a digit
main                   // main is a reserved keyword in C++
```

LITERALS

Literals are often referred to as *constants*. A constant is an entity with a fixed value. Literals can be divided into characters, string, integer numbers and floating point numbers.

String and Character Constants

To define a character constant we specify a character within single quotes (`' '`), for example `'T'` or `'f'`. To define a string constant we specify one or more characters in double quotes (`" "`). For example, `"True"`, `"false"` and `"Hello"` are valid string constants.

Escape sequences

C++ defines several escape codes using character constants. These codes represent operations such as newline (`\n`) and tab (`\t`). A list of escape codes is given below with their descriptions:

Escape code	Description
\n	Newline consists of Carriage Return (CR) and Line Feed (LF)
\r	Carriage return
\t	Tab
\v	Vertical tabulation
\b	Backspace
\f	Page feed
\a	Alert (beep)
\ ' '	Single quote (')
\ "	Double quote (")
\ ?	Question mark (?)
\ \	Inverted slash (\ )

We use the escape sequences in our string constants to output the desired action. For example, the use of ' \t ' escape sequence in our output string results in setting the cursor to the next tab position before outputting the next character. Similarly, the use of ' \n ' advances the cursor to the beginning of the next line (CR/LF—Carriage Return/Line Feed).

Integer Constants

Integer constants represent the integers that cannot be modified by the program code. For example, the use of numbers such as 100, −345, 34 in our program code is treated as declaring integer constants. The following program statement declares two integer constants: 36 and 64.

```
int sum = 36 + 64;
```

The arithmetic expression, 36 + 64 is called *constant expression* as the value of this expression remains constant throughout the program body.

The default numbering system used for representing integers is decimal. Thus, in the above program statement, both 36 and 64 are treated as decimal numbers.

We may define integer constants in octal or hexadecimal notation. The octal constants are represented by prefixing the number with a 0 (zero character). Thus, 0232 and 0125 are examples of valid octal constants.

Note that both the above numbers are octal numbers. The constant declaration 018 is invalid because 8 is not a valid digit in the octal number system.

To represent hexadecimal constants in the program, we prefix the number with 0x or 0X. Thus, 0xABC, 0X200, and 0x100 are all hexadecimal constants.

Floating Point Constants

The numbers specified with decimals or exponents are called floating point numbers or floating point constants. Examples of floating point constants are:

```
3.14159
40.0
6.02e23 // expressed in scientific notation.
```

KEYWORDS

As mentioned earlier, C++ language defines several keywords. You cannot create variables with the name same as the keyword. A list of keywords in C++ is given below:

asm	auto	break	case
catch	char	class	const
continue	default	delete	do
double	else	enum	extern
float	for	friend	goto
if	inline	int	long
new	operator	private	protected
public	register	return	short
signed	sizeof	static	struct
switch	template	this	throw
try	typedef	union	unsigned
virtual	void	volatile	wchar_t
while			

The following variable declarations would generate compilation error as they use reserved keywords.

```
int virtual;    // virtual is a reserved keyword.
char private;   // private is a reserved keyword.
```

DATA TYPES

C++ defines several data types. The list of data types along with the size and range of values for each data type, is given in the Table 2.1:

Table 2.1 List of data types

Data type	Bytes	Description	Range signed	Range unsigned
char	1	Represents ASCII character set.	−128 to 127	0 to 255
short int (or short)	2	Is larger than or equal to the size of char type	−32768 to 32767	0 to 65535
int	2	The range for this data type is system dependent.	−32,768 to 32,768	0 to 65,535
bool	1	Can have one of the two values (True or False).		True or False

(Contd.)

Table 2.1 List of data types (*Contd.*)

Data type	Bytes	Description	Range signed	Range unsigned
long int	4	Is larger than or equal to the size of int data type.	2147483648 to −2147483647	0 to 4294967295
float	4	Is the smallest floating type.		3.4E–38 to 3.4E+38
double	8	Has size larger than or equal to the type float, but smaller than or equal to the long double type.		1.7E–308 to 1.7E+308
long double	8	Is a floating type.		3.4E–4932 to 1.1E+4932
wchar_t	2	Represents a wide character or multi-byte character type.		0 to 65,535
enum	16	Enum is a user-defined type consisting of a set of named constants called enumerators.		−32,768 to 32,767

OPERATORS IN C++

C++ defines several types of operators: arithmetic, increment and decrement, relational, logical, and so on. These operators are listed further in their logical groups:

Mathematical/Arithmetic Operators

Mathematical or arithmetic operators are used in performing mathematical operations. The various arithmetic operators are listed here:

```
+   Addition

-   Subtraction

/   Division

*   Multiplication

%   Modulo
```

Listing 2.3 illustrates the use of arithmetic operators:

Listing 2.3: Use of arithmetic operators

```
#include "stdafx.h"
#include <iostream>
using namespace std;

int main()
{
    int a=20;
    int b=12;
    int c=25;
```

```
    int d=20;
    int result;

    result = a+b;
    cout << "Addition: " << a << " + " << b << " = " << result << '\n' ;
    result = a-b;
    cout << "Subtraction: " << a << " - " << b << " = " << result << '\n' ;
    result = a*b;
    cout << "Multiplication: " << a << " * " << b << " = " << result<< '\n' ;
    result = a/b;
    cout << "Division: " << a << " / " << b << " = " << result << '\n' ;
    result = a%b;
    cout << "Modulo Division: " << a << " % " << b << " = "   << result<< '\n' ;
    return 0;
}
```

When we run this program, we will see the following output:

```
Addition: 20 + 12 = 32
Subtraction: 20 - 12 = 8
Multiplication: 20 * 12 = 240
Division: 20 / 12 = 1
Modulo Division: 20 % 12 = 8
```

Increment and Decrement Operators

These operators help in incrementing or decrementing the value of a variable by 1.

++   Auto-increment

--   Auto-decrement

The program in Listing 2.4 illustrates the use of increment and decrement operators with both post- and pre-operations.

Listing 2.4: Use of increment, decrement operators

```
#include "stdafx.h"
#include <iostream>
using namespace std;

int main()
{
    int a =10, b = 10;
    cout << "Using increment operator:\n";
    cout << "Pre-increment: a = ++b\n";
    cout << "Initial value of b: " << b << endl ;

    a = ++b ;
    cout << "Value of a now:" << a << endl;
    cout << "Value of b now:" << b << endl ;
```

```
    a =10; b = 10;
    cout << "Post-increment: a = b++\n";
    cout << "Initial value of b: " << b << endl ;

    a = b++;
    cout << "Value of a now:" << a << endl;
    cout << "Value of b now:" << b << endl ;

    a =10; b = 10;
    cout << "\nUsing decrement operator:\n";
    cout << "Pre-decrement: a = - -b\n";
    cout << "Initial value of b: " << b << endl ;

    a = --b ;
    cout << "Value of a now:" << a << endl;
    cout << "Value of b now:" << b << endl ;

    a =10; b = 10;
    cout << "Post-decrement: a = b--\n";
    cout << "Initial value of b: " << b << endl ;

    a = b--;
    cout << "Value of a now:" << a << endl;
    cout << "Value of b now:" << b << endl ;
    return 0;
}
```

When we run the program, we will see the following output:

```
Using increment operator:
Pre-increment: a = ++b
Initial value of b: 10
Value of a now:11
Value of b now:11
Post-increment: a = b++
Initial value of b: 10
Value of a now:10
Value of b now:11

Using decrement operator:
Pre-decrement: a = --b
Initial value of b: 10
Value of a now:9
Value of b now:9
Post-decrement: a = b--
Initial value of b: 10
Value of a now:10
Value of b now:9
```

Carefully study the effect of post- and pre-operations by examining the program output. Also, note the use of endl keyword. The endl keyword when output to cout stream results in a CR/LF (carriage return /line feed) on the console. Thus, it is equivalent to printing ' \n ' on the terminal.

Relational Operators

Relational operators are used to compare two values. The comparison value is either true or false.

<	Less than
>	Greater than
<=	Less than or equal to
>=	Greater than or equal to
==	Equivalent
!=	Not equivalent

Logical Operators

Logical operators are used to combine and test two or more expressions.

&&	AND
||	OR
!	NOT

Bitwise and Bitshift Operators

Bitwise operators are used to test, set or shift actual bits in a byte or a word which corresponds to the char and int data types. These operators cannot perform operations on data types such as float, double, bool, etc.

&	AND
|	OR
^	XOR
~	Negation
<<	Left-shift
>>	Right-shift

Program in Listing 2.5 illustrates the use of bitwise and bitshift operators.

Listing 2.5:   Use of bitwise and bitshift operators

```cpp
#include "stdafX.h"
#include <iostream>
using namespace std;

int main()
{
    int a = OXFFFFFFFF;
    int b = 0X80000000;
    int result;
```

```
    result = a & b;
    printf("Logical AND: %X & %X = %X\n", a, b, result);

    a = 0X0000FFFF;
    b = 0XFFFF0000;
    result = a | b;
    printf("Logical OR: %08X | %X = %X\n", a, b, result);

    a = 0X8000FFFF;
    b = 0XFFFF8000;
    result = a ^ b;
    printf("Logical XOR: %08X ^ %X = %X\n", a, b, result);

    a = 0X7FFF0000;
    result = ~a;
    printf("Logical NOT: ~%08X = %08X\n", a, result);

    a = 0xFFFF0000;
    result = a<<4;
    printf("Left Shift: %08X << 4 = %08X\n", a, result);

    a = 0xFFFF0000;
    result = a>>4;
    printf("Right Shift: %08X >> 4 = %08X\n", a, result);

    return 0;
}
```

When we run the program, we will see the following output:

```
Logical AND: FFFFFFFF & 80000000 = 80000000
Logical OR: 0000FFFF | FFFF0000 = FFFFFFFF
Logical XOR: 8000FFFF ^ FFFF8000 = 7FFF7FFF
Logical NOT: ~7FFF0000 = 8000FFFF
Left Shift: FFFF0000 << 4 = FFF00000
Right Shift: FFFF0000 >> 4 = FFFFF000
```

Unary Operators

Unary operators are operators that work only on one operand.

−	Unary minus
+	Unary plus
&	address-of; provides the internal location of the variable.
*	de-reference; returns the value of the variable located at the address that follows it.
new	Memory allocation operator
delete	Memory release operator

The following operators that we studied earlier are also the unary operators:

++   Increment

−−   Decrement

Conditional or Ternary Operator (?:)

The syntax for the conditional or ternary operator is as follows:

```
Syntax: Condition ? expression1 : expression2
```

```
e.g.: s = (x<0) ? -1 : x*x
```

The program tests the `condition`, if it is true the value of `expression1` is assigned to the LHS otherwise the value of `expression2` is assigned.

Program in Listing 2.6 illustrates the use of the ternary operator.

Listing 2.6:   Use of ternary operator

```
#include "stdafx.h"
#include <iostream>
using namespace std;

int main()
{
    int a = 10;
    int b = 20;
    int max;

    max = (a > b) ? a : b;
    cout << "max of " << a << " and " << b << ": " << max << endl;
    b = 5;
    max = (a > b) ? a : b;
    cout << "max of " << a << " and " << b << ": " << max << endl;
    return 0;
}
```

When we run the program, we will see the following output:

```
max of 10 and 20: 20
max of 10 and 5: 10
```

Comma Operator (,)

The `comma` operator is used to separate an expression.

```
e.g.: A = (B++, C++, D++, E++);
```

Cast Operator (())

The `cast` operator helps to force an expression to be of a specific type by using () `cast` operator.

e.g.: A = (int) B;

Program in Listing 2.7 illustrates the use of cast operator.

Listing 2.7:   Use of cast operator

```
#include "stdafX.h"
#include <iostream>
using namespace std;

int main()
{
    float f = 12.25f;
    int i = -200;
    char c = 'A';

    i = (int) f;
    cout <<"float type " << f <<
        " assigned to an int produces " << i << endl;

    f = i;
    cout <<"int type " << i <<
        " assigned to a float produces "<< f << endl;

    i = c;
    cout <<"char type " << c <<
        " assigned to an int produces " << i << endl;

    i = 66;
    c = (char)i;
    cout <<"int type " << i <<
        " assigned to a char produces " << c << endl;
}
```

When we run the program, we will see the following output:

```
float type 12.25 assigned to an int produces 12
int type 12 assigned to a float produces 12
char type A assigned to an int produces 65
int type 66 assigned to a char produces B
```

The size of Operator (sizeof())

The sizeof operator is a unary operator which is used to retrieve the length in bytes.

e.g.: cout << sizeof(double);

PROGRAM STATEMENTS

Every C++ program contains several program statements. A program statement may be a simple variable declaration statement; an output statement or it may be a complex statement like the one for evaluating conditions, defining program loops, etc. We will study the different types of program statements in this section.

Variable Declaration Statements

We create variables for the use of our program code according to the following general format:

```
datatype variable1, variable2;
```

The datatype specifies the data type of the declared variables. We may declare multiple variables of the same data type in a single program statement. A variable may be initialized at the time of its declaration. The following is a declaration for two integer variables that are initialized at the time of declaration.

```
int IntegerVar1 = 10, IntegerVar2 = 200;
```

Conditional Statements

The conditional statements allow us to control the program flow based on the result of evaluation of some condition.

The *if* statement

The if statement is a conditional statement used for controlling the program flow based on the result of evaluation of a specified condition.

Syntax:

```
if (condition)
    statement1;
statement2;
```

If the condition given in parentheses is satisfied, statement1 is executed. If the condition is not satisfied, program does not execute statement1 and proceeds with statement2.

The program in Listing 2.8 illustrates the use of if statement.

Listing 2.8: Use of if construct

```
#include "stdafX.h"
#include <iostream>
using namespace std;

int main()
{
    char c;

    cin >> c;
```

```
    if (c=='q' || c=='Q')
        cout << "Quitting gracefully ...\n";
    return 0;
}
```

If the user inputs the character 'q' or 'Q', the program prints the message "Quitting gracefully ..." on the console and then terminates. If the user enters any other character, the program terminates without printing any message on the terminal.

When we run the program and enter q or Q on the keyboard, we will see the following output on the console.

```
Q
Quitting gracefully ...
```

We now consider one more example on the use of if statement. The Listing 2.9 uses multiple if statements:

Listing 2.9:   The if construct illustration program

```
// IF.cpp

#include "stdafx.h"
#include <iostream>

using namespace std;

int main()
{
    int num1, num2;
    cout << "Enter number 1: ";
    cin >> num1;
    cout << "Enter number 2: ";
    cin >> num2;
    if(num1 > num2)
        cout << "number 1 is greater" << endl;
    if(num2 > num1)
        cout << "number 2 is greater" << endl;
    if(num1 == num2)
        cout << "Both numbers are equal" << endl;
    return 0;
}
```

In this program, we ask the user to enter two numbers. The program compares if the first number is greater than the second one and if so prints an appropriate message to the user. Then the program tests again to see if the first number is less than the second one and finally conducts one more test to see if both numbers are equal. Depending on the result of the if condition checking, the program prints an appropriate message to the user.

A typical output for one of the conditions is shown below:

```
Enter number 1: 200567
Enter number 2: 342782
number 2 is greater
```

Notice that the above program does all the three condition checks even if the first condition is satisfied. It is obvious that if the first condition is satisfied there is no need to carry out the remaining two checks as they would be definitely false. This problem is resolved with the help of `if-else` construct described next.

The *if-else* statement

The `if-else` construct is a conditional statement that executes a specified statement if the result of evaluation of the specified condition returns true, else it evaluates another statement given in the `else` clause.

Syntax:

```
if (condition)
    statement1;
else
    statement2;
```

If the `condition` given in parentheses is satisfied, `statement1` is executed and `statement2` is skipped. If the condition is not satisfied, `statement1` is skipped and `statement2` is executed.

The program in Listing 2.10 illustrates the use of `if-else` construct.

Listing 2.10: **The if-else construct illustration program**

```cpp
// IF ELSE.cpp

#include "stdafx.h"
#include <iostream>

using namespace std;

int main()
{
    int num;
    cout << "Enter number: ";
    cin >> num;
    if(num >= 0)
        cout << "Number is positive" << endl;
    else
        cout << "Number is negative" << endl;
    return 0;
}
```

In this program, we ask the user to input a number and then test whether it is positive or negative. The program prints the appropriate message on the console depending on the result of the test condition. Note that the program executes either the body of `if` or `else` condition, unlike the previous program which does the multiple checking. Thus, the use of this `if-else` construct would result in a more efficient code compared to the use of multiple `if` blocks.

A typical output for a positive input number is shown below:

```
Enter number: 256734
Number is positive
```

The if-elseif-else statement

This is yet another construct for conditional statements.

Syntax:
```
if (condition1)
    statement1;
elseif (condition2)
    statement2;
else
    statement3;
```

If the `condition1` given in parentheses is satisfied, `statement1` is executed and `statement2` and `statement3` are skipped. If the `condition1` returns `false`, `statement1` is skipped and `condition2` is tested. If `condition2` is satisfied, `statement2` is executed and `statement3` is skipped. If both the conditions `condition1` and `condition2` return `false`, `statement3` is executed.

We may put any number of `elseif` clauses between `if` and `else` clause as in:

```
if (condition1)
    statement1;
elseif (condition2)
    statement2;
elseif (condition3)
    statement3;
elseif (condition4)
    statement4;
...
else
    statement5;
```

If any of the conditions `condition1`, `condition2`, etc. is satisfied the corresponding statement is executed and the program execution continues with the next statement following the `if-elseif-else` block. If none of the conditions are satisfied then only `statement5` is executed.

Listing 2.11 illustrates the use of `if-elseif-else` construct.

Listing 2.11:   The if-else-if construct illustration program

```
// IF ELSE IF.cpp

#include "stdafx.h"
#include <iostream>
```

```
using namespace std;

int main()
{
    int num;
    cout << "Enter a number 1: ";
    cin >> num;
    if(num > 0)
        cout << "Number is greater than zero" << endl;
    else if(num < 0)
        cout << "Number is lesser than zero" << endl;
    else
        cout << "Number equal to zero" << endl;
    return 0;
}
```

In this program, we test the user input number for a positive or negative value. If both these conditions are not satisfied then the number is obviously zero. Note that the use of this construct avoids multiple condition checking resulting in an efficient code.

The program output for a typical positive input number is shown below:

```
Enter a number 1: 5645
Number is greater than zero
```

We may embed multiple `elseif` statements between `if` and `else` clauses. The program execution bubbles through all such conditions until the condition is satisfied, or else finally it will execute the `else` clause. This too can result in inefficient coding as the execution requires multiple conditions to be evaluated. This problem is overcome with the introduction of `switch` statement discussed next.

The *switch* statement

The multiple `elseif` statements as shown in the above syntax cause performance degradation, as the program may have to evaluate several conditions before a given condition is satisfied. In such situations, the use of `switch` statement is advisable.

Syntax:
```
switch (expression)
{
    case 'value1':
        statement1;
        ...
        break;
    case 'value2':
        statement2;
        ...
        break;
```

```
        case 'value3' :
            statement3;
            ...
            break;
        ...
        default:
            statementN;
            break;
    }
```

The program evaluates the expression specified inside the parentheses of the switch construct. The value of the expression is then compared with the value specified in each case statement. If the value matches, the body of the corresponding case is executed. Thus, if the expression evaluates to a value that equals value1 in the above code, the program executes statement1 followed by the remaining statements until a break statement is encountered.

Each case can contain one or more program statements. A case is normally terminated with a break statement. When a break statement is encountered, the program comes out of the switch construct and continues execution following the switch construct. Sometimes, you may not terminate a case with a break statement on purpose. In such a case the program execution falls through the body of the next case until it encounters a break statement somewhere. If the value of the expression does not match any of the case values, the default case is executed. Note that the last case statement need not have a break statement at the end as the program control automatically falls through the statement following the switch construct.

The use of switch construct results in a more efficient code compared to multiple if-elseif constructs since it eliminates the need to evaluate several conditions as in the case of multiple elseif statements.

We will now develop a program example that illustrates the use of switch construct.

The program code shown in Listing 2.12 requests the user to enter the day of the week, and prints its value in words as Monday, Tuesday, etc.

Listing 2.12:   The switch construct illustration program

```cpp
// SwitchCase.cpp
// Switch ..case example

#include "stdafx.h"
#include <iostream>
using namespace std;

void main()
{
    int day;

    cout << "Enter the day of the Week: ";
    cin>> day;
```

```
switch(day)
{
case 1:
    cout << "The day is Monday"<<endl;
    break;
case 2:
    cout << "The day is Tuesday"<<endl;
    break;
case 3:
    cout << "The day is Wednesday"<<endl;
    break;
case 4:
    cout << "The day is Thursday"<<endl;
    break;
case 5:
    cout << "The day is Friday"<<endl;
    break;
case 6:
    cout << "The day is Saturday"<<endl;
    break;
case 7:
    cout << "The day is Sunday"<<endl;
    break;
default:
    cout << "You have entered incorrect day"<<endl;
}
}
```

The `main` function prints a message on the console requesting the user to enter the day of the week.

```
cout << "Enter the day of the Week: " << endl;
```

The `endl` in the above code serves the same purpose as the escape sequence `'\n'` seen earlier.

The user input is accepted using the following program line:

```
cin >> day;
```

As seen earlier, `cin` represents an input stream that is used for accepting user input from the keyboard. The user input value is stored in a variable listed on the right-hand side. In this case, the user input number is stored in the integer variable `day`.

The `switch` statement now compares this `day` value with the various `case` values.

```
switch(day)
```

If a matching `case` is found, the corresponding `case` body is executed and an appropriate message specifying the name for the day of week is printed on the user console. If the `switch` value does not match any of the `case` values, the `default` case is executed giving an appropriate message to the user.

The program output is shown below. The output illustrates two examples; in the first example a matching `case` value is found. In the next example, the expression value does not match any of the `case` values and thus the default `case` is executed.

```
Enter the day of the Week: 1
The day is Monday

Enter the day of the Week: 8
You have entered incorrect day
```

Loops

C++ provides `while`, `do-while` and `for` constructs for creating program loops.

The `while` statement

Syntax:

```
while (condition)
    statement;
```

The program evaluates the `condition` given in the `while` construct. If the `condition` returns true, the `statement` is executed. If the condition returns false, the `statement` is skipped and the statement following the `while` construct is executed. The `statement` shown above may consist of a compound statement. We create a compound statement by enclosing the desired statements in braces as illustrated below:

```
while (condition)
{
    statement;
    ...
}
```

The program in Listing 2.13 computes the square of a number input by the user. The program sets up a `while` loop to accept user input values until the user decides to quit.

Listing 2.13: The `while` construct illustration program

```
//program to demonstrate while loop
#include "stdafx.h"
#include <iostream>
using namespace std;

void main()
{
  char reply = 'y';
  int num;
  while(reply == 'y' || reply == 'Y')
  {
     cout<< "Enter a number: ";
     cin>>num;
```

```
    cout<< "The square of "<< num <<"is"<< num*num <<endl;
    cout<< "Do you want to continue (y/n)?";
    cin>>reply;
  }
}
```

The `main` function declares a `char` type variable and initializes it to value `'y'`. It also declares an integer variable called `num` to store the user input number.

The `while` condition tests the value of `reply` variable.

```
    while(reply == 'y' || reply == 'Y')
```

If the `reply` variables holds either lower case or upper case `'y'` value, we enter the `while` body. Note that the || symbol is a conditional logical OR between the two expressions.

If the condition evaluates to true, we prompt the user to input a number and copy the user input value into the variable `num`.

```
    cout<< "Enter a number :";
```

```
    cin>>num;
```

The program computes the square of the given number and prints the result on the console.

```
    cout<< "The square of "<< num <<" is "<< num*num <<endl;
```

We now ask the user whether he or she wants to continue.

```
    cout<< "Do you want to continue (y/n)?";
```

We copy the user response to reply variable.

```
    cin>>reply;
```

The `while` body ends with the above statement. The program now goes to the top of the while body to test the while `condition` once again.

If the user has input a character other than `'y'` or `'Y'`, the condition returns false and the program comes out of the `while` block. If the user input evaluates the condition to true, the program enters the `while` block one more time requesting the user to input a new number, computes its square and prints it on the console.

A typical program output is shown below:

```
Enter a number: 5
The square of 5 is 25
Do you want to continue (y/n)? Y
Enter a number: 10
The square of 10 is 100
Do you want to continue (y/n)? y
Enter a number: 20
The square of 20 is 400
Do you want to continue (y/n)? n
```

Thus, `while` loops may be used for repeating a block of code until the condition specified (in the `while` block) is satisfied. For the condition to get satisfied, the body of the `while` block must provide appropriate program statements; no statement external to `while` block can satisfy the condition once the program enters the `while` block.

We will now study another construct: `do-while`.

The do-while statement

In the `while` construct, if the `condition` returns false on first evaluation, the body of `while` statement never executes. In some situations, we may like to execute `while` body at least once, even if the `condition` returns `false` on the first evaluation itself. In the above program example, had we initialized the value of `result` variable to anything other than `'y'` or `'Y'`, the program would never prompt the user for the number input. We have to ensure that the `while` body is executed at least once by checking the condition after executing the body. To achieve this, we need to use the `do-while` construct. The syntax of `do-while` construct is shown below:

```
do
    statement1;
while (condition);
```

The `condition` is tested after executing the `statement1`. If the `condition` evaluates to `false`, the program continues with the next statement following `do-while` construct. The `statement1` is guaranteed execution at least once. If the `condition` returns `true`, the program iterates through the loop one more time. At the end of the loop, the `condition` is tested once again. The `statement1` is executed multiple times until the `condition` returns `false`.

The program code in Listing 2.14 is a modified version of the square computation program discussed in the previous section. The program illustrates the use of `do-while` construct that ensures that the `while` body is executed at least once.

Listing 2.14:   The do-while construct illustration program

```
//program to demonstrate do while loop

#include "stdafx.h"
#include <iostream>
using namespace std;

void main()
{
    char reply;
    int num;
    do
    {
        cout<< "Enter a number: ";
        cin>>num;
        cout<< "The square of "<<num <<" is " <<num * num<<endl;
        cout<< "Do you want to continue (y/n)?";
        cin>>reply;
    }  while(reply != 'n');
}
```

The implementation code inside the `do-while` body is identical to the one discussed in the `while` construct above. During each iteration of the loop, the user is asked whether he or she wants to continue. The user breaks out of the loop by entering `'n'` on the terminal. Note that in the earlier program code, we checked for a value of `'y'` for the user input. In this case, we check for `'n'`.

A typical output when we run the above program is shown below.

```
Enter a number: 36
The square of 36 is 1296
Do you want to continue (y/n)?y
Enter a number: 25
The square of 25 is 625
Do you want to continue (y/n)?y
Enter a number: 125
The square of 125 is 15625
Do you want to continue (y/n)?n
```

In the above example, if the user does not know the appropriate character for quitting the loop, the application would never terminate. In such a case, we can enforce the maximum number of iterations for a program loop, so that even if the user does not quit the loop voluntarily, the loop will be terminated after a predetermined number of iterations. This is achieved by using the `break` construct in a loop as discussed next.

Infinite loops

We may set up an infinite loop using the `while` or `do-while` statement by ensuring that the condition is never satisfied. A simple technique of creating an infinite loop by using the `while` statement is shown further:

```
while (true)
{
    ...
}
```

In the above statement, the value of the condition is always true and cannot be made false anytime. Thus, the body of the `while` statement will execute infinite number of times.

Breaking infinite loops

It is possible to break such infinite loops by the use of a `break` statement in the body of the `while` statement.

```
while (true)
{
    ...;
    if (condition)
        break;
    ...;
}
```

Somewhere in the body of the `while` statement, we test for some condition using an `if` statement. If this condition returns `true`, we execute the `break` statement. The `break` statement breaks the `while` loop and continues with the statement following the `while` statement. The infinite loops and conditional breaking of such loops is illustrated with a program example.

The program in Listing 2.15 allows the user to compute the square of a given number for a maximum of three times. The user may quit earlier than this by inputting 'n' at the user input request.

Listing 2.15: The break construct illustration program

```
//program to demonstrate break statement in loops

#include "stdafx.h"
#include <iostream>
using namespace std;

void main()
{
    char reply;
    int count;
    int num;

    count = 1;
    do
    {
        cout<< "Enter a number: ";
        cin>>num;
        cout<< "The square of "<<num <<" is "<<num * num<<endl;
        count ++;
        if (count > 3)
            break;
        cout<< "Do you want to continue (y/n)?";
        cin>>reply;
    }   while(reply!='n');
}
```

We use the do-while loop that is identical to the example discussed in the previous section. To terminate the loop after a predetermined count, we set up a variable called count to keep track of the number of iterations. At each iteration, the program increments count and tests its value for 3. If the count reaches a value greater than 3, the loop is terminated. The user may quit the loop earlier by inputting 'n' after the first or the second iteration.

The program output for the case when the program terminates on its own after three iterations is shown below:

```
Enter a number: 25
The square of 25 is 625
Do you want to continue (y/n)?y
Enter a number: 36
The square of 36 is 1296
Do you want to continue (y/n)?y
Enter a number: 45
The square of 45 is 2025
```

The *for* loop

The use of while and do-while constructs require setting up a loop variable, incrementing the variable and testing its value against a desired loop count during each iteration. A for loop provides an alternate and a more elegant syntax for setting up such loops.

Syntax:

```
for (initialization; condition; expression)
    statement;
```

The for construct contains three elements, initialization, condition and expression.

The initialization is done at the beginning of the for loop before the condition is evaluated. The initialization may contain multiple program statements. In this section, you typically initialize the variables required within the for body.

After the initializations are done, the condition is evaluated. If the condition returns false, the body of the for statement is skipped and the program execution continues with the statement following the for construct. If the condition returns true, the body of the for construct is executed.

After the execution of the body, the last portion of for construct, that is, the expression is evaluated. This may be used for incrementing/decrementing the loop count used to control the number of iterations of for loop. The expression may contain more than one program statement. After the expression is evaluated, the condition is tested once again. If the condition returns false, for loop is terminated and the program execution continues with the statement following the for construct. The body of for will be executed multiple times until the condition evaluates to false.

The program in Listing 2.16 illustrates the use of the for construct.

Listing 2.16:   The *for* construct illustration program

```
//program to demonstrate for loop

#include "stdafx.h"
#include <iostream>
using namespace std;

void main()
{
    cout<<"The squares of first 10 Natural Numbers are "<<endl;
    cout << "Number \t Square" << endl;
    for(int i=1;i<=10;i++)
    {
        cout<<i<<'\t'<<i * i<<endl;
    }
}
```

The program computes the squares of the first 10 natural numbers and prints the result on the user console. Note the declaration of the loop count variable i in the initialization portion of for construct. The condition part of for construct tests the value of loop count i against 10. The loop terminates as soon as the count reaches the value of 10. The expression portion of for construct increments the loop count at the end of each iteration.

When we run the program we will see the following output on the console:

```
The squares of first 10 natural numbers are
        Number              Square
           1                   1
           2                   4
           3                   9
           4                   16
           5                   25
           6                   36
           7                   49
           8                   64
           9                   81
          10                  100
```

Infinite loops using for construct

It is easy to set up an infinite loop using a for construct. If we do not specify a condition in the conditional block of the for statement, an infinite loop would be created. The following syntax for the for statement construct illustrates this:

```
for (initialization;; expression)
```

Note the use of two semicolons. These are mandatory in the for construct. Similarly, we may omit statements in the expression and initialization parts of for statement. Omitting the expression portion may result in an infinite loop if we do not modify the loop count within the body of for loop. Typically, we will find the following for construct used for setting up an infinite loop:

```
for (;;)
```

Note that in this case, the initialization, the condition and the expression portions, all are omitted. They do not contain any program statements.

The continue statement

So far we have studied how to set up a loop that executes a given block of code until some desired condition is satisfied. We also saw the use of break statement that enables us to come out of a loop when a desired condition is satisfied in the body of the loop. Sometimes, we may like to continue with another iteration of the loop by skipping the rest of the code in the loop, whenever a certain condition that is tested within the loop is satisfied. For this, C++ language provides the continue statement.

The `continue` statement skips the remaining program statements in the loop and jumps to the beginning of the loop for the next iteration. We will write a program to print the square root of a number input by the user. If the user inputs a negative number, we ignore the number and jump to the beginning of the loop requesting the user to input another number. If the user inputs a positive number, we will print its square root.

The program code in Listing 2.17 that computes the square of a given positive number.

Listing 2.17: The `continue` construct illustration program

```
//program to demonstrate continue statement in loops

#include "stdafx.h"
#include <iostream>
using namespace std;

void main()
{
    char reply;
    int num;

    for (int i=0;i<3;i++)
    {
        cout<< "Enter a number: ";
        cin>>num;
        if (num < 0)
            continue;
        cout<< "The square of "<<num <<" is :" <<num * num<<endl;
    }
}
```

Note the use of `if` condition within the loop body.

```
        if (num < 0)
            continue;
```

If the condition is satisfied, we execute the `continue` statement to jump to the beginning of the loop requesting the user to input another number.

The program output is shown below for three different input values.

```
Enter a number: 5
The square of 5 is :25
Enter a number: -2
Enter a number: 10
The square of 10 is :100
```

Note: The `continue` statement can only be used inside `for`, `while` and `do-while` loops.

The goto statement

The goto statement is a type of unconditional branching. The goto statement allows you to transfer program control from the current line of execution to any other desired program line marked with a label. This is illustrated in the following code snippet:

```
/*Line 10:*/ sum = num1 + num2;
/*Line 11:*/ goto PRINTRESULT;
/*.
  .
  .*/
/*Line 15:*/ PRINTRESULT:
/*.  : */ cout << "Result"<< sum;
```

The program code executes line 10 to evaluate the sum of two numbers. On line 11 the program executes a goto statement. The goto statement contains a label called PRINTRESULT. This label is declared at line 15. Note that for declaring labels at any line of code in the program, we suffix the label with a colon (':'). The execution of goto statement at line 11 causes the program to jump to line 15 containing the desired label. The program execution now continues from line 15 onwards.

The goto statement is used for transferring control to another location in the program. This location may be a forward or a backward location with respect to the current line of execution.

Syntax:

The general syntax of a goto statement is as follows:

```
goto <label>;
```

The label specifies the destination for the goto statement. The destination point must have a valid identifier followed by a colon (:).

```
<label>:
```

The program code in Listing 2.18 illustrates the use of goto statement:

Listing 2.18:   The goto construct illustration program

```
// Program to illustrate use of goto statement

#include "stdafx.h"
#include <iostream>
using namespace std;

void main ()
{
    int sum=0, i=0;
    int num;

    while (true)
    {
        cout<< "Enter a number: ";
        cin>>num;
```

```
        if (num == -1)
            goto END;
        cout << "you entered number " << num << endl;
    }
END:
    cout << "You entered -1, Quitting ..." << endl;
}
```

The program sets up an infinite loop for accepting an input from the user. The program loop simply prints the number input by the user. If the user inputs –1, the program quits. This is achieved by using a goto statement in an if statement.

```
        if (num == -1)

            goto END;
```

If the condition is satisfied, the program executes the goto statement that transfers the program control to a statement marked with END label.

```
        END:
            cout << "You entered -1, Quitting ..." << endl;
```

Note the declaration of the label. The label name is suffixed with a colon. The execution of goto statement transfers the program control to the cout statement following the END label.

Note: The use of goto statement is generally considered a bad programming practice.

A typical output is shown below:

```
Enter a number: -5
you entered number -5
Enter a number: 2
you entered number 2
Enter a number: -1
You entered -1, Quitting ...
```

SUMMARY

In this chapter, we started learning the C++ language. We started out with a simple "Hello World" program that prints a greeting message on the user console. The general program structure was discussed. Every executable C++ program contains a main function. The program execution begins with the first line of main function. The implementation code in the main function calls other functions in the program and decides the sequence in which these functions are called.

We use cout class defined in the class libraries to write to the console. We use cin class to accept input from the user. We learned how to accept keyboard input from the user using cin class and how to output on the console using cout class.

The chapter discussed the basic constructs of C++ language. We learned how to create valid identifiers in C++ and studied the list of reserved keywords that cannot be used as identifiers in a program code. We talked about literals and integer constants in different numbering systems.

The chapter discussed the various data types and their sizes. This was followed by a discussion on the program structure and statements. A C++ program consists of several functions. Each function may contain multiple program statements. The types of program statements consist of simple variable declaration statements, conditional statements, loops, and so on.

We discussed various conditional statements such as if, if-else, if-elseif-else and switch. The switch is preferred over multiple if-elseif statements as it helps in most cases in reducing the program execution time.

This was followed by a discussion on setting up the program loop. We use while, do-while constructs for creating program loops. The do-while construct guarantees execution of the while body at least once.

We saw the use of for construct for creating the program loops. The for construct contains three parts—initialization, condition and expression.

In the context of loops, we talked about infinite loops where the loop body is executed infinite number of times. We discussed the use of break construct for breaking the infinite loops. We also talked about continue construct that allows us to jump back to the beginning of the loop by skipping the rest of the code in the loop. We also talked about goto statement that allows us to transfer the program control to any predetermined location. The use of goto statement is generally discouraged.

This chapter covered the basic constructs of C++ language. Most of the concepts are common with C programming language. In the next chapter, we will study some advanced constructs such as creating arrays, declaring and using pointers, and so on.

EXERCISES

1. Give the output of the following program:

```cpp
#include "stdafx.h"
#include <iostream>
using namespace std;

void main()
{
    int num = 20;
    num = num + 10;
    cout<< num<< endl;
    num -= 2;
    cout<< num<<endl;
    num*=2;
    cout<<num<<endl;
    num /= 2;
    cout<<num<<endl;
    num %=2;
    cout<<num<<endl;
}
```

2. Give the output of the following program:

```
#include "stdafx.h"
#include <iostream>
using namespace std;

void main()
{
    int num = 20;
    cout<< num<< endl;
    cout<< --num<<endl;
    cout<< num++<<endl;
    cout<<++num<<endl;
    cout<<num--<<endl;
}
```

3. Write a program to calculate the square of a number entered by the user.

4. Write a program to calculate the factorial of a number entered by the user.

5. Write a program to calculate the cubes of the numbers from 1 to 10.

6. Write a program to display the multiplication table of a number entered by the user.

7. Write an infinite `for` loop that breaks when the count reaches 200.

8. Write a `for` loop without a body that counts from 0 to 1000.

9. Write a program to accept an integer from a user and display all the prime numbers up to the user input number.

10. Write a program to display a Fibonacci series of numbers.

11. Write a program to accept a year from the user and check if it is a leap year. (*Hint:* A year that is divisible by 4 and not a century except every 400th century is considered a leap year.)

12. Write a C++ program to add three integers using functions. Also, find the weighted average using a function.

13. Which of the following statements are valid?
    (a) `Integer` num = 100;
    (b) `int` num = 100;
    (c) `int` num(10);
    (d) `int` num = {10};

14. Identify all the correct syntax that moves the cursor to next line:
    (a) `cout` << \n;
    (b) `cout` << \endl;
    (c) `cout` << "\n";
    (d) `printout` <<endl;

15. Which of the following statements are valid in case of an `if-else` statement?
    (a) If the `condition` given in parentheses is satisfied, `statement1` is executed and `statement2` is skipped. If the condition is not satisfied, `statement1` is skipped and `statement2` is executed.

(b) If the condition given in parentheses is satisfied, `statement1` is executed and then `statement2` is executed. If the condition is not satisfied, `statement1` is skipped and `statement2` is executed.

16. Which of the following statements are valid in case of `switch` statement?

(a) `switch` syntax cause performance degradation, as the program may have to evaluate several conditions before executing the appropriate program statement.

(b) The use of `switch` construct results in more efficient code as compared to multiple `if-elseif` constructs.

(c) Termination of a `case` in switch statement using a `break` statement is mandatory.

(d) The `default` case must appear at the end of all the cases.

(e) The `default` case must be terminated with a `break` statement.

17. Which of the following statements are valid in case of the `while` statement?

(a) The `while` loop is executed at least once.

(b) In `while` construct, if the `condition` returns `false` on first evaluation, the body of `while` statement never executes.

(c) The `while` loop is executed only when the `condition` is `true`.

(d) In `while` loop `condition` is tested after its body is executed.

18. Which of the following statements are valid in case of the `do-while` statement?

(a) In `do-while` loop `condition` is tested before its body is executed.

(b) If the `condition` evaluates to `false`, the program continues with the next statement following `do-while` construct.

(c) The loop body is executed only when the condition is `true`.

(d) The body of a `do-while` loop is executed at least once.

19. Which of the following statements are valid in case of `for` loop statement?

(a) The `for` construct contains three elements, initialization, condition and expression.

(b) During execution of the `for` loop the `condition` is checked first and then initialization is done.

(c) If the condition returns `false`, the body of the `for` statement is skipped and the program execution continues with the statement following the `for` construct.

(d) The body of the `for` will be executed multiple times until the condition evaluates to `false`.

20. Identify the correct syntax of a `for` loop.

(a)
```
int i=0;
for(i< 100;i++)
{
}
```
(b)
```
for(int i=0; i< 100;i++)
{
}
```

(c)
```
int i=0;
for(i=0, i< 100,i++)
{
}
```

(d)
```
for(int i=100; if(i > 100);)
{
    i++;
}
```

21. Which of the following statements are valid in case of the `continue` statement?

    (a) The `continue` statement is used to skip the rest of the instructions in the current loop.
    (b) The `continue` statement is used to jump to the next iteration of the loop.
    (c) Is used to move from one line in the program to another without any condition specified with it.
    (d) The `continue` statement can only be used inside `for`, `while` and `do  while` loops.

22. Identify the correct statement relating to the `goto` statement.

    (a) The `goto` statement is not recommended because its execution ignores any type of loops or nesting limitations.
    (b) The destination point must have a valid identifier followed by a semicolon (;).
    (c) Is used to move from one line in the program to another with any condition specified with it.
    (d) The destination point must have a valid identifier followed by a colon (:).

23. Give the output of the following program:
```
#include <iostream.h>
void main()
{
    int a = 25, b= 5, c = 10, d = 7;

    cout << a%b << endl;
    cout << a%c/b << endl;
    cout << a/b << endl;
    cout << a%b-c << endl;
    cout << c%b << endl;
    cout << a/d*d + a%b << endl;
}
```

24. Write a program to calculate the 200th triangular number using a `for` loop. (Triangular number *n* equals summation *n*.)

25. Write a program to find the Greatest Common Divisor of two non-negative integer values.

26. Write a program to reverse the digits of a number.

27. Write a program to determine if a number is even or odd.

28. Write a program to determine if a number is positive or negative.

29. Write a program to accept a single character from the user and check if the entered character is an alphabet, number or a special character.

30. State whether the following statements are true or false.

    (a) C++ provides the keyword `static` to declare variables whose values cannot be changed during runtime.

    (b) `switch` control statement supports `float` type in its expression.

    (c) C++ does not allow equating two variables of different types.

    (d) If we want to fall through the case of a `switch` statement, we use the `break` keyword at the end of the case.

3

Advanced Constructs

In Chapter 2, we studied the basic C++ syntax. In this chapter, we will study more about the C++ syntax.

We will learn the following in this chapter:

- Declaring arrays
- Accessing/modifying array elements
- Runtime and compile time initialization of arrays
- Multidimensional arrays
- Declaring pointers
- Initializing pointer variables and using them to access the variables
- Complex declarations such as pointer to a pointer
- Creating structures
- Accessing structure elements using a dot operator and/or a pointer variable
- Aggregate structures.

ARRAYS

When we want to create several variables of the same data type, we use arrays. An *array* is essentially a collection of elements of the same data type. These elements are accessed individually using unique index values. Thus, an array of integers will contain several elements each of `int` type and an array of float will contain several elements each of `float` type. As array elements are accessed using a single variable name, we do not need to create several unique variable names in our program code to store and access many variables having the same data type. We will begin with basic array operations as applied to single-dimensional arrays.

Declaring Arrays

The general syntax for declaring an array is as follows:

```
datatype ArrayName[array_size];
```

The `datatype` specifies the type of element that the array is going to store. The `array_size` specifies the number of elements that array will hold. The `ArrayName` is the name of the variable by which different elements of the array are accessed.

Example:

```
int numbers[5];
```

The above statement declares an array of integers holding 5 integer values. The elements of the array will be accessed using the variable name `numbers`.

To declare an array of `float` having 10 elements, you will use the following declaration:

```
float floatNumbers [10];
```

The name of the array is `floatNumbers` and each element of the array holds a floating-point number.

Accessing and Modifying Array Values

We use an index to access the elements of an array. Each element of the array has a unique index value. An element of an array is accessed by using the array name followed by its index in the array in square brackets. The general syntax of accessing an array element is as follows:

```
ArrayName[index_value];
```

For example, consider the declaration of an array of integers as follows:

```
int numbers[10];
```

There will be totally 10 elements in the `numbers` array declared above. The index in the array starts with a value of zero. Thus, the first element of the array is accessed using the following syntax:

```
numbers[0]
```

The subsequent elements will be accessed using syntax `numbers[1]`, `numbers[2]`, ..., and so on. The last element is accessed using syntax `numbers[9]`. Note that using an index value of 10 will be illegal as `numbers[10]` will try to access the 11th element that is out of bounds for the given array.

The array elements are always stored in a block of contiguous memory. Figure 3.1 shows the memory allocation for an integer array consisting of 5 elements declared using the following statement:

```
int numbers[5];
```

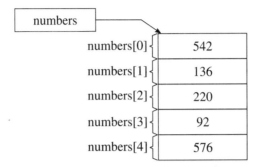

Figure 3.1 Scheme of memory allocation for an array.

To modify the element value, we use the same syntax as above and place it on the left-hand side of an assignment statement. The general syntax for modifying array elements is as follows:

```
ArrayName[index_value] = data ; //new data value
```

Example:

```
numbers[2] = 300;
```

The above statement assigns a value of 300 to an array element at an index value of 2, the array being addressed by name `numbers`. This will modify the third element in the array.

Initializing Arrays

The declaration of an array does not result in the initialization of its elements. When you declare an array, the space for storing array elements is allocated. The contents of these memory locations remain un-initialized and will thus contain any random value they hold at the time of allocation.

After an array is declared, the individual elements of the array must be initialized to the desired values. There are two techniques for initializing the array elements. Elements of array may be initialized at runtime or at compile time.

Runtime initialization

An array element may be initialized at run time using its index value as discussed in the previous section. Consider the following declaration for an array of integers:

```
int numbers[10];
```

The above declaration results in creating a contiguous block of memory for storing 10 integers. Assuming that an `int` data type occupies 4 bytes of memory, the declaration made above will result in allocating 40 bytes of contiguous memory. After declaration, each array element will be in un-initialized state. Thus, each element will hold some random value. Each element may now be initialized to a desired value by using a block of code as illustrated below:

```
numbers[0] = 10;
numbers[1] = 5;
numbers[2] = 145;
...
numbers[9] = 24;
```

If we decide to initialize all the elements of the array to the same value, we may use one of the loop constructs discussed in Chapter 2. For example, the following for loop will initialize all the elements of the preceding array to zero.

```
for (int i=0; i < 10; i++)
    numbers[i] = 0;
```

Compile time initialization

Elements of the array may be initialized at the same time as it is declared. The following statement declares an array of integers containing 5 elements and also initializes those elements to the values specified in curly braces:

```
int numbers[5] = {10, 20, 30, 40, 50};
```

The array size is five. The values of elements are specified in the curly braces. The memory representation of the above declaration is shown in Figure 3.2.

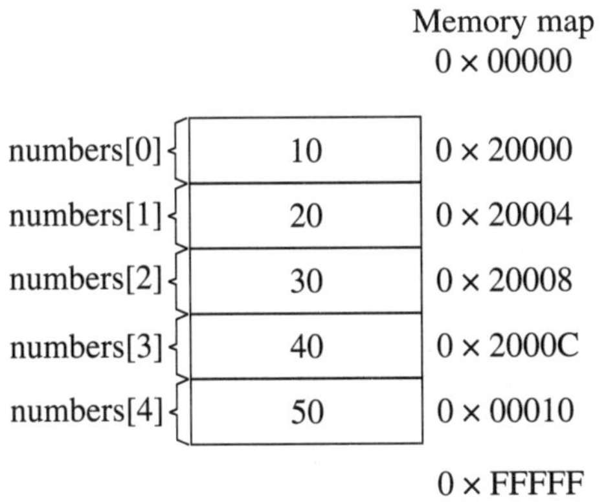

Figure 3.2 Memory representation of an array declaration.

A partial initialization of the array at the compile time is allowed. Thus, the following statement is legal:

Example:

```
int numbers[5] = {10, 20, 30};
```

The above statement results in initializing the first 3 elements of the array to the respective values specified in the curly braces. The rest of the array elements remain un-initialized, which means they will hold some value at random.

If we use the compile time initialization with data items specified in curly braces, we may not skip any element. Thus, the following declaration that tries to initialize elements with index value 1 and above will be illegal.

Example:

```
int numbers[5] = {, 10, 20, 30};
```

We may omit the array size in the declaration statement if we use compile time initialization. In such cases, the compiler creates an array of size equal to the number of data items specified in curly braces. The following declaration results in creating an array of integers having size equal to 3:

```
int numbers[] = {10, 20, 30};
```

The three elements will be initialized to values 10, 20 and 30 in that order.

We will now develop a simple program that declares and uses an array of integers for storing the marks scored by students in their mathematics test. The program prompts the user to enter the marks obtained by each student. The input data is stored in the integer array. After accepting the scores of all students, the program computes the class average by accessing the scores stored in the array.

The program code in Listing 3.1 illustrate the use of Arrays.

Listing 3.1: Program to illustrate the use of Arrays

```
// program to illustrate use of single dimensional array.
#include "stdafx.h"
#include <iostream>
using namespace std;

void main ()
{
    const int NUMBER_OF_STUDENTS=10;
    int numbers[NUMBER_OF_STUDENTS];
    int Total=0;

    for (int i=0; i<NUMBER_OF_STUDENTS; i++)
    {
        cout << "Enter marks for student ID " << i << " : ";
        cin >> numbers[i];
    }

    for (int j=0; j<NUMBER_OF_STUDENTS; j++)
        Total += numbers[j];
    cout << "Avg marks for the class : " <<
        (float)Total/NUMBER_OF_STUDENTS << endl;
}
```

In the `main` function, we first create a constant for defining the number of students in the class.

```
const int NUMBER_OF_STUDENTS=10;
```

It is always a good practice to create a constant in such situations, as in the future if the number of students in a class changes, we will need to modify only one statement and the rest of the program would remain unaffected. In C++, we create constants using the `const` keyword or by using #define as follows:

```
#define NUMBER_OF_STUDENTS 10
```

We then declare an array of integers called `numbers` having size equal to the NUMBER_OF_STUDENTS.

```
int numbers[NUMBER_OF_STUDENTS];
```

For accepting marks obtained by each student, we set up a `for` loop:

```
for (int i=0; i<NUMBER_OF_STUDENTS; i++)
```

In the loop body, we request the user to enter marks for each student by specifying the student ID on the command line.

```
cout <<"Enter marks for student ID" << i <<":";
```

The user input is directly assigned to the appropriate array element using the following statement:

```
cin >> numbers[i];
```

In the above statement, we use the value of loop variable `i` as an index in the numbers array.

Once all the marks are input by the user, we set up another `for` loop to retrieve the elements of the array for computing the class total:

```
for (int j=0; j<NUMBER_OF_STUDENTS; j++)

    Total += numbers[j];
```

Note that `Total` variable was initialized to zero at the time of declaration. The marks will be aggregated in the variable `Total`. Note the use of `numbers[index]` syntax for accessing the elements of the `numbers` array.

Finally, we compute the class average and print its value on the user console:

```
cout << "Avg marks for the class : " <<

    (float)Total/NUMBER_OF_STUDENTS << endl;
```

This simple program has illustrated the declaration of a single-dimensional array, initializing the array elements and accessing the elements later in the program code.

The program output for a typical user input is shown below:

```
Enter marks for student ID 0 : 98
Enter marks for student ID 1 : 56
Enter marks for student ID 2 : 78
Enter marks for student ID 3 : 85
Enter marks for student ID 4 : 95
Enter marks for student ID 5 : 30
Enter marks for student ID 6 : 88
Enter marks for student ID 7 : 85
Enter marks for student ID 8 : 69
Enter marks for student ID 9 : 50
Avg marks for the class : 73.4
```

We will now take one more program example to illustrate the use of a single-dimensional array. We will develop a program that generates Fibonnaci numbers. We will create the first 15 Fibonnaci numbers. We will use a single-dimensional array to store these numbers. After the array is filled with the numbers, we will print the entire array on the user console. The Listing 3.2 provides the complete program code to generate the Fibonnaci numbers.

Listing 3.2:   Fibonnaci number generation program using arrays

```
#include "stdafX.h"
#include <iostream>
using namespace std;

int main()
{
#define MAX 15
        int Fibonacci[MAX], i;

        Fibonacci[0] = 0; // by definition
        Fibonacci[1] = 1; // by definition

        for (i=2; i<MAX; i++)
            Fibonacci[i] = Fibonacci[i-2] + Fibonacci[i-1];
        cout << "Fibonacci Series: " << endl;
        for (i=0; i<MAX; i++)
            cout << Fibonacci[i] << '\t';
        cout << endl;
        return 0;
}
```

When we run the program, we will see the following output:

Fibonacci Series:									
0	1	1	2	3	5	8	13	21	34
55	89	144	233	377					

CHARACTER STRING ARRAYS

One of the major applications of arrays is in the creation of character strings. A character string consists of a series of characters and thus can easily be declared as an array of char data type. In this section, we will discuss a few applications of string manipulations.

String Reversal

First, we will write a program that accepts a string from the user, stores it in a character array, reverses its contents and then prints the resultant string on the console. The full program is given in Listing 3.3.

Listing 3.3:   String reversal program

```
// String Reverse.cpp : main project file.

#include "stdafx.h"
#include <iostream>
```

```
using namespace std;

int main()
{
    char str[20],temp;
    int len,i;
    cout<<"Enter a string (Max 20 characters)\n";
    gets(str);
    len = strlen(str);
    cout<<"Entered string = "<<str<<endl;
    for(i=0;i<len/2;i++)
    {
        temp = str[i];
        str[i] = str[len-1-i];
        str[len-1-i] = temp;
    }
    cout<<"Reverse string = "<<str<<endl;;
    return 0;
}
```

To store the user input string, we first declare a character array using the following statement:

char str[20];

The user string is accepted by calling the gets function.

gets(str);

The gets method allows the user to enter a string containing even the spaces. The input string is stored in the character array specified in the function parameter which is str in the above case.

Note: If we use cin class as in the earlier examples to accept input from the user, the call gets terminated whenever the user enters a space. Thus, we cannot use the cin class for accepting the strings containing spaces.

After obtaining the string from the user, we determine its length by calling the strlen method.

len = strlen(str);

The strlen method takes a character array as an argument and returns the length of the string stored in this character array. We assign the length to the len variable.

We now reverse the string contents using the following for loop:

```
for(i=0;i<len/2;i++)
{
    temp = str[i];
    str[i] = str[len-1-i];
    str[len-1-i] = temp;
}
```

Note that the for loop is executed only till the center of the string. Each character from the beginning of the array is first copied to a temporary variable. The contents of the temporary variable are then copied starting at the end of the array. This process is repeated till the array center is reached. When the loop completes, the `str` array will contain the reversed string. We print this on the user console using `cout`.

```
cout<<"Reverse string = "<<str<<endl;;
```

A typical program output is shown below:

```
Enter a string (Max 20 characters)
this is a string
Entered string = this is a string
Reverse string = gnirts a si siht
```

String Word Count

Next, we will write a program that accepts a string from the user, counts the number of words in it and prints the count on the user console. The complete program is given in Listing 3.4.

Listing 3.4:   Program to count the number of words in a string

```cpp
// Word Count.cpp : main project file.

#include "stdafx.h"
#include <iostream>

using namespace std;

int main()
{
    char str[50];
    int count = 0;
    cout<<"Enter string: "<<endl;
    gets(str);
    for(int i=0 ; i<strlen(str) ; i++)
    {
        if(str[i] != ' ')
        {
            count++;
            while(str[i] != ' ')
                i++;
        }
    }
    cout<<"Number of words in given string = "<<count<<endl;
    return 0;
}
```

The program first declares a character array called `str` of size 50.

```
char str[50];
```

The program accepts the string from the user using the `gets` method as in the previous example. To count the number of words in the string, we define a word as the sequence of characters that is terminated at the end with the space character. Thus, our program scans all the characters in the char array and for each occurrence of a space character, it increments the word count. This is done in the following for loop:

```
for(int i=0 ; i<strlen(str) ; i++)
{
    if(str[i] != ' ')
    {
        count ++;
        while(str[i] != ' ')
            i++;
    }
}
```

When the for loop terminates, the count variable will hold the number of words in the given string. We print this number on the user console:

```
cout<<"Number of words in given string = "<<count<<endl;
```

A typical program output is shown below:

```
Enter string:
this is a test string
Number of words in given string = 5
```

Concatenating Strings

Now, we will write a program to concatenate strings. Assume that we ask the user to input his first name, middle name and the last name in three different requests. We will now like to combine these three names to create the user's full name. The program that does this is given in Listing 3.5.

Listing 3.5:   String concatenation program

```
// String Concatenation.cpp

#include "stdafx.h"
#include <iostream>

using namespace std;

int main()
{
    char first_name[20],middle_name[20],last_name[20],name[63];
    int len1,len2,len3,i;
    cout<<"Enter first name: ";
    gets(first_name);
    cout<<"Enter middle name: ";
    gets(middle_name);
    cout<<"Enter last name: ";
    gets(last_name);
```

```
    len1 = strlen(first_name);
    len2 = strlen(middle_name);
    len3 = strlen(last_name);
    for(i=0;i<len1;i++)
        name[i] = first_name[i];
    name[i++] = ' ';
    len1++;
    for(;i<len1+len2;i++)
        name[i] = middle_name[i-len1];
    name[i++] = ' ';
    len2++;
    for(;i<len1+len2+len3;i++)
        name[i] = last_name[i-(len1+len2)];
    name[i] = '\0';
    cout<<"Full Name is: "<<name<<endl;
    return 0;
}
```

The program first declares four character arrays:

```
    char first_name[20], middle_name[20], last_name[20], name[63];
```

The first three arrays have a length of 20 characters and will be used for storing the user input first name, middle name, and last name, respectively. The last declaration name array is of size 63. This is to account for two spaces between the three names (first, middle, last) and the string termination character.

We accept the three names from the user using the gets method as in the previous examples. We determine the length of each input name by calling the strlen method. Now, to concatenate three strings, we first copy the contents of the first string into the name string:

```
    for(i=0;i<len1;i++)
        name[i] = first_name[i];
```

We now append a space after the first name using the following statement:

```
    name[i++] = ' ';
```

Next, we append the contents of the second string:

```
    len1++;
    for(;i<len1+len2;i++)
        name[i] = middle_name[i-len1];
    name[i++] = ' ';
```

And finally we append the contents of the third string:

```
    len2++;
    for(;i<len1+len2+len3;i++)
        name[i] = last_name[i-(len1+len2)];
    name[i] = '\0';
```

At this time, the name array contains the combined string which we print on the user console using the following statement:

```
    cout<<"Full Name is: "<<name<<endl;
```

A typical program output is shown below:

```
Enter first name: Vinay
Enter middle name: Gajanan
Enter last name: Rana
Full Name is: Vinay Gajanan Rana
```

We will now consider one more program based on character arrays.

Palindromic Strings

A string is considered `palindromic` when it produces the same string on its reversal. The example of a `panadromic` string is "madam". Note that reversing the contents of this string produces the same string. We will now write a program to determine if the user input string is `palindromic`. The full program is given in Listing 3.6.

Listing 3.6: Determining palindromic strings

```cpp
// Palindrome.cpp

#include "stdafx.h"
#include <iostream>
using namespace std;

int main()
{
    char str[20];
    int len, i, flag=1;
    cout<<"Enter string (Max 20 characters)\n";
    gets(str);
    len = strlen(str);
    for(i=0;i<len/2;i++)
    {
        if(str[i] != str[len-1-i])
        {
            flag = 0;
            break;
        }
    }
    if(flag)
        cout<<"Palindromic"<<endl;
    else
        cout<<"Not Palindromic"<<endl;
    return 0;
}
```

As in the earlier programs, we create a character array for storing the string, use a `gets` method to accept the string from the user, and use `strlen` method to determine its length. To determine if the string is `palindromic`, we use the following `for` loop:

```
    for(i=0;i<len/2;i++)
    {
        if(str[i] != str[len-1-i])
        {
            flag = 0;
            break;
        }
    }
```

In each iteration of the `for` loop, we test a character from the start of the string with the corresponding character from the end of the string. If the characters compare equal, we proceed to the next iteration of the `for` loop and continue such iterations till the middle of the string. If the two characters do not compare equal, we set the flag and break the loop.

After the `for` loop completes, we test the condition of the flag and print an appropriate message to the user. If the flag has been set to zero in the `for` loop, it indicates that the given string is not `palindromic`.

```
    if(flag)
        cout<<"Palindromic"<<endl;
    else
        cout<<"Not Palindromic"<<endl;
```

A typical program output is shown below:

```
Enter string (Max 20 characters)
nitin
Palindromic
```

So far we have discussed single-dimensional arrays, now we shall discuss multidimensional arrays.

MULTIDIMENSIONAL ARRAYS

Multidimensional arrays are arrays with more than one dimension. An array may consist of any number of dimensions, of course, subject to the restrictions put by a compiler implementation within the scope of language specifications.

We shall begin our study of multidimensional arrays with two-dimensional arrays.

Two-dimensional Arrays

A two-dimensional array may be visualized as a table consisting of rows and columns. Each cell of the table will denote an array element.

Syntax:
The general syntax to declare a two-dimensional array is as follows:

```
    <DataType> <array_name> [<row>][<col>];
```

The `DataType` specifies the type of data that each array element will hold. The `array_name` specifies the name for the array. The `row` specifies the number of rows in the tabular array and the `col` specifies the number of columns in the table.

Suppose we have to write a program to store the marks obtained by each student in a class in various subjects. Let us assume that each student takes 5 subjects and there is a total of 50 students in a class. We will create a two-dimensional array using the following declaration:

```
const int NUMBER_OF_SUBJECTS = 5;
const int NUMBER_OF_STUDENTS = 50;
int marks [NUMBER_OF_SUBJECTS] [NUMBER_OF_STUD-ENTS];
```

The first dimension of the array or the rows specifies the subjects and the second dimension specifies the student ID. You could have interchanged rows and columns in the above declaration easily by changing their order in the declaration as shown in the statement below:

```
int marks [NUMBER_OF_STUDENTS] [NUMBER_OF_ SUBJECTS];
```

In the above statement, the first dimension specifies the student ID while the second dimension specifies subject ID. The memory layout for this second declaration is shown in Figure 3.3.

To assign the marks obtained by student with ID equal to 5 in subject number equal to 3, we will use the following syntax:

```
marks [5][3] = 78;
```

Note that row-index value of 5 indicates the sixth row in the table as the index always starts with zero. This implies that we assume that the student IDs start with zero. If student IDs were to start with 1, we would use an index value of 4 to denote the 5th student. The same applies to subject numbers. We assume that different subjects are numbered starting with zero. As another example, the syntax `marks[0][0]` would denote the marks obtained by a student with ID 0 in subject designated by subject ID 0. Similarly, `marks[49][4]` would denote the marks obtained by the last student in the class (ID 49) in the last subject (Subject ID 4).

marks	subject ID 0	subject ID 1	subject ID 2	subject ID 3	subject ID 4
student ID 0					
student ID 1					
student ID 2					
student ID 3					
..	..	..	..	..	..
..	..	..	..	..	..
~	~	~	~	~	~
student ID 49					

Figure 3.3 Memory representation of an array declaration.

Initializing Two-dimensional Arrays

Just as with a single-dimensional array, we can initialize a two-dimensional array by two techniques, by using runtime or compile time. We will discuss both these methods below.

Runtime initialization

We will use the usual syntax discussed above for accessing the element of a two-dimensional array and use it on the left-hand side of the assignment statement as follows:

```
arrayname [row][col] = data;
```

For example, consider the following declaration for a two-dimensional array of integers:

```
int marks [5][50];
```

The individual elements of the above array may be initialized using the following program statements:

```
marks [0][5] = 78;
marks [2][10] = 56;
```

The first statement initializes the value of the array element addressed by row 0 and column 5 to value 78. The second statement initializes the array element addressed by row 2 and column 10 to value 56.

Like in the earlier case, we may use a nested `for` loop to initialize each element of a two-dimensional array to a constant value.

```
for (int row=0; row < MAX_ROWS < row++)
    for (int col=0; col < MAX_COLS < col++)
        marks [row] [col] = 0;
```

Compile time initialization

We may define the values of individual array elements in curly braces on the right-hand side of assignment operator during the array declaration. The general syntax for initializing elements of two-dimensional array using this method is shown as:

```
int marks[5][50] = {
    { 10, 50, 78, ... },
    { 47, 23, 18, ...},
    ...
};
```

The three dots (' . . . ') in the above statement indicate the place for the rest of the array element values. Note the use of nested curly braces to separate out the different rows of the data declarations. We may avoid the use of nested braces and list out all the elements of the array in single braces in the desired order. The data elements, as they appear in the declaration, will now be assigned to individual elements of the array, row-wise. When one row is filled, we advance to the next row, column 0 and assign the next data element to it. Such a declaration is shown below:

```
int marks [5][50] = {10, 50, 78, 85, 23, 11, ... };
```

Though we can use the single brace declaration as above, it is advantageous to use the nested braces. When we use nested braces, the organization of data becomes more systematic obviating the possibility of leaving out any element. In single brace declaration, if we miss out a single data item in between, all the rest of the elements will be assigned to the array element prior to the desired one. This effect is undesirable and could be difficult to debug.

If we use the nested brace method for initialization, we may skip some of the elements in each row. As each row is clearly terminated with a brace, the compiler knows that at the beginning of the next brace, the first data item should be assigned to the new row at column 0. For example, consider the following declaration:

```
int marks[5][50] =
    {
        {10, 50, 78},
        {47, 23},
    };
```

In the above declaration, only the 5 array elements listed below are initialized to their individual values as shown by the following assignment statements:

```
marks [0][0] = 10;
marks [0][1] = 50;
marks [0][2] = 78;
marks [1][0] = 47;
marks [1][1] = 23;
```

The rest of the array elements are non-initialized holding random values.

We will now develop a program for storing and displaying the marks obtained by all the students in a class in the various subjects. As explained in the previous section, we will create a two-dimensional array for storing the students' scores. The program will demonstrate how to declare, initialize and access a multidimensional array. The complete program is given in Listing 3.7.

Listing 3.7:   Program to demonstrate use of two-dimensional arrays

```
// Program to demonstrate use of multi-dimensional array

#include "stdafx.h"
#include <iostream>
using namespace std;

void main ()
{
    const int NUMBER_OF_STUDENTS = 5;
    const int NUMBER_OF_SUBJECTS = 3;

    int marks [NUMBER_OF_STUDENTS][NUMBER_OF_ SUBJECTS];

    int StudentID =0;
    int SubjectNumber = 0;

    // Adding data to the array
    for (StudentID=0;StudentID<NUMBER_OF STUDENTS;StudentID++)
```

```
    {
        for (SubjectNumber=0;
                SubjectNumber<NUMBER_ OF_SUBJECTS;
                SubjectNumber++)
        {
            marks[StudentID][SubjectNumber]=
                100.0* (SubjectNumber+1)/
                (StudentID+NUMBER_OF_ STUDENTS);
        }
    }

    // Printing Array
    cout << "\t\t\t";
    for (SubjectNumber=0;
            SubjectNumber<NUMBER_ OF_SUBJECTS;
            SubjectNumber++)
            cout << "Subject " << SubjectNumber << "\t";
    cout << endl;

    for (StudentID=0; StudentID<NUMBER_OF STUDENTS; StudentID++)
    {
        cout << "Student " << StudentID << '\t';
        for (SubjectNumber=0;
                SubjectNumber< NUMBER_OF_SUBJECTS;
                SubjectNumber++)
        {
            cout << '\t' <<
                marks[StudentID] [SubjectNumber]<< '\t';
        }
        cout << endl;
    }
}
```

We first create two constants for defining the array size:

```
        const int NUMBER_OF_STUDENTS = 5;
        const int NUMBER_OF_SUBJECTS = 3;
```

In practice, both the above constants may contain larger values than those used here for simplicity. Next, we declare a two-dimensional array of integers:

```
        int marks [NUMBER_OF_STUDENTS] [NUMBER_OF_SUBJECTS];
```

Note that the first dimension is used for tracking students—each row will correspond to a unique student ID. The second dimension tracks subjects—each column will correspond to a unique subject number.

We will now add some data to the array. Rather than asking the user to input the scores for each subject and each student, we will enter a few values in the array programmatically. We first set up a loop to iterate through all student IDs as follows:

```
        for (StudentID=0; StudentID < NUMBER_OF_STUDENTS; StudentID++)
```

For each student ID, we will iterate through all subject IDs by setting up an inner `for` loop:

```
for (
        SubjectNumber=0;
        SubjectNumber<NUMBER_OF_SUBJECTS;
        SubjectNumber++)
```

We will now initialize the individual array elements using the following statement:

```
marks[StudentID][SubjectNumber]=
        100.0*(SubjectNumber+1)/(StudentID+NUMBER_ OF_STUDENTS);
```

Note that to access an `[i,j]`th element of the array, we use the syntax `marks[i,j]`. The nested `for` loops ensure that we visit all rows and columns of the array and initialize each individual element of the array. Once the entire array is filled with some values, we will print the array values on the user console.

Once again, we set up the nested `for` loops to iterate through all the rows and columns. The individual array elements are accessed and printed on the console using the following statement:

```
cout << '\t' << marks[StudentID][SubjectNumber] << '\t';
```

We print a TAB after each cell value to separate out the columns. The program prints TABs at appropriate places to format the output. The program output is shown below:

	Subject 0	Subject 1	Subject 2
Student 0	20	40	60
Student 1	16	33	50
Student 2	14	28	42
Student 3	12	25	37
Student 4	11	22	33

We will now consider another program that uses two-dimensional arrays. We will write a program to add two 2-dimensional matrices.

Matrix Addition Program

A two-dimensional matrix is represented in the program by using a two-dimensional array. If A_2, B_2 are the two square matrices, then the addition of these two matrices is given by

$$C_{ij} = A_{ij} + B_{ij}$$

where $A_{ij} + B_{ij}$ are the (i, j)th elements of matrices A and B, and C_{ij} is the corresponding element of the resultant matrix C. The complete program that does this addition is shown in Listing 3.8.

Listing 3.8: Matrix addition program

```
// Matrix Addition.cpp
#include "stdafx.h"
#include <iostream>

using namespace std;
```

```cpp
int main()
{
    int mat1[10][10], mat2[10][10], matAns[10][10];
    int N;
    cout << "Enter size of square matrix: ";
    cin >> N;
    cout << "Enter value into matrix 1" << endl;
    for(int i=0 ; i<N ; i++) {
        for(int j=0 ; j<N ; j++)
        {
            cout << "Enter value of " << i+1 << "," << j+1 <<": ";
            cin >> mat1[i][j];
        }
    }
    cout << "Enter value into matrix 2" << endl;
    for(int i=0 ; i<N ; i++) {
        for(int j=0 ; j<N ; j++)
        {
            cout << "Enter value of " << i+1 << "," << j+1 <<": ";
            cin >> mat2[i][j];
        }
    }
    for(int i=0 ; i<N ; i++) {
        for(int j=0 ; j<N ; j++)
        {
            matAns[i][j] = mat1[i][j] + mat2[i][j];
        }
    }
    cout << "Result of addition of the two matrices is" << endl;
    for(int i=0; i<N; i++)
    {
        for(int j=0 ; j<N ; j++)
        {
            cout << matAns[i][j] << " ";
        }
        cout << endl;
    }
    return 0;
}
```

The program first declares three two-dimensional arrays using the following statement:

```cpp
int mat1[10][10], mat2[10][10], matAns[10][10];
```

Each array declaration is of size 10 × 10. The mat1 and mat2 arrays would store the user input arrays and matAns would store the resultant array after the addition of two matrices. We first ask the user to enter the matrix dimension; this should not exceed size 10.

```cpp
cout << "Enter size of square matrix: ";
cin >> N;
```

Next, we accept the elements of the first array using the following `for` loop.

```
for(int i=0 ; i<N ; i++) {
    for(int j=0 ; j<N ; j++)
    {
        cout << "Enter value of " << i+1 << "," << j+1<<": ";
        cin >> mat1[i][j];
    }
}
```

The values entered by the user are stored in `mat1` matrix. Note, how each element of the matrix is accessed using the `[i][j]` notation. The `mat1[i][j]` refers to `[i,j]`th element of the matrix. Likewise, we also accept the elements of the second array.

We now perform the addition of the two matrices using the following `for` loop:

```
for(int i=0 ; i<N ; i++) {
    for(int j=0 ; j<N ; j++)
    {
        matAns[i][j] = mat1[i][j] + mat2[i][j];
    }
}
```

Again, note the notation for accessing the array elements. Finally, we print the resultant array on the user console using the following code fragment:

```
cout << "Result of addition of the two matrices is" << endl;
for(int i=0; i<N; i++)
{
    for(int j=0 ; j<N ; j++)
    {
        cout << matAns[i][j] << " ";
    }
    cout << endl;
}
```

A typical program output is shown below:

```
Enter size of square matrix: 2
Enter value into matrix 1
Enter value of 1,1: 1
Enter value of 1,2: 2
Enter value of 2,1: 3
Enter value of 2,2: 4
Enter value into matrix 2
Enter value of 1,1: 2
Enter value of 1,2: 3
Enter value of 2,1: 4
Enter value of 2,2: 5
Result of addition of the two matrices is
3 5
7 9
```

Matrix Multiplication Program

We will now write a program to multiply two matrices. The full program that does this is given in Listing 3.9.

Listing 3.9:   Matrix multiplication program

```cpp
// Matrix Multiplication.cpp

#include "stdafx.h"
#include <iostream>

using namespace std;

int main()
{
    int mat1[10][10], mat2[10][10], matAns[10][10];
    int N;
    cout << "Enter size of square matrix: ";
    cin >> N;
    cout << "Enter value into matrix 1" << endl;
    for(int i=0 ; i<N ; i++)
        for(int j=0 ; j<N ; j++)
        {
            cout << "Enter value of " << i+1 << "," << j+1<<": ";
            cin >> mat1[i][j];
        }
    cout << "Enter value into matrix 2" << endl;
    for(int i=0 ; i<N ; i++)
        for(int j=0 ; j<N ; j++)
        {
            cout << "Enter value of " << i+1 << "," << j+1<<": ";
            cin >> mat2[i][j];
        }

    //perform multiplication here
    for(int i=0 ; i<N ; i++)
    {
        for(int j=0 ; j<N ; j++)
        {
            matAns[i][j] = 0;
            for(int k=0 ; k<N ; k++)
            {
                matAns[i][j] += mat1[i][k]*mat2[k][j];
            }
        }
    }
```

```
cout << "Result of multiplication of the two matrices is"<< endl;
for(int i=0; i<N; i++)
{
    for(int j=0 ; j<N ; j++)
    {
        cout << matAns[i][j] << " ";
    }
    cout << endl;
}
return 0;
}
```

As in the earlier program, after accepting the matrix dimension, the program accepts the values of elements for two matrices. We assume the use of only square matrices. The matrix multiplication is performed in the following `for` loop:

```
//perform multiplication here
for(int i=0 ; i<N ; i++)
{
    for(int j=0 ; j<N ; j++)
    {
        matAns[i][j] = 0;
        for(int k=0 ; k<N ; k++)
        {
            matAns[i][j] += mat1[i][k]*mat2[k][j];
        }
    }
}
```

Note, how the different elements of three matrices are accessed using the two indices on each matrix. The program prints the resultant matrix on the user console by using another `for` loop as in the previous example.

A typical program output is shown below:

```
Enter size of square matrix: 2
Enter value into matrix 1
Enter value of 1,1: 1
Enter value of 1,2: 2
Enter value of 2,1: 3
Enter value of 2,2: 4
Enter value into matrix 2
Enter value of 1,1: 2
Enter value of 1,2: 3
Enter value of 2,1: 4
Enter value of 2,2: 5
Result of multiplication of the two matrices is
10 13
22 29
```

n-dimensional Arrays

So far, we have discussed single-dimensional and two-dimensional arrays. The same concepts may be extended to represent and access *n*-dimensional arrays. For example, to declare a three-dimensional array, we will use following syntax:

```
int x = 5;
int y = 15;
int z = 10;
int Matrix [x][y][z];
```

The above declaration creates a 3-dimensional array, the size of the first dimension is 5, that of the second dimension is 15 and of the third dimension is 10. Each element of the array will store an integer. The total number of elements for this array is 5 × 15 × 10, i.e. 750. The memory allocations for the entire array will be 750 × size of `int` data type. Assuming size of `int` data type to be 4, the byte allocation will be 3000.

To access the `[i,j,k]`th element, we will use the syntax: `Matrix[i][j][k]`. The array elements may be initialized by using either the runtime or compile time techniques discussed earlier.

The concepts may be extended further to create and access arrays having more than three-dimensions.

We will now study pointers in C++.

POINTERS

Whenever you declare a variable in your program code, the compiler reserves a space for the variable in the memory map. When the program loader loads the executable code in memory, the space in physical memory will be allocated to each declared variable. The amount of space allocated depends on the variable type. For example, an integer variable may occupy 4 bytes of memory space while a double type of variable may occupy 8 bytes of memory space. Each such memory allocation will have a unique address in the memory map. To access this memory address, the pointer type variables are provided. A pointer variable holds the address of a variable in the program code.

Declaring/Initializing Pointers

In this section, we will learn to declare pointer type variables and how to initialize them so that they point to the desired program variables.

Declaring pointers

The following statement declares a pointer type variable that holds the address of `int` type variable:

```
int *intptr;
```

The `intptr` is the name of pointer type variable. The `int *` indicates that `intptr` variable is used for holding the address of the `int` type variable.

The memory map for this pointer declaration is shown in Figure 3.4.

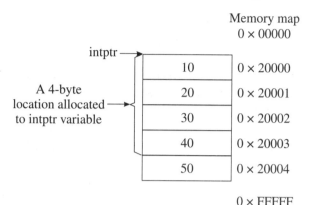

Figure 3.4 Memory map for a pointer declaration.

Just as we create pointer variables to integer data types, we may create pointer variables to other data types as well. To create a pointer variable that holds the address of float type variable, we will use the following syntax:

```
float *floatptr;
```

To create a pointer variable that holds the address of double type variable, we use the following syntax:

```
double *doubleptr;
```

To create a pointer to a char type variable, we use the following syntax:

```
char *charptr;
```

The size of the pointer type variable remains always constant and is independent of the type of variable it points to. This is because each pointer type variable holds the address of some other variable. As the address of a variable is independent of the size of the variable, the size of the pointer type variable always remains constant. This size is mainly decided by the addressing scheme used by the CPU and/or the operating system.

The addressof operator

We have learned to create pointer type variables. Now, how do we initialize such variables so that they point to the desired variable in our program code?

Our next task is to obtain the address of a program variable and assign it to the appropriate pointer type variable. To extract the address of a variable, C++ provides addressof operator ('&'). Thus, if we have a variable called intvar of type' int in our program code, its address can be retrieved using syntax &intvar. If the variable of type double has name doublevar, its address is obtained using syntax &doublevar.

Assigning

After declaring a pointer type variable and obtaining the address of another desired variable, a simple assignment statement will initialize the pointer. Consider the following program snippet:

```
int intvar = 100;
int *intptr;
intptr = &intvar;
```

The first statement declares an integer type variable called `intvar`. The variable is initialized to value 100. The second statement declares a pointer type variable. This variable is currently un-initialized; it means that it does not point to any other variable. In other words, it does not hold the address of any other variable. The third statement now initializes the pointer variable by using the assignment statement. The right-hand side of the expression extracts the address of `intvar` and assigns it to the pointer type variable `intptr`.

A typical memory map for the above declarations is shown in Figure 3.5:

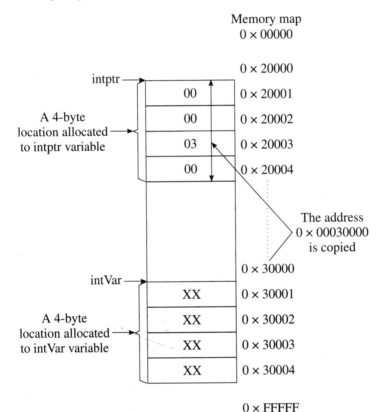

Figure 3.5 Memory map for initialized pointer declaration.

Accessing Variables Using Pointers

Once we create a pointer variable and initialize it, it may be used to access the contents of the variables that the pointer is pointing to. For this, we use the de-reference operator (' * '). In the above declarations, we will obtain the value of the `intvar` by using syntax `*intptr`. The following program statements use this syntax to modify the contents of the `intvar` variable and later print its value on the console:

```
    *intptr = 200;

    cout << *intptr;
```

We will now develop a program that declares pointer type variables to various data types. We will assign these variables to appropriate data types and use them to access the contents of those variables.

Program in Listing 3.10 demonstrates how to declare pointer type variables; how to initialize them and how to use them in your program code for modifying/accessing variables.

Listing 3.10:   Program to demonstrate use of pointers

```
// Program to demonstrate use of pointers
#include "stdafx.h"
#include <iostream>
using namespace std;

void main ()
{
    int intVar = 10;
    float floatVar = 1.5;
    char charVar = 'c';
    int *intptr = &intVar;
    float *floatptr = &floatVar;
    char *charptr = &charVar;

    cout << "intVar = " << *intptr << endl;
    cout << "floatVar = " << *floatptr << endl;
    cout << "charptr = " << *charptr << endl;
    cout << endl;

    cout << "Modifying variables using pointers ..."<< endl << endl;
    *intptr = 200;
    *floatptr = 34.23;
    *charptr = 'a';

    cout << "Modified variables: " << endl;
    cout << "intVar = " << intVar << endl;
    cout << "floatVar = " << floatVar << endl;
    cout << "charptr = " << charVar << endl;
    cout << endl;
}
```

The program first creates three variables of type int, float and char. These variables are initialized at the time of declaration.

```
    int intVar = 10;
    float floatVar = 1.5;
    char charVar = 'c';
```

Next, we create a pointer type variable called `intptr`. The `intptr` variable will hold the address of an integer variable.

```
int *intptr = &intVar;
```

We initialize this variable at the time of declaration by using an assignment operator. The right hand side of the assignment uses an `addressof` operator to extract the address of `intVar` variable. After the execution of this statement, the `intptr` variable will point to `intVar` variable and can be used for modifying/accessing the contents of `intVar` variable.

Likewise, we declare two more pointer type variables called `floatvar` and `charvar`.

```
float *floatptr = &floatVar;

char *charptr = &charVar;
```

The two variables are initialized to the addresses of other variables of the corresponding data types. We will now use these pointer variables to access the contents of the three variables to which they point and print their values on the user console.

```
cout << "intVar = " << *intptr << endl;

cout << "floatVar = "  << *floatptr << endl;

cout << "charptr = " << *charptr << endl;
```

We use the de-reference operator ('*') as discussed above to access the contents of the variables pointed to by the respective pointers.

Next, we will use the de-reference operator to modify the contents of these variables. We use the de-reference operator along with the pointer variable on the left hand side of the assignment statement:

```
*intptr = 200;
*floatptr = 34.23;
*charptr = 'a';
```

The above statements modify the contents of the variables pointed to by the respective pointers. We print the modified values of the variables on the console using the following program code:

```
cout << "intVar = " << intVar << endl;
cout << "floatVar = " << floatVar << endl;
cout << "charptr = " << charVar << endl;
```

Note that, we use the variable name directly in the above statements rather than accessing those variables through the pointers.

The program output is shown below:

```
intVar = 10
floatVar = 1.5
charptr = c

Modifying variables using pointers ...
Modified variables:
intVar = 200
floatVar = 34.23
charptr = a
```

Printing Pointer Value

In some situations, you may wish to examine the contents of the pointer variable itself. This can be done using a simple console output statement by passing the pointer variable as the argument. This is shown in the statement below:

```
cout << "Address of intvar : " << (int) intptr << endl;
```

The output value printed on the console is the address of the variable to which the pointer currently points.

Alternatively, we may use the `addressof` operator to extract the address of a variable and pass it as an argument in the print statement:

```
cout << "Address of intvar : " << (int) &intVar << endl;
```

A typical output is shown below:

```
Address of intvar : 0 x 0012FF70
```

Note that the address consists of 4 bytes as shown in the above output. The actual value for this address will vary with machine and the instance of time when the program is run.

Address of Pointer Variable

The code discussed in the previous section prints the address of the variable held by the pointer type of variable. What if we want to know the address at which the pointer variable itself is created? The address of the pointer variable may be extracted using the `addressof` operator. The following program statement will print the value of the `intptr` pointer discussed in the above code.

```
cout << "Address of intptr : " << (int) &intptr << endl;
```

The program in Listing 3.11 creates an integer type pointer variable, assigns it to some integer variable, and prints the contents of the pointer variable and the address of the pointer variable.

Listing 3.11:   Displaying pointer address

```
#include "stdafx.h"
#include <iostream>
using namespace std;

void main ()
{
    int intVar = 10;
    int *intptr = & intVar;

    cout << "intVar = " << intVar << endl;
    cout << endl;

    cout << showbase << hex;
    cout << "Address of intVar: " << (int)intptr << endl;
    cout << "Address of intptr: " << (int)&intptr << endl;
    cout << endl;
}
```

The showbase and hex in the above program format the output. They are called manipulators. These manipulators ensure that the subsequent integer numbers output to the console will be printed in hex format. Manipulators are discussed in detail in Chapter 13.

The program output is shown below:

```
intVar = 10

Address of intVar: 0x12ff7c
Address of intptr: 0x12ff78
```

The memory map for the above allocations is shown in Figure 3.6.

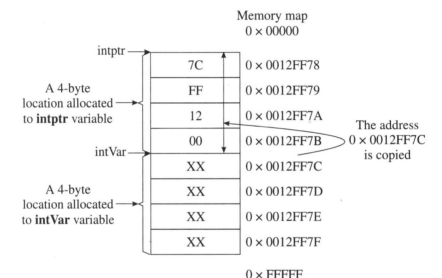

Figure 3.6 Memory map showing the addresses and contents of pointer variable.

Pointer to Pointer

In the proceding program (Listing 3.11), we extracted and printed the address of a pointer type variable. This may be assigned to another pointer type variable. This new variable may now be used to access the contents of the variable pointed by the first pointer. Such a pointer is called a *double pointer* or a *pointer to a pointer*. How do we declare such variables of double pointer type?

Consider the declaration of a char type variable as follows:

```
char charVar;
```

The following code declares a pointer variable to char data type and assigns it the address of charVar declared above.

```
char *charptr = &charVar;
```

We now create another pointer that holds the address of charptr.

```
char **charptr2 = &charptr;
```

Note the use of double asterisk to declare a pointer to a pointer. To access the variable using the double pointer, we use following syntax:

```
cout << **charptr2;
```

Listing 3.12 demonstrates how to declare a double pointer and how to use it to access the original variable.

Listing 3.12:   Using double pointers

```
#include "stdafx.h"
#include <iostream>
using namespace std;
void main ()
{
    char charVar = 'A';
    char *charptr = &charVar;
    char **charptr2 = &charptr;
    cout << "Accessing charVar directly: " << charVar << endl;
    cout << "Accessing charVar through first pointer: " << *charptr << endl;
    cout << "Accessing charVar through double pointer: "<< **charptr2 << endl;
    cout << endl;
    cout << showbase << hex;
    cout << "Address of charVar: " << (int)&charVar << endl;
    cout << "Address of charptr: " << (int)&charptr << endl;
    cout << "Address of charptr2: " << (int)&charptr2 << endl;
}
```

The program creates a `char` type variable and assigns some value to it. We create a `charptr` variable of type `char pointer` and set it to point to our `char` variable.

```
char *charptr = &charVar;
```

We then declare a double pointer and set it to point to the above pointer.

```
char **charptr2 = &charptr;
```

We can now use the original variable name, that is, the first pointer or the double pointer to access the `char` variable contents.

The program prints the value of the original variable by using the variable name (`charVar`), the first pointer (`*charptr`) and the double pointer (`**charptr2`).

The program also prints the memory address at which the `charVar` and the two pointer variables are created.

The program output is shown below.

```
Accessing charVar directly: A
Accessing charVar through first pointer: A
Accessing charVar through double pointer: A

Address of charVar: 0 × 12ff7c
Address of charptr: 0 × 12ff78
Address of charptr2: 0 × 12ff74
```

Figure 3.7 shows the memory map for the above allocations.

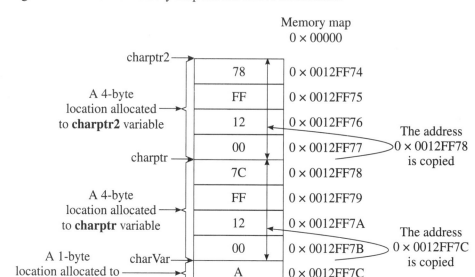

Figure 3.7 Memory map representing double pointer declaration.

Having discussed various types of pointers and their use in accessing the program variables indirectly, we now proceed to discuss structures in C++.

STRUCTURES

Several times, we need to logically group the related data. C++ uses data structures for combining such logically related data under a single unit. The individual data items in a structure may be of any of the primary data types or other pre-defined data structures.

The general syntax to declare a data structure is given below:

```
struct structure_name
{
    data_type element1;
    data_type element2;
    data_type element3;
} object_name;
```

The structure_name specifies the unique name for the new data type. The element1, element2 and element3 are the elements of this new type. Each element may be of any of the pre-defined or user-defined data types. The object_name is the name of the object variable. The above statement defines a structure data type with the specified name (structure_name) and also creates an object of this type with the name specified by object_name variable.

We may create multiple objects at the time of structure declaration with several object_names separated with commas as shown below:

```
struct structure_name {
    // element definitions
    // ...
} object1, object2, object3, ...;
```

We may create additional objects later in your program code by using the declared `structure_name`.

```
structure_name object1, object2, ...;
```

We may not create objects at all, at the time of structure definition and choose to create objects of structure type as and when required. The following is a structure definition with no objects created at the time of definition.

```
struct structure_name {
    // element definitions
    // ...
};
```

If we decide to create all your object variables of the structure type at the time of its definition, we may omit the structure name altogether in its declaration as follows:

```
struct {
    // element definitions
    // ...
} object1, object2, object3, ...;
```

In the above declaration, we will not be able to create objects of the above structure type later in the code as there is no name available for the newly created data type.

We will now define a structure for representing an employee record. Each employee has values for name, age, and gender and draws some salary. The employee may be a full time or a part time employee. We define the `Employee` structure as follows:

```
struct Employee
{
    char name[50];
    int age;
    char gender;
    double basic_salary;
} FullTimeEmp, PartTimeEmp;
```

The above declaration defines a structure called `Employee` having four data fields. The `name` field is a character array and stores the employee name. The `age` is an integer field and represents the employee age. The `gender` field is of `char` type and can take the value of 'M' or 'F' to represent male or female. The `basic_salary` field designates the basic employee salary.

We also declared two variables `FullTimeEmp` and `PartTimeEmp` having the defined structure. We may also create additional variables later in the program by using the structure name as follows:

```
Employee emp1;

Employee emp2;
```

Accessing Structure Elements

So far we have learned how to create a user-defined data type using the struct keyword. A structure contains several data elements. How do we access these elements? The fields or elements of the structure can be accessed by using a dot operator or by using a pointer to the structure data type. We will discuss both the techniques here.

Accessing using dot (.) operator

We can access and modify the structure fields using the dot operator. The syntax is as follows:

```
<structure_name>.<field_name>
```

To set the name and salary of the FullTimeEmp object as declared in the previous section, we write

```
FullTimeEmp.name = "Santosh";
FullTimeEmp.basic_salary = 1000;
```

To retrieve the values of the structure elements, we once again use the dot operator and also the resulting expression on the right-hand side of the assignment expression:

```
cout << "Name: " << FullTimeEmp.name;
cout << "Salary: " << FullTimeEmp.basic_salary;
```

The program in Listing 3.13 illustrates how to define a structure and use it in your application program.

Listing 3.13: Program to demonstrate use of structures

```
// Program to demonstrate the use of structures

#include "stdafx.h"
#include <iostream>
using namespace std;

struct Employee {
    char name [50];
    int age;
    char gender;
    double basic_salary;
} emp1, emp2;

void printEmployeeDetails (Employee emp);

void main ()
{
    cout << "Initializing Employee structure variables ..." << endl << endl;
    strcpy ( emp1.name, "Santosh");
    emp1.age = 35;
    emp1.gender = 'M';
    emp1.basic_salary = 20000;
```

```
        strcpy ( emp2.name,"Rahul");
        emp2.age = 28;
        emp2.gender = 'M';
        emp2.basic_salary = 15000;

        cout << "Printing Employee details:\n";
        printEmployeeDetails (emp1);
        printEmployeeDetails (emp2);
}

void printEmployeeDetails (Employee emp)
{
        cout << endl;
        cout << "Name: " << emp.name << endl;
        cout << "Age: " << emp.age << endl;
        if (emp.gender == 'M')
            cout << "Gender: Male" << endl;
        else
            cout << "Gender: Female" << endl;
        cout << "Salary: Rs." <<emp.basic_salary << endl;
}
```

The above program first defines a structure called Employee as follows:

```
        struct Employee {
            char name [50];
            int age;
            char gender;
            double basic_salary;
        } emp1, emp2;
```

The Employee structure contains four fields viz. name, age, gender and basic_salary. We also create two variables called emp1 and emp2 during structure declaration.

We now set the name for the emp1 object by using a string copy operation in the following statement:

```
        strcpy ( emp1.name, "Santosh");
```

Note the use of dot operator for referring the name element of the Employee object. Likewise, we set the remaining fields of the emp1 object by using the dot operator. Similarly, we initialize the fields of emp2 object.

In the printEmpDetails method, we print all the element values of the two objects. The elements are accessed using the dot operator as in the previous case.

```
        cout << "Name: " << emp.name << endl;
```

The program output is shown below:

```
Initializing Employee structure variables ...

Printing Employee details:

Name: Santosh
Age: 35
Gender: Male
Salary: Rs.20,000
Name: Rahul
Age: 28
Gender: Male
Salary: Rs.15,000
```

Accessing using pointer

We can also use pointers to access elements of a structure data type. First, we need to create a pointer to a structure data type. We declare such a pointer variable as follows:

```
Employee *ptrEmp;
```

The `empptr` is a pointer variable that will hold the address of `Employee` data type. Next, we will assign this variable to the desired `Employee` variable. We do so using the following syntax:

```
ptrEmp = &emp1;
```

Once the above assignment is done, we will use the following syntax to access the elements of `Employee` data type.

```
ptrEmp -> name;
ptrEmp -> basic_salary;
```

This refers to the `name` and `basic_salary` fields of `emp1` object.

We will now demonstrate the use of structures by considering an example that uses array of structures.

Array of Structures

A structure is a user-defined data type that contains a group of logically related entities. Several times, we are required to create a number of such entities having the same structure. We do this by creating an array of structures. As an example, consider that you are required to maintain the average grades of each student in a class. We could declare a structure for this purpose as follows:

```
struct Student
{
    char name[30];
    float avgMarks;
};
```

The `Student` structure contains two elements name of `char` array type and `avgMarks` of `float` type. An instance of `Student` structure will hold data for one student in the class. For storing data of all the students in a class, we will need to declare an array of `Student` types. This is done in the following declaration:

```
Student S[10];
```

To access the ith element of this array, we will use the syntax `S[i]`. To access the name of the ith student in the array, we will use the syntax `S[i].name` and to access the `avgMarks` for the same student we use the syntax `S[i].avgMarks`.

We will now write a program that accepts the student data from the user, stores it in an array of structure, sorts the array in the descending order of average marks, and finally prints the sorted data on the user console. The full program is given in Listing 3.14.

Listing 3.14: Array of structure element

```cpp
// Array of Structure.cpp

#include "stdafx.h"
#include <iostream>

using namespace std;

struct Student
{
    char name[30];
    float avgMarks;
};

int main()
{
    Student S[10];
    int N;
    cout << "Enter the number of students: " ;
    cin >> N;
    cout << "Enter details of " << N << " students" << endl;
    for(int i=0;i<N;i++)
    {
        cout << "Enter name of student " << i+1 << ": ";
        getchar();
        gets(S[i].name);
        cout << "Enter average marks of student " << i+1 << ": ";
        cin >> S[i].avgMarks;
    }
    for(int i=0;i<N-1;i++)
    {
        for(int j=0;j<N-i-1;j++)
        {
            if(S[j].avgMarks < S[j+1].avgMarks)
```

```
            {
                float temp = S[j].avgMarks;
                S[j].avgMarks = S[j+1].avgMarks;
                S[j+1].avgMarks = temp;
            }
        }
    }
    cout << "The list of students rank wise is:" << endl;
    for(int i=0;i<N;i++)
    {
        cout << "Name = " << S[i].name << "\t\tAverage Marks = "
            << S[i].avgMarks << endl;
    }
    return 0;
}
```

Note, how the different elements and the sub-elements of the array of structures are accessed. A sample program output is shown below:

```
Enter the number of students: 4
Enter details of 4 students
Enter name of student 1: Sameer
Enter average marks of student 1: 89
Enter name of student 2: Nisha
Enter average marks of student 2: 76
Enter name of student 3: Manisha
Enter average marks of student 3: 90
Enter name of student 4: Rajiv
Enter average marks of student 4: 67
The list of students rank wise is:
Name = Sameer          Average Marks = 90
Name = Nisha           Average Marks = 89
Name = Manisha         Average Marks = 76
Name = Rajiv           Average Marks = 67
```

Structures Containing Other Structure Data Types

C++ allows us to embed the variables of other structure data types within a structure definition. For example, each company has a few employees. We can create a data structure for representing company objects that contains data elements of Employee structure type. Such a definition is shown below:

```
struct Company {
    char name[50];
    Employee FullTimeEmp;
    Employee PartTimeEmp;
} ABCOM;
```

For such definitions, how do we access the elements of Employee structure object? In the above declaration, we have created an object called ABCOM of Company type. Thus, to access FullTimeEmp data member of this structure, we will use the syntax ABCOM.FullTimeEmp. Now, to access the name element, say, within the Employee structure, we will use another dot operator as follows:

ABCOM.FullTimeEmp.name

Likewise, we will be able to access the rest of the elements of FullTimeEmp or PartTimeEmp objects defined within a Company object.

We may declare a pointer to a Company structure and set it to point to ABCOM object. This declaration is shown below:

Company *ptrCompany = &ABCOM;

Using this pointer, how do we resolve the elements of inner Employee objects? To access the age field of FullTimeEmp object, we will use the following syntax:

ptrCompany->FullTimeEmp.age = 50;

Note the use of indirection ('->') to access the Employee object and the dot operator to access the age element of the Employee object.

We will now consider an example of structures containing other structures. Look at the complete program given in Listing 3.15.

Listing 3.15:   Nested structures

```cpp
// Structure in Structure.cpp

#include "stdafx.h"
#include <iostream>

using namespace std;

struct Date
{
    int dd;
    int mm;
    int yy;
};

struct Employee
{
    char name[30];
    Date date;
};

int main()
{
    Employee E[10];
    int N;
    cout << "Enter number of employees: ";
```

```
    cin >> N;
    cout << "Enter details of " << N << " employees" << endl;
    for(int i=0 ; i<N ; i++)
    {
        cout << "Enter name of employee " << i+1 << ": ";
        getchar();
        gets(E[i].name);
        cout << "Enter joining date of employee" << i+1 << endl;
        cout << "Day [dd]: ";
        cin >> E[i].date.dd;
        cout << "Month [mm]: ";
        cin >> E[i].date.mm;
        cout << "Year [yy]: ";
        cin >> E[i].date.yy;
    }
    cout << "Details of employees are:" << endl;
    cout << "Name\t\t\t\tJoining Date" << endl;
    for(int i=0 ; i<N ; i++)
    {
        cout << E[i].name << "\t\t\t\t" << E[i].date.dd << "/"
            << E[i].date.mm << "/" << E[i].date.yy << endl;
    }
    return 0;
}
```

The following program declares a `Date` structure as follows:

```
struct Date
{
    int dd;
    int mm;
    int yy;
};
```

It also declares another structure called `Employee` as follows:

```
struct Employee
{
    char name[30];
    Date date;
};
```

Note that the `Employee` structure contains `Date` structure as an element. The `main` function asks the user for the number of employees for which the data is to be entered. We accept the name of each employee using the `gets` method as follows:

```
        gets(E[i].name);
```

Note how the name element of the ith employee is accessed. For accepting the date (which could be the joining date) for each employee, we use three `cin` calls. For example, to accept date we use the following code fragment:

```
cout << "Day [dd]: ";
cin >> E[i].date.dd;
```

Note how the `dd` element within the date sub-element is accessed. After accepting all the user details, we print the list of employees along with their joining dates on the user console using a `for` loop.

A sample program output is shown below:

```
Enter number of employees: 4
Enter details of 4 employees
Enter name of employee 1: Sameer
Enter joining date of employee1
Day [dd]: 12
Month [mm]: 10
Year [yy]: 97
Enter name of employee 2: Smita
Enter joining date of employee2
Day [dd]: 11
Month [mm]: 05
Year [yy]: 99
Enter name of employee 3: Nitin
Enter joining date of employee3
Day [dd]: 05
Month [mm]: 02
Year [yy]: 93
Enter name of employee 4: Vijay
Enter joining date of employee4
Day [dd]: 09
Month [mm]: 08
Year [yy]: 99
Details of employees are:
Name            Joining Date
Sameer          12/10/97
Smita           11/5/99
Nitin           5/2/93
Vijay           9/8/99
```

SUMMARY

In this chapter, we studied some of the advanced constructs of C++ language. We learned how to declare arrays of different data types and how to access the elements of the array. Whenever an array is declared, the elements of the array remain un-initialized and contain values at random.

We initialize the array elements at runtime by assigning a value to each array element by using the assignment statements. The array elements may be initialized at compile time by listing the values of each element in curly braces at the time of declaration.

An array may contain more than one dimension. To create an *n*-dimensional array, we need to specify the sizes for all the *n*-dimensions at the time of declaration. To access the elements of an *n*-dimensional array, we need to specify the index value for each dimension.

After discussing arrays, we talked about creating pointer type variables. A pointer type variable holds the address of another variable. The address of a variable may be extracted using `addressof` operator. The extracted address may be assigned to a pointer type variable. We also talked about double pointers or pointer to a pointer that allows us access to the contents of a variable pointed by another pointer.

This was followed by a discussion on creating user-defined data types using the `struct` keyword. A structure groups together logically related data items under a common heading. The individual data elements of structure consist of basic data types or other user-defined data types. The elements of a structure are accessed using a `dot` operator or a variable of pointer type to a structure.

In the next chapter, we will learn the most important feature of C++ language, which is object-oriented programming.

EXERCISES

1. Write a program statement for each of the following data types: `float`, `int`, `char` pointers.
2. Write a program to reverse the elements of an input string.
3. Write a program to display the month name by accepting the month number. (*Hint:* use arrays)
4. Write a program to check if a string is a palindrome. (Palindrome is a string when reversed forms the same string; for example, *radar.*)
5. Write a program to accept the sales turnover for a company for the last 5 months into an array. Calculate the average sales for this period and print the result on the console.
6. Write a program to accept numbers in an array and sort them in ascending order.
7. Write a program to traverse a `char` array using pointers.
8. Write a program to read scores obtained in 4 different subjects by 10 students in a class. Calculate the average score of each subject and print the result.
9. Write a structure representing a student. The structure should hold the student's roll number, name, address and scores obtained in 3 subjects during the last semester.
10. Write a program to change the contents of an integer variable using pointers. Display the address value and the variable contents.
11. Write a program to accept a few positive numbers from the user, store them in an array and after filling the array, determine the maximum and the minimum number in the array.
12. Write a program to represent two matrices of dimension 2×3 in an array. Write functions for adding and subtracting these two matrices.
13. Write a program to perform multiplication of two matrices.

14. Write a program to create a structure called date (month, day, year). Accept today's date and determine tomorrow's date. (Note: You need to consider end of month and end of year.)
15. Which of the following statements are correct with respect to data structures?
    (a) A data structure is a user-defined data type.
    (b) A data structure is a primitive data type.
    (c) A data structure is a class type.
    (d) A data structure consists of data members and member functions.
16. Which of the following statements are correct with respect to arrays?
    (a) An array is a collection of elements of the same data type.
    (b) An array is a collection of elements of multiple data types.
    (c) Arrays are accessed individually using the unique index values.
    (d) Arrays are accessed using the base value, not starting from 1.
17. A valid syntax to declare an array variable is:
    (a) `int []` number;
    (b) `int` number(10);
    (c) `int` number[10];
    (d) `int` number[] = 10;
18. Declaring a pointer to the structure we can access the structure fields using the:
    (a) `arrow` operator (->)
    (b) `new` operator
    (c) dot operator (.)
    (d) * operator
19. State whether the following statements are true or false
    (a) Array elements are accessed using the `dot` operator.
    (b) An array can store data of different types.
    (c) Structures are a flexible way of grouping a diverse collection of data types into a single entity.
    (d) Pointer is a variable that holds a variable's contents.
    (e) A pointer variable may hold the address of any memory location.
    (f) The new operator is used for dynamic de-allocation of memory.
    (g) The delete operator is used for dynamic de-allocation of memory.
    (h) The & operator is used for extracting the contents of a variable.

4

Classes in C++

The major strength of C++ lies in its support for object-oriented programming. In the earlier chapters we gave a quick overview of the C++ syntax and procedure-oriented programming in C++. The syntax discussed in the last two chapters overlapped with the C language syntax and served as a refresher course for those who already knew C language programming. In this chapter, we will learn about some new features of C++ language that are not found in C language. We will introduce the object-oriented features of C++ language.

We will learn the following in this chapter:
- Defining the new data type—the class
- Declaring classes
- Creating objects based on class footprint
- Accessing/modifying data members of an object
- Creating objects dynamically
- Defining methods within a class
- Defining methods outside class definition
- Inline functions
- Public and private scope for data member access.

We begin our learning by defining the new data type—the class.

INTRODUCTION

In Chapter 3, we discussed the use of structure data types for grouping logically related data under a single heading. Data in the real world can usually be combined into logical groups that are associated with real objects in the world. For example, a company employee has a first name, surname, age, gender, etc. To represent employee information in our program code, we would create a structure such as:

```
struct employee
{
    char firstname[15];
    char lastname[15];
    int age;
    char gender;
    ...
};
```

Generally, we will also create various methods that operate on this data. For example, we will have methods to set/retrieve the employee name, age, and so on. We may have methods that compute employees' monthly salary, etc. These methods essentially operate on the data contained within the structure. Such methods and the data on which they operate can be logically grouped together under a single heading. However, C language does not allow us to combine the data and such methods under one group. For a large program, it becomes difficult on the part of the application developer to maintain the relationship between data and the several methods that the application program may contain. C++ solves this problem by allowing the programmer to logically group together the data and the related methods. This is done with the help of a new data type called class. As discussed in Chapter 1, this feature is called *encapsulation*.

DATA TYPE—CLASS

C++ provides a new data type called class that allows us to combine data and the methods that operate on data, under a single logical unit. To represent the employee structure discussed in the earlier section, we will define a class called employee as follows:

```
class employee
{
    char firstname[15];
    char lastname[15];
    int age;
    char gender;
    // methods
    char *getFirstname();
    char *getLastname();
    int getAge();
    char getGender();
};
```

A class definition begins with the keyword `class` followed by its name. The name must follow the standard rules for defining identifiers in C++.

```
class employee
```

The body of the class is enclosed in braces. The closing brace must be terminated with a semicolon to indicate the end of class definition.

```
class employee
{
    ...
};
```

Within braces, we first declare the data that the class is going to hold. Thus, we will declare variables of various data types. For example, the above class definition contains a variable called `lastname` of type `char` array and an integer variable called `age`, besides other variable declarations.

```
char lastname[15];
int age;
```

The variable declarations are followed by the method declarations. We define several methods here that operate on the above-declared data. For example, our above class definition contains the following two methods besides other methods.

```
char *getLastname();
int getAge();
```

Note that each method declaration is terminated with a semicolon, indicating that it is simply a method declaration. The body of each such method must be defined elsewhere. We will talk about method definitions later in the section Defining Member Functions. It suffices to say now that the newly introduced class data type allows us to combine the data and the related methods under a single logical heading. This helps in organizing our large applications into smaller manageable logical units.

DECLARING AND USING CLASSES

We will now learn how to define classes and use them in our program code.

General Form of Class Declaration

The general form of a class declaration is shown as:

```
class name
{
    private:
        variable declarations;
        ...;
```

```
public:
      function declarations;
      ...;
};
```

As discussed in the earlier section, a class declaration starts with the `class` keyword followed by its name. The braces define the class body that encloses the data and method declarations. Note that the general syntax shown above uses the keywords, `private` and `public`. For a class definition, we can control the visibility of its data and methods. For example, we may define a `salary` datafield in employee class. This field should be modifiable only by the methods of the `employee` class and the outside program code should not gain access to this field for modifications. To achieve this, the `private` keyword is designed. Such fields may be marked as private ensuring that they are not visible to any methods that do not belong to the current class. Any of the methods defined in the current class will be able to access such private variables. If we wish to expose a data or a method publicly, we define these with the `public` scope. To define a data or a method with public scope, we use the `public` keyword. Generally, most of the class methods would be defined under `public` scope as the outside objects would use these methods to effectively use the given object.

Besides, `private` and `public` keywords for defining scope, there is another keyword available which is called `protected`. The complete explanation of `private` and `public` keywords is given in a later section. The `protected` keyword is discussed in Chapter 8.

We will now learn how to define classes and use them in program code. We will start with a simple class declaration that contains only data members. We will learn how to declare classes in your program code. We will expand on this basic bare-minimum class definition to add more functionality as we proceed further.

Declaring Classes

The following example shows a declaration for a `Point` class.

```
class Point
{
public:
    int x;
    int y;
};
```

The class definition begins with the keyword `class` followed by its name, `Point`.

```
class Point
{
    ...
};
```

The class definition is enclosed in braces. Note that the definition is terminated with a semicolon. In the body of the class, we create variables for storing data items specific to this class. The `public` keyword creates a section for creating variables that can be publicly accessed. In this simple example, we will declare our class variables with the public scope. In further examples, we will use `private` keyword whenever we want to hide the variables from the code defined outside the class definition.

In the variable declaration section, we declare two variables x and y of type integer as follows.

```
public:
    int x;
    int y;
```

This simple `Point` class definition does not contain any methods.

As shown in the example in this section, it is possible to create a class that does not contain any methods and with only public data types. This is equivalent to the C structure data type.

Using Classes

A class definition serves as a template based on which we create objects for the use of our application code. For example, by using our class definition of `Point`, we can create several `Point` objects. Each `Point` object will be characterized by two distinct variables x and y, which specify the x-coordinate and y-coordinate of the point. Each `Point` object will have its own copy of the data elements x and y. The process of creating an object from a class definition is also called class *instantiation*. We say that a class is instantiated to create an object.

To create an object, we use the following declaration:

```
Point p;
```

This is similar to declaring a variable of any other data type in C++. When we run the program, the runtime will create a variable called p having two data members, x and y. The values of these data members are undefined and will contain some random value at the time of object creation. The memory representation of the `Point` object is as shown in Figure 4.1.

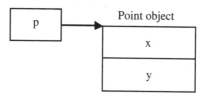

Figure 4.1 Memory representation of a point object.

We may create multiple `Point` objects by declaring several variables of `Point` class type. For each variable declaration, an independent memory block will be allocated. The following program statement declares three variables of type `Point`.

```
Point p1, p2, p3;
```

The memory allocations for the proceding declaration are as shown in Figure 4.2. Note that each `Point` variable declaration receives its own copy of class variables x and y. Though the figure shows three allocations as contiguous, this may not be always the case.

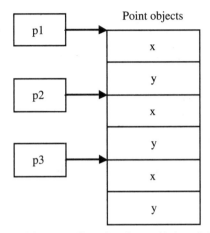

Figure 4.2 Memory allocation for multiple point objects.

Accessing/modifying class variables

To access the data members declared with the public scope, as in the above example, is simple. We use the same syntax that we used for accessing the structure variables in C language, that is, the dot operator. To access the x-coordinate of point p1, we use the syntax p1.x and to access the y-coordinate we use the syntax p1.y.

The program in Listing 4.1 declares a class called Point. The class definition is the same as the one discussed earlier. The class contains two public data members and no methods. The main method in the program creates an object of Point class by declaring a variable p of type Point. The two data members of the Point object are set to value zero by using the dot operator. The values of these data members are printed to the console using cout class. We use the same dot notation to retrieve the values of the data member as shown in Listing 4.1.

Listing 4.1: Demonstration of class construct

```
//Declaring and using classes

#include "stdafx.h"
#include <iostream>
using namespace std;

class Point
{
public:
     int x;
     int y;
};

void main()
{
     cout << "Creating a Point object ... " << endl << endl;
     Point p;
     p.x = 0;
```

```
    p.y = 0;
    cout << "Dumping Point object" << endl;
    cout << "Point p (" << p.x << ", " << p.y << ")" << endl;
}
```

The program output is shown below:

```
    Creating a Point object ...
    Dumping Point object
    Point p (0, 0)
```

DYNAMIC OBJECTS

In the program code of Listing 4.1 the memory allocation for the Point object is done at the compile time. At certain times, we may wish to create objects dynamically at run time and delete those as and when they are no more required by the application. This results in better memory usage. To allow for the dynamic allocation and de-allocation of objects at runtime, C++ provides keywords called new and delete.

Creating Objects Using new

The new keyword allows you to create objects dynamically at runtime. To access the objects created at runtime in your application code, we must assign the reference to the dynamically created object to a variable. Thus, we first need to declare a pointer type variable for this purpose. The following declaration creates a variable with name p that will hold a reference to an object of type Point.

```
    Point *p;
```

After declaration of the variable, we use new keyword to instantiate Point class and assign the dynamically created instance to the variable p. This is shown in the statement below:

```
    p = new Point();
```

Note that when the above statement is executed, the object is created dynamically at runtime rather than at the compile time as in the earlier case. At compile time, only the pointer type variable p is created. The memory allocation for these two statements is as shown in Figure 4.3.

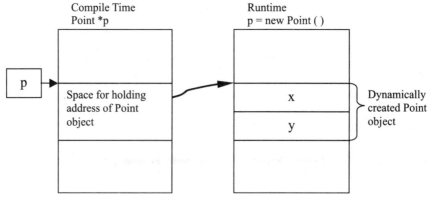

Figure 4.3   Memory map representing dynamic creation of point object.

Deleting Dynamically Created Objects

To conserve the system resources, an object that is created dynamically at runtime should be deleted as soon as it is no longer required by the running code. If we do not delete such dynamic objects, the runtime does not assume any responsibility for freeing the resources used by such dynamic objects. This can result in several memory allocations for the object of this type when we call the same allocation code repeatedly in your application. As the resources used by such memory allocations are not freed, the system performance may degrade over a period of time. This problem is called *memory leak*. To avoid memory leaks in our program, we should delete the objects that are no more required by our application.

We use the `delete` keyword to delete a previously created object. Thus, in the previous program code, the `Point` object referred to by the pointer variable p could be deleted using the following program statement:

```
delete p;
```

This will free the memory associated with the object p. If we do not delete the unused objects, the running application will consume resources on our machine resulting in poor application performance after some use. Sometimes, our code may even loose all the references to a dynamically created object. We lose a reference to the object whenever the variable that holds the reference goes out of scope and gets destroyed. Sometimes, we may explicitly set the variable to `null`. For example, the execution of the following program statement results in losing the reference to the object that the variable p is pointing to:

```
p = 0;
```

When we lose all the references to a dynamically created object, the object cannot be accessed by further code in our application. However, the object is not automatically destroyed and continues to leave resulting in memory leak. We must ensure that all the un-referenced objects are destroyed in your program code to avoid memory leaks in the application.

So far, we have learned to create classes that contain only data members. Now we will learn to add methods to the class definition. Such methods would operate on the data members of the class.

DEFINING MEMBER FUNCTIONS

A member function is a function that belongs to a given class definition and generally operates on the data members of the class. We will write two member functions for our previous class definition to *get* and *set* the value of data member x.

The methods that belong to the class may be defined within the class body or outside the class body. However, the methods must be *declared* within the class body. When we say that a method is *declared*, we mean that we write its prototype and suffix it with semicolon. There is no implementation for the method provided in such declarations. When we say that a method is *defined*, we mean that the code contains the implementation or the full body of the method. First, we will look at the methods *defined* within the class body.

Methods Defined within Class Definition

The modified class declaration is shown below:

```
class Point
{
public:
    int x;
    int y;
public:
    int getx(void)
    {
        return x;
    }
    void setx (int x1)
    {
        x = x1;
    }
};
```

We create a new `public` modifier section and add the two member function definitions. Both methods are declared with public scope and will be accessible from outside the class.

The method `getx` does not take any parameter and returns the value of data member x to the caller. The method `setx` accepts an integer argument and sets the value of the data member x to the value of the parameter received in the method call.

Now, we will see how to declare a method outside the class body.

Scope Resolution Operator

The modified `Point` class definition that defines two methods `getx`, `setx` outside the class body is shown below:

```
class Point
{
public:
    int x;
    int y;
public:
    int getx(void);
    void setx(int);
};

int Point::getx(void)
{
    return x;
}
void Point::setx (int x1)
{
    x = x1;
}
```

Here, we declare the prototypes for the two methods in the class body. Both the methods are declared in public section as in the earlier case. The method definitions are put outside the class body. As there could be several methods belonging to different classes defined outside the body of any of those classes, we need to relate each method with the corresponding class to which it belongs. This is done with the help of a scope resolution operator (' : : '). On the left of scope resolution operator, we write the class name and on the right we write the method name. This associates a class and the method with each other. The parameter list and return type are written as in the case of a normal method declaration.

Inline Functions

Whenever a program makes a function call, the runtime saves the return address on the stack so that the program can return to the next statement following the function call after the function body has been successfully executed. If the function body constitutes a small amount of code—just a few lines of code—the time spent on the call and return statements becomes comparable to the time spent in the execution of the function body. If this function is called several times in our program code, this can affect the application performance severely in terms of execution speed. Thus, for small functions, it is sometimes preferred to embed the function body in the calling program rather than using the call syntax. The compiler does this if we declare the function using inline keyword.

Inline functions are short functions declared with an inline directive. By default, the functions defined inside the class body become inline. For example, in the following class definition, the AddMethod will be an inline function.

```
class MyClass
{
    public:
    int AddMethod(int num1, int num2)
    {
        return num1 + num2;
    }
};
```

The inline directive specifies that the function body should be inserted in the compiled code at the point where it is called. The compiler replaces the function call with a copy of the function body. This results in faster execution of the program, as there is no overhead involved in calling the function. However, at the same time this increases the program size. Thus, if we declare a function with large code as inline and if our function is called several times in our program, it would result in a significantly large size for the binary code.

The syntax for declaring an inline function is as follows:

```
inline <type> <method_name> ( <arguments> )
{
    <implementation>
}
```

We call the `inline` function just the same way as we would call any other function in our program.

The program in Listing 4.2 defines a class called `Point` that defines a few member functions, some of which are `inline` and some are not.

Listing 4.2: Inline functions in classes

```cpp
// Program to demonstrate use of inline keyword
#include "stdafx.h"
#include <iostream>
using namespace std;
class Point
{
public:
    int x;
    int y;
public:
    // Implicit Inline functions
    void setX(int X)
    {
        x=X;
    }
    int getX()
    {
        return x;
    }
    //  Method declarations
    void setY(int Y);
    int getY();
};
//   Outside method implementation that is not inline.
void Point :: setY(int Y)
{
    y=Y;
}
//   Outside method implementation is made inline
//   using the 'inline' keyword
inline int Point :: getY()
{
    return y;
}
void main()
{
    Point p;
    p.setX(20);
    p.setY(40);
    cout << "Point p (" << p.getX() << ", " << p.getY() << ")" << endl;
}
```

The functions, `setX` and `getX` are defined in the class body and thus become `inline` by default. The function `setY` and `getY` are declared in the class definition and are defined outside the class body and thus become usual class functions by default. However, we have preceded the declaration of `getY` function by `inline` keyword. Thus, `getY` becomes an inline function. It is possible to examine the intermediate output of the compiler, i.e. the generated assembler code. The assembler code would clearly show that the calls to `setX`, `setY` and `getY` functions in the `main` function are replaced with the actual corresponding function bodies. The call to `setY` is a normal method call and will contain an assembler code for pushing the return address on the stack.

Variable Scope—Public, Private

Inside a class definition, the data members and functions can be declared with a `public` or `private` scope. There is also a `protected` scope available that will be discussed in Chapter 8.

The general syntax for creating the `private` and `public` scope regions in the class definition is shown below:

```
class classname
{
private:
    data member declarations;

public:
    data member declarations;

private:
    function declarations;

public:
    function declarations;
}
```

Inside the class definition, we use `private` and `public` identifiers to mark the beginning of the respective sections. The data members and functions declared in their respective `private` sections will be accessible only within the class body and not from outside the class body. Thus, these are totally `private` to the class. The data members and functions defined in their respective `public` sections are accessible to any code defined within the class body and the code outside the class body.

To illustrate this further, we will take an example. The code in Listing 4.3 shows definition of an `Employee` class and the `main` function that instantiates this class and uses the `Employee` object.

Listing 4.3: Demonstration of private and public declarations in classes

```
#include "stdafx.h"
#include <iostream>
using namespace std;
```

```cpp
class Employee
{
private:
    double Salary;
    double BasicSalary;
public:
    char name[50];
private:
    double ComputeBonus (void)
    {
        return BasicSalary*0.10;
    }
public:
    void setName (char *empname)
    {
        strcpy (name, empname);
    }
    double ComputeSalary()
    {
        Salary = BasicSalary + ComputeBonus();
        return Salary;
    }
    double getSalary()
    {
        return Salary;
    }
    void setBasicSalary(double salary)
    {
        BasicSalary = salary;
    }
};

int main()
{
    cout << "Creating Employee object ..." << endl;
    Employee *e = new Employee();
    cout << "Calling setName public method ..." << endl;
    e ->setName("Santosh");
    cout << "Calling setBasicSalary public method ..." << endl;
    e ->setBasicSalary(1000);
    cout << "Calling ComputeSalary public method ..." << endl;
    e->ComputeSalary();
    cout << "Calling getSalary public method ..." << endl;
    cout << "Employee: " << e->name << " Salary: Rs. "
        << e->getSalary() << endl;
    return 0;
}
```

The class declares two private data members:

```
private:
    double Salary;
    double BasicSalary;
```

Both members `Salary` and `BasicSalary` are visible within the class scope and not accessible from outside the class definition. The `name` variable of type `char` array is declared with `public` scope. Thus, any program code within your application will be able to access this variable.

```
public:
    char name[50];
```

The variable declarations are followed by the method declarations. First, we create a `private` section for defining the private methods of our `Employee` class. We declare and define a single method called `ComputeBonus` in this section. The method as it is declared with `private` modifier will be accessible to the code only within the current class definition.

```
private:
    double ComputeBonus (void)
    {
        return BasicSalary*0.10;
    }
```

After the private method declarations, we create few public methods. These methods are declared under the `public` heading as follows:

```
public:
    void setName (char *empname)
    {
        strcpy (name, empname);
    }
    ...
```

In all, we declared four methods—`setName`, `ComputeSalary`, `getSalary` and `setBasicSalary` in this section. All the four methods have `public` scope and can be called by a code outside the current class definition.

Having defined the `Employee` class, we now write a `main` method for instantiating the `Employee` class and verifying the scope of various class variables and methods. The scheme for this is depicted in Figure 4.4.

In the `main` method, we create an instance of the `Employee` class and assign the object reference to the variable e.

```
Employee *e = new Employee();
```

This reference is used for accessing the public data members and methods of the class. Using this object reference, we will not be able to access the private members of the class. Thus, the declaration e –>Salary or e –>BasicSalary results in compile-time error.

The private variables declared in the class are accessible to all the class methods irrespective of whether they are declared inside or outside the class body.

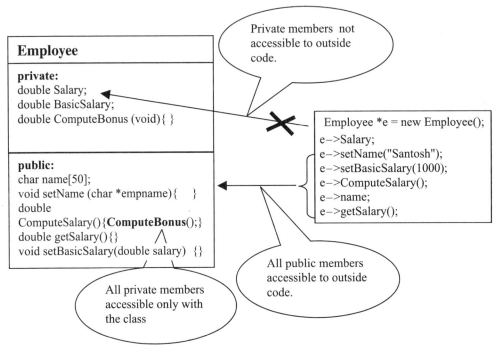

Figure 4.4 An Employee class representation with private/public declarations.

The Employee class declares one variable called name with the public scope. As this variable has public scope, it can be accessed using the object reference e created in the main program. Thus, e ->name will be a valid reference.

The Employee class declares ComputeBonus method with private scope. This method can be invoked only from within the body of the other class methods. The class method ComputeSalary invokes this private method. The invocation of the ComputeBonus method using the earlier created e object reference would be invalid. Thus, e ->ComputeBonus () is an invalid method call.

The Employee class declares few public methods, setName, ComputeSalary. getSalary and setBasicSalary. As these methods are declared with public scope, they can be invoked from outside the bodies of the class methods. Thus, the main function in the above code can invoke any of these methods.

For example, the following statement that outputs the employee name and the salary on the user console accesses the public name variable directly using the pointer reference and calls public getSalary method to access the private salary data member.

```
cout << "Employee:" << e ->name << "Salary: Rs."
      << e ->getSalary() << endl;
```

The program output is shown below:

```
Creating Employee object ...
Calling setName public method ...
Calling setBasicSalary public method ...
Calling ComputeSalary public method ...
Calling getSalary public method ...
Employee: Santosh Salary: Rs. 1100
```

STATIC DATA MEMBERS AND FUNCTIONS

In the previous sections, we discussed how to define a class and the data members and functions for a class. Whenever we instantiate a class, the runtime allocates memory for these maps. Each object holds its own copy of such data members, which are not shared between different objects of the same type. There could be situations where we may like to share a data member across all the objects of the same type. Similarly, we may also like to invoke a method defined in a class without instantiating the class. This can be achieved with the help of static keyword.

Static Data Members

We may declare a data member by prefixing the declaration with a static keyword. In case of static data members, only one copy of the data is maintained for all objects of the class. The data members have class scope i.e. they are visible only within the class but their lifetime is the entire program.

The static data members are defined using the scope resolution operator as shown below:

```
class ClassA
{
private:
    static int static_variable;
public:
    ...;
};
int ClassA::static_variable;
```

Here, the variable static_variable is of type int and declared to be a static member of the class.

```
static int static_variable;
```

By defining a static data member outside the class, we actually allocate a storage for it and link it to a class.

```
int ClassA::static_variable;
```

A static data member definition within the class is just a logical construct of the member. All static variables are initialized to zero at runtime.

The concept of static data members will be easily understood from the following example. The example demonstrates how we can keep a track of the number of objects created from a particular class definition. We will create a variable called `counter` in our class definition and make it static. A single copy of `counter` variable is now maintained by the runtime. This copy is accessible to all the instances of our class. The scheme is depicted in Figure 4.5.

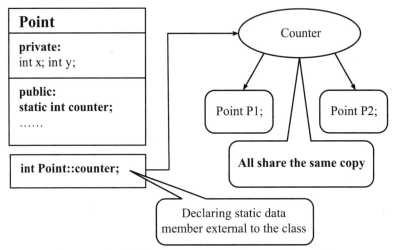

Figure 4.5 Multiple instances sharing a static variable.

We define our `Point` class as follows:

```
class Point
{
private:
    int x, y;
```

The `Point` class defines two private data members `x` and `y` of type integer. In the `public` access specifier we define the `static` data member `counter` of type `int`. We will increment the value of this variable every time an object of this type is constructed.

```
public:
    static int counter;
```

We write a no-argument constructor for the class.

```
Point()
{
    counter++;
}
```

In the body of the constructor, we access the static variable `counter` and increment its value. As explained earlier we also need to declare the static data member outside the class using the scope resolution operator with its data type.

```
int Point::counter;
```

In the `main` method, we will simply create object of `Point` class as follows:

```
Point p1;
Point p2;
Point p3;
```

Each time the object of `Point` class is created, the `counter` variable is incremented. As only a single copy of `counter` variable is maintained and shared among all the objects, the value of the `counter` is properly incremented during each object construction.

After constructing an object, we print the value of the `counter` variable for user information.

```
cout <<"Number of objects created: "
    <<Point::counter<<endl<< endl;
```

Note the syntax used for accessing the `counter` variable. We do not use the object reference to access the static member `counter`; rather we use the class name and the scope resolution operator to access its value.

The full program is shown in Listing 4.4.

Listing 4.4:   The static data members in classes

```cpp
// Static data members
#include "stdafx.h"
#include <iostream>
using namespace std;

class Point
{
private:
    int x, y;

public:
    static int counter;
    Point()
    {
        counter++;
    }
};

int Point::counter;
```

```
void main()
{
    cout <<"Creating FIRST object of Point class ..."<<endl;
    Point p1;
    cout <<"Number of objects created:
        "<<Point: :counter<<endl << endl;
    cout <<"Creating SECOND object of Point class ..."<<endl;
    Point p2;
    cout<<"Number of objects created: "<< Point::counter <<endl << endl;
    cout <<"Creating THIRD object of Point class ..."<<endl;
    Point p3;
    cout <<"Number of objects created: "<<Point: :counter<<endl;
}
```

The program output is shown below:

```
Creating FIRST object of Point class ...
Number of objects created: 1

Creating SECOND object of Point class ...
Number of objects created: 2

Creating THIRD object of Point class ...
Number of objects created: 3
```

As seen from the above output, the value of counter variable is incremented as expected.

Static Member Functions

Static member functions are based on the same concept as that of static data members. The static member functions have class scope and can use only static data members in their implementation. The procedure followed to define static member functions is similar to that for static data members. A static member function is declared as follows:

```
class ClassA
{
private:
    ...
public:
    static void staticMemberFunction()
    {
        // implementation
    }
};
```

The following rules apply while declaring static functions:

Rules for defining static member function

- The function declaration is prefixed with `static` keyword
- The function name must be unique. We cannot create another non-static function with the same name.
- We may define an overloaded static function. (Function overloading is discussed in Chapter 1.)
- Static member functions may not be defined as `virtual`. (Virtual functions are discussed in Chapter 1.)

Let us discuss an example that demonstrates the use of the static member function. We will use the same `Point` class discussed in the previous section and add a `static` member function to it. In the previous example, we used the data member to show the number of objects created. In this example we will implement `ShowCounter` static member function to display the value of `counter` variable.

The scheme of this example is depicted in Figure 4.6.

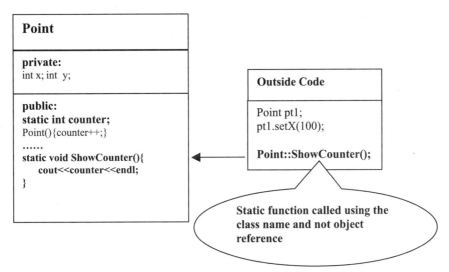

Figure 4.6   Declaring and calling static class methods.

We add a new member function `ShowCounter` to the `Point` class. We define this function as `static` as shown below:

```
static void ShowCounter()
```

In the method implementation, we output the `counter` value to the console.

```
cout <<"Number of objects created: "<<counter <<endl << endl;
```

In the `main` function, we call this static method as follows:

```
Point::ShowCounter();
```

We use the scope resolution operator to resolve the method call. Note that we do not use an object reference for invoking the method. The full program is given in Listing 4.5.

Listing 4.5: **The static methods in classes**

```cpp
#include "stdafx.h"
#include <iostream>
using namespace std;

class Point
{
private:
    int x, y;

public:
    static int counter;
    Point ()
    {
        counter++;
    }
    static void ShowCounter()
    {
        cout <<"Number of objects created: "<<counter<<endl<< endl;
    }

};

int Point::counter;

void main()
{
    cout <<"Creating FIRST object of Point class ..."<<endl;
    Point p1;
    Point::ShowCounter();
    cout <<"Creating SECOND object of Point class ..."<<endl;
    Point p2;
    Point::ShowCounter();
    cout <<"Creating THIRD object of Point class ..."<<endl;
    Point p3;
    Point::ShowCounter();
}
```

The program output is shown below:

```
Creating FIRST object of Point class ...
Number of objects created: 1

Creating SECOND object of Point class ...
Number of objects created: 2

Creating THIRD object of Point class ...
Number of objects created: 3
```

SUMMARY

In this chapter, we introduced the most important feature of C++ language—the *class* that is a foundation of object-oriented programming. A class encapsulates the data and the methods that operate on this data. We learned how to define classes containing data and the methods. A class acts like a template on which the objects are based upon. When we create an object of a class, we say that the class is instantiated. We learned creating objects at compile time and dynamically at runtime using new keyword. We accessed the data members of the class using the dot operator.

A class may contain several methods. Such methods may be defined within the class body or may be defined outside the class body. The methods defined outside the class body require the use of scope resolution operator to associate them with a particular class. The methods defined outside the class body may be preceded with an inline keyword to save the overhead of function calling whenever such methods are called. For the inline methods, the compiler includes the function body whenever it encounters a call to such methods in the source program. The functions defined in the class body are implicitly inline. Generally, the function having small body is declared inline. For such small functions, the method execution time is comparable to the time for calling and returning from a method. By making such methods inline, we save on the overhead of calling and returning from the method at the cost of increase in code size.

Both data and methods declared inside the class may have a public or private scope of access. The access visibility is controlled with the use of public and private keywords. A private data member or a method is visible only to the code within the current class definition. Any method that does not belong to the current class definition cannot access the private data members or methods of the current class. In contrast to this, a public data member or a method is publicly available to the entire application code. We learned how to control the access to the class data members and methods by creating public and private sections in the class definition.

We also studied the use of static keyword for creating static data members and methods for the class. The runtime maintains a single copy of a static data member that is shared between all the instances of the class. A static method is invoked without a reference to the class instance.

In the next chapter, we will learn more about class methods.

EXERCISES

1. Describe a class. Write a class definition for representing a colour point object.
2. Describe what do you understand by *data members* and *member functions of a* class.
3. Explain the access modifiers and their importance in writing classes.
4. What is data encapsulation?
5. What do you understand by *static data members*? Explain using an example.
6. What do you understand by *static member functions*? Explain using an example.
7. Write a Clock class that displays time. Implement the required data members and member functions.
8. Write a class representing a Customer and implement its data members and member methods to store and display member data.

9. Design a class `Person` that contains appropriate members for storing name, age, gender, and telephone number. Write member function that can individually change these data members. Write a member function `printInfo()` that prints a person's data nicely formatted.

10. Write a class `Triangle` that stores the length of the base and height of a right-angled triangle. Define two functions `Hypotenuse()` that returns the length of the hypotenuse and `Area()` that returns area of the triangle.

11. Write a class called `Machine` with data member (`current_ cycle as int`), and member functions (`start(), next()`). We need to define constants such as `idle = 0, gear1 = 1, gear2 = 2, gear3 = 3, gear4 = 4` and `gear5 = 5`. The start function acts as the starter of the machine where we set the initial `current_cycle` value. The next method changes the `current_ cycle's` value using the constants' value. Write the appropriate class and the main function to start the machine and change the machine gears accordingly.

12. Write a class called `Student` with data members (`char` name, `int` rollnumber, `int` marks). Write the appropriate program statement to create the `Student` class object at compile time. Using this object set the values of the data members and print them.

13. Using the above created class, write the appropriate program statement to create the `Student` class object dynamically. Using this object set the values of the data members and print them.

14. Write a class called `Student` with data members (`char` name, `int` rollnumber, `int` marks). Write appropriate `inline` member functions to enter and access the student data.

15. Modify the `Student` class of Ex. 14 to provide the function implementation outside the class.

16. Using the `Student` class of Ex. 14, write a member function to calculate the average marks for a student and print it on the console.

17. State whether the following statements are true or false:
    (a) Data members of a class are usually defined with a public access specifier.
    (b) Member functions of a class specified with `private` specifier are accessible to the member functions of that class.
    (c) Member functions have access to an object's `private` data.
    (d) A separate copy of the data members is created for each object that is created from a class but only one copy of member functions exists.
    (e) Member functions of a class are `public` by default.
    (f) Class name and the constructor name can be different.
    (g) Data member can be restricted to a single instance for all objects of a class by defining it as `static`.
    (h) A `friend` function of one class may be declared as a friend of another class.

5

Member Functions

In Chapter 4, we studied how to define a class, and how to add data members and functions to it. In this chapter, we will elaborate further on member functions. More specifically, we will learn the following:

- Defining member functions that take parameters by value
- Defining member functions that take parameters by reference
- Defining constant parameters for your class methods
- Setting default values for the method parameters
- Defining friend functions.

Some of the above features are common to C language programming syntax. The other features such as creating friend functions or function overloading (function overloading is discussed in Chapter 6) are unique to C++ language and are not supported by C language.

We will begin our study of various kinds of member functions by first learning how to pass parameters to a function.

PASSING PARAMETERS

A class method may or may not take any parameters. Such parameters may consist of built-in data types or user-defined data types. There are two ways of passing parameters to a method:

- By value
- By reference

Pass by Value

Consider the following function declaration:

```
void functionA (int a);
```

The functionA takes one parameter and does not return anything. The parameter is of type integer and is sent by value. For example, you may call the method as follows:

```
int intVariable = 5;
functionA (intVariable);
```

During a call to functionA, the runtime makes a copy of intVariable and pushes it on the stack. What the function receives is a copy of the variable intVariable. Within the body of the function, this copy is referred by the variable name a. The function body, if it modifies the contents of this variable, will do so on the received copy and the original variable contents remain unaffected. The function does not receive the address of the original variable. Thus, any changes made to the variable using parameter a do not affect the original variable.

The program in Listing 5.1 demonstrates the effect of calling a method that takes an integer parameter by value.

Listing 5.1:   Passing method parameters by value

```
//program to demonstrate Call by Value

#include "stdafx.h"
#include <iostream>
using namespace std;

class TestClass
{
public:
    int functionA (int a);
};

int TestClass::functionA (int a)
{
    cout << "------" << endl;
    cout << "Inside functionA: " << endl;
    cout << "Parameter value: " << a << endl;
    cout << "Modifying Parameter: " << endl;
    a = 10;
    cout << "Modified Value: " << a << endl;
    cout << "------" << endl;
    return a;
}

void main()
{
    TestClass TestObject;
```

```
int tempVar = 5;
cout << "Initial Value:" << tempVar << endl;
cout << "Calling functionA" << endl;
int temp = TestObject.functionA(tempVar);
cout << "After returning from function call" << endl;
cout << "Original variable:" << tempVar << endl;
cout << "Function returned value:" << temp << endl;
}
```

The program defines a class called `TestClass`. The `TestClass` defines a single public method `functionA` that takes an integer type of parameter.

```
int functionA (int a);
```

In the method body, we print the parameter value.

```
cout << "Parameter a: " << a << endl;
```

After printing the received parameter value, we modify its value.

```
a = 10;
```

Now, the value of variable a within the method body becomes 10. We print this modified value on the console.

```
cout << "Modified Value: " << a << endl;
```

The function now returns the value of variable a to the caller. The calling function (the `main` function) prints the method returned value and the value of the original variable on the console.

```
cout << "After returning from function call" << endl;
cout << "Original variable:" << tempVar << endl;
cout << "Function returned value:" << temp << endl;
```

The program output is shown below:

```
Initial Value: 5
Calling functionA

Inside functionA:
Parameter value: 5
Modifying Parameter:
Modified Value: 10

After returning from function call
Original variable: 5
Function returned value: 10
```

Note that the value of the original variable remains unmodified even after the function call is completed. This indicates that what the function has received is a copy of the variable and not its address. Thus, the function works on the copy all the time within its body and changes made to it do not affect the original variable.

What if we want the function to modify the value of the original variable? In this case, we need to pass the address of the variable as a parameter to the function call. We study how to achieve this in the next section.

Pass by Reference

To pass the variable by reference, we declare a pointer to the variable and pass the pointer variable as a parameter to the function. We will declare our function as follows:

```
void functionB (int *a);
```

While calling the method, we will extract the address of the variable by using the addressof operator ('&') and pass this as a parameter to the method. Thus, the method call will look like:

```
int intVariable = 5;
functionB (&intVariable);
```

Since we pass a pointer to the variable, the changes made by the function to the variable contents using this pointer would be retained even when we return from the method call.

The program code in Listing 5.2 demonstrates the effect of passing parameters by reference.

Listing 5.2: Passing method parameters by reference

```
//program to demonstrate Call by Reference

#include "stdafx.h"
#include <iostream>
using namespace std;

class TestClass
{
public:
     void functionB (int *a);
};

void TestClass::functionB (int *a)
{
     cout << "------" << endl;
     cout << "Inside functionB: " << endl;
     cout << "Parameter a: " << *a << endl;
     cout << "Modifying Parameter: " << endl;
     *a = 10;
     cout << "Modified Value: " << *a << endl;
     cout << "------" << endl;
}

void main()
{
     TestClass TestObject;
```

```
        int tempVar = 5;
        cout << "Initial Value:" << tempVar << endl;
        cout << "Calling functionB" << endl;
        TestObject.functionB(&tempVar);
        cout << "After returning from function call" << endl;
        cout << "Original variable: " << tempVar << endl;
}
```

The `TestClass` declares a method called `functionB` that takes a single parameter of type pointer to an integer variable:

```
        void functionB (int *a);
```

In the method body, we print the contents of the original variable using pointer variable `a` as follows:

```
        cout << "Parameter a:" << *a << endl;
```

We now modify the contents of the variable using the received pointer variable:

```
        *a = 10;
```

Note that we use the de-reference operator on the pointer variable to access the variable pointed to by this pointer. We print the modified variable value on the user console.

```
        cout << "Modified Value: " << *a << endl;
```

The function now returns the execution control to the caller without returning any value to the caller.

In the `main` method, we declare an integer variable and print its value on the console:

```
        int tempVar = 5;
        cout << "Initial Value: " << tempVar << endl;
```

We now call the `functionB` by sending a pointer to `tempVar` as a parameter to the method call:

```
        TestObject.functionB(&tempVar);
```

After returning from the method call, we print the value of the original variable on the user console.

```
        cout << "After returning from function call" << endl;
        cout << "Original variable:" << tempVar << endl;
```

The program output is shown below:

```
    Initial Value: 5
    Calling functionB
    .................
    Inside functionB:
    Parameter a: 5
    Modifying Parameter:
    Modified Value: 10
    .................
    After returning from function call
    Original variable: 10
```

Note the value printed on the last line of the output. Clearly, the method has modified the original variable. By passing a pointer to a variable as a parameter to a method, we pass the address of the variable to a method. Thus, the method implementation is able to access the contents of the original variable directly and can modify its contents using the address of the variable that it has received as a parameter.

Alternate way of passing by reference

As the pointer syntax sometimes becomes cryptic, C++ provides another simpler syntax to pass variables by reference. In this case, we declare the function as follows:

```
void functionC (int &a);
```

Here, the parameter a is passed by its reference to the method. Inside the function, we do not need to use the de-reference operator (*). Instead, we use the variable name directly.

```
a = 10;
```

The above statement results in modifying the contents of the original variable. The complete program is given in Listing 53.

Listing 5.3:   Alternate syntax for passing by reference

```
//program to demonstrate Call by Reference

#include "stdafx.h"
#include <iostream>
using namespace std;

class TestClass
{
public:
    void functionC (int &a);
};

void TestClass::functionC (int &a)
{
    cout << "......" << endl;
    cout << "Inside functionC: " << endl;
    cout << "parameter a: " << a << endl;
    cout << "Modifying Parameter: " << endl;
    a = 10;
    cout << "Modified Value: " << a << endl;
    cout << "......" << endl;
}

void main()
{
    TestClass TestObject;

    int tempVar = 5;
    cout << "Initial Value:" << tempVar << endl;
    cout << "Calling functionC" << endl;
```

```
TestObject.functionC(tempVar);
cout << "After returning from function call" << endl;
cout << "Original Variable: " << tempVar << endl;
}
```

The program output is as shown below:

```
Initial Value: 5
Calling functionC
................
Inside functionC:
parameter a: 5
Modifying Parameter:
Modified Value: 10
...................
After returning from function call
Original Variable: 10
```

Once again, note the value printed on the last line. Clearly, the value of the original variable is modified. Also, note that nowhere in the method body we use the de-reference operator, resulting in a cleaner code.

CONSTANT PARAMETERS

When we send parameters to a function by reference, the function is able to modify the contents of the original variable using the obtained reference. In some situations, we would like to pass a parameter by its reference and yet we would like to make sure that function does not modify the variable value even unknowingly. Consider the following class definition:

```
class TestClass
{
private:
public:
    void PrintNumber (int &number)
    {
        cout << number << endl;
    };
};
```

The TestClass defines a function called PrintNumber that takes an integer number as an argument and prints its value on the user console. The sole purpose of this function is to print the value of the input parameter. Now, we will modify the method definition as follows:

```
void PrintNumber (int &number)
{
    cout << number << endl;
    number = 100;
};
```

The modified definition uses the reference to input variable and modifies its contents. This may happen unintentionally and may not be truly desired. So how do we prevent the function to modify the variable contents even when we pass a reference to it? We use the `const` keyword for creating constant parameters. We will modify the above function definition as follows:

```
void PrintNumber (const int &number)
{
    cout << number << endl;
    number = 100;
};
```

Now, if we try to compile the above code, the compiler will throw an error indicating that the input parameter is a constant object and cannot be modified. The compiler output is shown below:

```
C:\TC\BIN>cl test.cpp
Microsoft (R) 32-bit C/C++ Optimizing Compiler Version 12.00.8168 for 80x86
Copyright (C) Microsoft Corp 1984-1998. All rights reserved.

test.cpp
test.cpp(10) : error C2166: l-value specifies const object
```

If we wish to ensure that the function body does not unintentionally modify the external variables for which it receives the reference in a parameter, it should declare such parameters as const.

DEFAULT PARAMETERS

When we pass parameters to a function, we may set the default values for these parameters. During a method call, we need not specify such parameters in the method argument list. For example, consider the following method declaration:

```
void Add(int number1, int number2);
```

The `Add` method takes two parameters of integer type. The method adds these two numbers and prints the result on the user console. A call to this method must include values for these parameters. Thus, we would call this method using a statement similar to that shown below:

```
Add (100, 200);
```

Within the method, the `number1` parameter takes the value 100 and `number2` takes the value 200.

Sometimes, we may wish to add the same number repeatedly to another number. In other words, the value of `number2` parameter may remain constant while `number1` will change on every call to the method. We may now declare the `Add` method as follows:

```
void Add(int number1, int number2 = 100);
```

In the above declaration, the second parameter `number2` is assigned a default value of 100. To call this method, we may use the following program statement:

```
Add (500);
```

Note that we have specified only one parameter in the above method call. The call results in setting up the `number1` parameter value to 500 and `number2` parameter value to a default of 100. What if we wish to add, say 500 to 300? In this case, we will use the following program statement:

```
Add (500, 300);
```

In the above call, the value specified for `number2` parameter, that is, 300, would override its default value. Within the function, `number1` parameter assumes value of 500 and `number2` parameter assumes value of 300.

The default parameters help in keeping the function calling code simple by eliminating the need to specify all the parameters in each and every call to a function.

Default Parameter Order

If a method takes multiple parameters, we may set default values for none, partial or all parameters. If we set the default values for a partial list of parameters, all such parameters must appear at the end of the list. Thus, the following function declaration would be invalid:

```
void Add(int number1 = 200, int number2);
```

So also, the following declaration is invalid:

```
void MyFunction(
    int param1 = 200,
    int param2,
    int param3 = 100);
```

However, the following declaration that takes three parameters, two of which assume default values is valid:

```
void MyFunction(
    int param1,
    int param2 = 200,
    int param3 = 100);
```

When we call a function by using its default parameter values, we cannot skip-in-between parameters in the parameter list and override only the values for the end parameters. For example, the following call would be invalid:

```
MyFunction (50, 300);
```

In the above case, we wish to use the default value for the second parameter and override the default value of the third parameter. This is not permitted. The correct method call for the above situation is shown below:

```
MyFunction (50,200,300);
```

In the above call, we explicitly mention the default value for the second parameter. The value for the third parameter is overridden.

You may override the values of the default parameters that appear first in the list and assume default values for the rest of the parameters. Thus the following call is valid.

```
MyFunction (50,400);
```

Here, we override the default value for the second parameter and use the default value for the third parameter.

The program code in Listing 5.4 demonstrates the use of default parameters:

Listing 5.4: Program to illustrate use of default parameters

```
//program to demonstrate default arguments to a function

#include "stdafx.h"
#include <iostream>
using namespace std;

class TestClass
{
public:
    void Add(int number1=400, int number2=200);
};

void TestClass::Add(int number1, int number2)
{
    cout<< number1 << " + " << number2 << " = "
    << number1+number2<<endl;
}

void main()
{
    TestClass TestObject;

    cout << "Using Default values for both parameters" << endl;
    TestObject.Add();
    cout << "Using Default value for second parameter" << endl;
    TestObject.Add(100);
    cout << "Overridding Default values for both parameters" << endl;
    TestObject.Add(50, 50);
}
```

The `TestClass` defines a method called `Add` that takes two parameters of integer type. For both the parameters, we set the default values:

```
void Add(int number1=400, int number2=200);
```

In the body of the `Add` method, we simply print the sum of the values of two parameters on the user console. The `main` program first calls the `Add` method with no parameters specified.

```
TestObject.Add();
```

The above call will print a value of 600 on the user console. This is the sum of two numbers 400 and 200, which are the default parameter values as specified in the function declaration. The next call to the `Add` method specifies value for the first parameter.

```
TestObject.Add(100);
```

This results in adding 100 to 200 (default value of `number2` parameter) and printing the result on the console. In the last call to the `Add` method, we specify both the parameter values.

```
TestObject.Add(50, 50);
```

This prints the sum of 50 and 50 on the user console, overriding the default values for both the parameters. The program output is shown below:

```
Using Default values for both parameters
400 + 200 = 600
Using Default value for second parameter
100 + 200 = 300
Overridding Default values for both parameters
50 + 50 = 100
```

FRIEND FUNCTIONS

We have seen that a class definition encapsulates data and the functions that operate on that data. As discussed earlier, the data is generally made private so as to avoid a direct access from outside the class definition. However, for pre-developed classes, we may like an outside function to access the private data of the class. For this purpose, C++ provides a `friend` keyword. Just the way we allow your friend to share your private data, a function that is declared as a friend of a class will be able to access the private data of the class.

In this section, we will study how to declare an external function as a `friend` in the class definition so that it can access the private data members defined within the class.

To treat an external function as a friend of a class, the function declaration must precede with the keyword `friend`. The function must be declared within the class definition to which the access is desired. The function implementation is external to the class body and does not constitute a part of class definition. The function is not treated as a member of the class. This is shown in Figure 5.1.

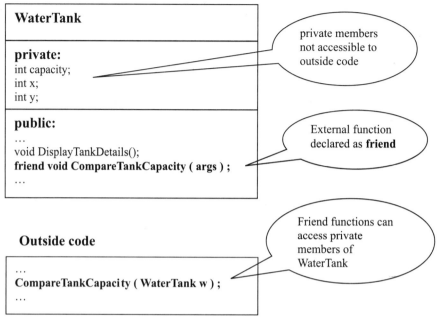

Figure 5.1 Friend functions.

We will now discuss a program example to illustrate the use of friend functions. Consider the class definition for a class called `WaterTank`:

```
class WaterTank
{
private:
    int capacity;
    int id;
```

The `WaterTank` class defines two private variables, called `capacity` and `id`. As these variables are declared private, the access to these variables is totally restricted to the methods defined in the class. The class defines a constructor (Constructors are discussed in detail in Chapter 7.) that takes two parameters and initializes these two private members while creating a `WaterTank` object.

```
WaterTank(int tankID, int tankCapacity);
```

The class also defines another method that prints the tank capacity on the user console.

```
void DisplayTankDetails();
```

We would also like to develop another method that compares the capacities of two tanks and prints the result on the user console. Obviously, such a method does not fit properly in the definition of our `WaterTank` class, since comparing its own capacity with some other tank object does not become the responsibility of a `WaterTank` object. Thus, we will develop a function external to the `WaterTank` class definition and allow it to access the private data members of our `WaterTank` class. Such a function, as it does not belong to the `WaterTank` class, must be declared as a friend of the class.

In the method declaration section of this class, we will declare a function called CompareTankCapacity.

```
friend void CompareTankCapacity
(WaterTank &tank1, WaterTank &tank2);
```

The CompareTankCapacity function takes two parameters tank1 and tank2 of type WaterTank. During a call to this function, it receives two objects of type WaterTank as input parameters. The function itself is defined outside the scope of the class definition as follows:

```
void CompareTankCapacity
(WaterTank &tank1, WaterTank &tank2)
```

Note that we do not use the scope resolution operator (: :) while defining this function. It indicates that the current function does not belong to any class definition. The function receives the two parameters of WaterTank objects by reference. In the body of the function, we will access the capacity member of the two WaterTank objects, compare them and print the result on the console indicating which tank has higher capacity. Note that the capacity member is declared with a private scope and is theoretically accessible only to class methods.

In the CompareTankCapacity method, we call the following statement to compare capacities of two tank objects.

```
if(tank1.capacity > tank2.capacity)
```

The method accesses the private member called capacity of the two input objects. This is permitted only because the function is declared as a friend of WaterTank class in the class definition.

A complete program that illustrates the use of friend function is given in Listing 55.

Listing 5.5:   Demonstration on the use of Friend function

```
// Program to demonstrate Friend function
#include "stdafx.h"
#include <iostream>
using namespace std;

class WaterTank
{
private:
    int capacity;
    int id;

public:
    WaterTank(int tankID, int tankCapacity);
    void DisplayTankDetails();
    friend void CompareTankCapacity(
            WaterTank &tank1,
            WaterTank &tank2);
};
```

```
WaterTank::WaterTank
(int tankID, int tankCapacity)
{
    id = tankID;
    capacity = tankCapacity;
}

void WaterTank::DisplayTankDetails()
{
    cout<< "Tank " << id <<" capacity is :\t"<< capacity<<endl;
}

void CompareTankCapacity
(WaterTank &tank1, WaterTank &tank2)
{
    if(tank1.capacity > tank2.capacity)
        cout<< "Tank1 has higher capacity than Tank2" << endl;
    else if (tank1.capacity == tank2.capacity)
        cout << "Both Tank1 and Tank2 has same capacity" << endl;
    else
        cout<< "Tank1 has less capacity than Tank2";
}

void main()
{

    WaterTank Tank1(1, 150);
    WaterTank Tank2(2, 100);
    cout << "Calling class member function" << endl;
    Tank1.DisplayTankDetails();
    cout << "Calling class member function" << endl;
    Tank2.DisplayTankDetails();
    // Friend function called
    cout << "Calling external friend function" << endl;
    CompareTankCapacity(Tank1, Tank2);
}
```

As discussed earlier, note that the CompareTankCapacity is declared with friend keyword within the class definition. The function is implemented outside the class body without the scope resolution operator. Note how the main function calls this friend function.

CompareTankCapacity(Tank1, Tank2);

The function is called without a reference to any object. This is because the function does not belong to any class. The function receives two object references. The function is a friend of the class of these objects and is thus allowed to access the private members of the two objects. The program output is shown below:

```
Calling class member function
Tank1 capacity is : 150
Calling class member function
Tank2 capacity is : 100
Calling external friend function
Tank1 has higher capacity than Tank2
```

Declaring a `Friend` Class

In the above example, we have considered how to declare an external function as a friend of a class. We may already have our classes developed and we may wish to access the private data members of one class directly from another class.

In the last example, we declared an external function as a friend to the class. We may even declare the entire class as a friend to some other class. In this case, the private members of the class will be accessible to the friend class. This is illustrated in Listing 5.5.

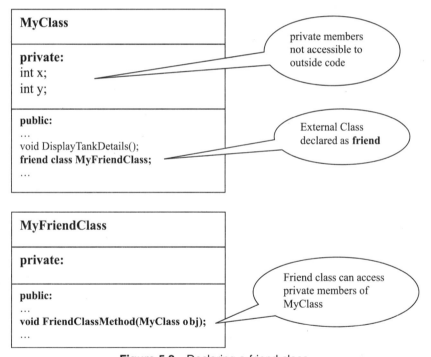

Figure 5.2 Declaring a friend class.

The program code in Listing 5.6 illustrates how to declare another class as a friend to a class. The friend class accesses the private members of the other class.

Listing 5.6: **Demonstration on the use of Friend class**

```
#include "stdafx.h"
#include <iostream>
using namespace std;
```

```
class MyClass
{
    private:
        int x;
        int y;
    public:
        MyClass()
        {
            x = 10;
            y = 20;
        }
    friend class MyFriendClass;
};

class MyFriendClass
{
    public:
        void FriendClassMethod(MyClass obj)
        {
            cout << "Accessing private members of MyClass object" << endl;
            cout << "The values of x and y are "<<obj.x<< ", " << obj.y << endl;
        }
};

void main()
{
    MyClass obj;
    MyFriendClass FriendObject;
    cout << "Invoking method on MyFriendClass" << endl;
    FriendObject.FriendClassMethod(obj);
}
```

The Listing 5.6 defines a class called MyClass that declares two private members x and y. The class declares another class as its friend.

```
        friend class MyFriendClass;
```

The members of MyFriendClass should now be able to access the private members x and y of MyClass. This is tested by writing a method called FriendClassMethod as follows:

```
        void FriendClassMethod(MyClass obj)
```

In the method body, we access the private members of MyClass object and print their values on the console.

```
        cout << "The values of x and y are" <<obj.x"<<,"
                << obj.y << endl;
```

In the main method, we create objects of two classes:

```
        MyClass obj;
        MyFriendClass FriendObject;
```

We invoke the method on `MyFriendClass` by passing an object reference to `MyClass` object.

```
FriendObject.FriendClassMethod(obj);
```

The method accesses and prints the private members of `MyClass` object on the user console. The program output is shown below:

```
Invoking method on MyFriendClass
Accessing private members of MyClass object
The values of x and y are 10, 20
```

SUMMARY

In this chapter we studied several variations of defining member methods to your class. A member function may take zero or more parameters. When we pass parameters to a method, we may choose to pass them by value. When we pass a parameter by its value, the method receives a copy of the parameter and the changes made to the parameter value within the method body remain local to the method and do not affect the value of the external variable. However, if we pass a reference to the variable as a parameter to a method, such reference variables can be used to change the value of the original external variables.

To pass a parameter by reference, we use pointer syntax. As pointer syntax is somewhat cryptic, C++ defines an alternate way of sending parameters by reference where we do not use the dereference operator that is normally used in pointers.

When a function receives a parameter by reference, it can inadvertently modify the value of the external variable using the received pointer. To avoid this, we can declare the parameter as constant using the `const` keyword in function declaration. By creating constant parameters, we ensure that the function cannot inadvertently modify the external variable using the reference parameter. Such attempts would be caught by the compiler resulting in compile-time errors.

A function definition may take several parameters. Every call to a function must specify the values for all these parameters. In some situations, some of the parameters may take the same values across several calls. To simplify the method calls in such cases, C++ allows us to define the default parameter values for any or all the parameters to a function. The default values are listed in the function declaration and not repeated while defining the function. All the default parameters must be specified at the end of the list and all other parameters that do not take default values must appear before any of the default parameters. While calling the function, the default parameters may not be specified in the call if we wish them to assume their default values. When we omit the default parameters in a method call, we cannot skip in-between default parameters while overriding the parameters listed at the end of a parameter list.

When we define a class, there could be an external method that wishes to operate on the private data members of the class; such external methods may not logically fit in the class definition and thus are not included in the class definition itself. Such methods may be declared as friend inside the class declaration to allow them access to its private members. We may even declare an entire external class as a friend. The members of the friend class will have access to the private members of the other class to which it has been declared as friend.

In the next chapter, we will study another important type of member function called overloading operator.

EXERCISES

1. What do you understand by "passing parameters to a function by value"?
2. What do you understand by "passing parameters to a function by reference"?
3. Write the syntax for member functions that take parameters by value.
4. Write the syntax for member functions that take parameters by reference.
5. Write the syntax for member functions that take parameters by reference (using the alternative method for pass by reference).
6. What do you understand by the following statements:
   (a) Passing constant parameters to a function
   (b) Setting default parameters for a function.
7. Write the syntax to define constant parameters for your class methods.
8. Write the syntax for setting default values for the method parameters.
9. What are `friend` functions and when are they used?
10. Write the syntax to define `friend` functions.
11. "When you define a `class`, there could be a method that operates on the `private` data members of the class and yet does not logically fit in the class definition." Write a program to include the details of the given statement.
12. Write a class that allows a non-member function access to the `private` members of a class. (Hint: `friend` keyword).
13. Write a program that accepts two integer values from the user. These integer values are passed to a function that calculates their squares. The program should make use of the same variables to display their calculated values.
14. The names of the arguments in the prototype, definition and call to function must be same. Prove with an example whether the given statement is true or false.
15. Write a recursive function to calculate the factorial of a number.
16. Write a function that ensures that the function cannot inadvertently modify the external variable using the pointer type parameter.
17. State whether the following statements are true or false.
    (a) A member function may take one or more parameters.
    (b) When passing parameters by value, the function receives a copy of the variable and not its address.
    (c) When passing parameters by reference, the function receives a copy of the variable and not its address.
    (d) When passing the variable by reference, we declare a pointer to the variable and pass the pointer variable as a parameter to the function.
    (e) When a function receives a parameter by reference, it can inadvertently modify the value of the external variable using the received pointer.
    (f) When we pass the parameter by its value, the method can modify the contents of the external variable.
    (g) If you pass a reference to the variable as a parameter to a method, such reference variables can be used to change the value of the original external variables.
    (h) Creating constant parameters, we ensure that the function cannot inadvertently modify the external variable.

6

Operator Overloading

In Chapter 5, we studied several variations of member method declarations for a class. We will extend our study of class methods further in this chapter by introducing methods that overload the pre-defined C++ operators.

In this chapter, we will learn the following:

- The meaning of operator overloading
- The benefits of operator overloading
- How to overload binary operators
- How to overload unary operators
- Overloading some of the complex operators such as array index operator, a function call operator, etc.

ADDING MEANING TO OPERATORS

Consider a class that defines a complex number. A complex number consists of real and imaginary parts. The arithmetic of complex numbers differs from the arithmetic of real numbers. Thus, the addition of two complex numbers cannot be represented equivalently to the arithmetic addition of two real numbers. To add two complex numbers, we would be required to write a function that probably takes two complex numbers as parameters and returns another complex number as a result. The function declaration may look like the following:

```
Complex AddComplex (Complex c1, Complex c2);
```

In the above declaration, Complex is a class that defines a complex number. A call to the above method would be as follows:

```
Complex c3 = AddComplex (c1, c2);
```

Since it is an addition of two numbers that we are representing in the above statement, the program code would be more readable if we could rewrite the above statement as:

```
Complex c3 = c1 + c2;
```

The above statement indicates clearly to the reader that we are adding two numbers c1 and c2. As the actual operation is more involved than a simple arithmetic addition between two numbers, we would be required to add more meaning to the '+' operator in the specified context. The C++ feature called *operator overloading* does this. Operator overloading allows us to override the default meaning assigned to the regular operators in a given context. We will study how to overload different kinds of operators in this chapter.

SYNTAX FOR OPERATOR OVERLOADING

The general syntax for declaring an operator overloading method is as follows:

```
return_type classname::operator# (argument-list)
{
    // operations;
}
```

Here the # sign is replaced by the operator to be overloaded and the return_type defines the return type of the method. This is best understood in a program. In the following sections, we will develop several program examples that override the default meaning of various operators.

OVERLOADING ARITHMETIC OPERATORS

First, we will consider overloading arithmetic operators such as the addition ('+') and the subtraction ('−') operators. These are binary operators; it means they require two operands.

Overloading Binary Operators

We will discuss the overloading of two binary operators, addition and subtraction operators in this section. First, we consider an addition operator.

Overloading addition operator

We will define a class called Complex to represent complex numbers. Complex numbers contain a real and an imaginary part. The class definition for our Complex class is shown as follows:

```
class Complex
{
private :
    float real,img;
public :
    Complex(float p = 0, float q = 0)
    {
        real = p;
        img = q;
    }

    // Overloading '+' operator
    Complex operator+(Complex complex);
    void dump ();
};
```

The class declares two data members, `real` and `img` to represent the real and imaginary parts of a complex number. We define a constructor (constructors are discussed in detail in Chapter 7) that receives two parameters of type float and assigns those values to the two data members of the class. Both parameters have default values of zero. So during the construction, if you do not specify the values for the two parameters, the object will be initialized with zero for both the values.

The class declares a method for overloading the + operator.

```
Complex operator+(Complex complex);
```

Note the syntax for overloading a + operator. We use the keyword `operator` and suffix it with the desired operator, in this case, it is a + operator. The method is declared to accept a single parameter. This will be the operand at the right side of the + operator during a call to this overloaded method. The other operand is implicit and appears on the left side of the overloaded + operator during a method call. After the addition operation, the method returns a complex number to the caller. Thus, in the above declaration, we specify the method return type as `Complex`. The method itself is defined outside the class body.

The class also declares another method called `dump` that dumps the contents of the two data members of the class on the console for user information.

The implementation of the overloaded + operator method is shown below:

```
// Overloading '+' operator
Complex Complex::operator+(Complex complex)
{
    Complex temp;
    temp.real = real + complex.real;
    temp.img = img + complex.img;
    return (temp);
}
```

The method receives a parameter of type `Complex` and returns another complex number to the caller. In the method body, we create a temporary variable called `temp` of `Complex` type. Next, we add the real portions of the two complex numbers.

```
temp.real = real + complex.real;
```

Note that the + operator implicitly operates on a complex number operand that appears on its left side. A call to this method would be of the following form:

```
C3 = C1 + C2;
```

When the program encounters the + operator in the above statement, it calls the overloaded method for the + operator. The method belongs to the `Complex` class and operates on complex numbers C1 and C2 in the above case. The method receives C1 implicitly, while C2 is passed as a parameter to the method as defined in the method declaration. Thus, the addition statement in the method body where we add the real portions of the two numbers translates into the following statement:

```
temp.real = this.real + complex.real;
```

Here, `this` represents the object on the left side of the operator on which the method operates. The object referred by `this` corresponds to the current object on which the operation is performed. The `complex.real` in the above statement represents the real portion of the complex number specified on the right side of the overloaded + operator. Thus, it represents the real portion of C2 in the above-mentioned statement.

Likewise, the method adds the imaginary part of the complex number on the left side of the operator to the imaginary part of the complex number on the right side of the operator.

```
temp.img = img + complex.img;
```

This statement is equivalent to the following program statement:

```
temp.img = this.img + complex.img;
```

After adding the real and imaginary parts of two operands, the method returns the complex number `temp` to the caller.

To test the overloaded function, we will write a `main` method where we first declare two complex numbers by calling the constructor for `Complex` class:

```
Complex A(10.5f,12.5f);
Complex B(8.0f,4.5f);
```

After dumping these two objects on the console, we will call our overloaded + operator to add the two complex numbers.

```
Complex C = A + B;
```

The resultant complex number is dumped on the user console to verify the addition operation. The program code in Listing 6.1 demonstrates how to overload addition operator.

Listing 6.1: Program to demonstrate overloading of addition operator

```cpp
// Program to demonstrate Operator Overloading

#include "stdafx.h"
#include <iostream>
using namespace std;

class Complex
{
private :
    float real,img;
public :
    Complex(float p = 0, float q = 0)
    {
        real = p;
        img = q;
    }

    Complex operator+(Complex complex);
    void dump ();
};

// Overloading '+' operator
Complex Complex::operator+(Complex complex)
{
    Complex temp;
    temp.real = real + complex.real;
    temp.img = img + complex.img;
    return (temp);
}

void Complex::dump ()
{
    cout<<"real: " << real << endl;
    cout<<"imaginary: "<< img <<endl;
}

void main()
{
    // create two complex numbers
    Complex A(10.5f,12.5f);
    Complex B(8.0f,4.5f);

    // print object A and B
    cout<<"Complex Number A"<<endl;
    A.dump();
    cout << endl;
    cout<<"Complex Number B"<<endl;
```

```
    B.dump();
    // add A and B, print result
    Complex C = A+B;
    cout<<endl;
    cout<<"After addition, Complex Number C = A + B: " << endl;
    C.dump();
}
```

The program declares two complex numbers, dumps them on the console, adds the two numbers using the overloaded + operator and dumps the result on the console. The program output is shown below:

```
Complex Number A
real: 10.5
imaginary: 12.5

Complex Number B
real: 8
imaginary: 4.5

After addition, Complex Number C = A + B:
real: 18.5
imaginary: 17
```

Overloading subtraction operator

Overloading subtraction operator is as straightforward as overloading addition operator. First, we declare the function prototype in the class declaration as follows:

```
    Complex operator-(Complex complex);
```

This declaration is similar to the one we used for addition operator, except that the operator sign has changed. The overloaded function takes a Complex number as an argument. This argument becomes the right-hand side operand of the subtraction operation. The left-hand side operand of the subtraction operation is passed implicitly to the function using this reference. The method returns a complex number that represents the difference between the two complex numbers.

The function implementation is similar to the implementation of the overloaded addition operator function. The function definition is shown below:

```
    // Overloading '-' operator
    Complex Complex::operator-(Complex complex)
    {
        Complex temp;
        temp.real = real - complex.real;
        temp.img = img - complex.img;
        return (temp);
    }
```

We declare a `temp` variable of type `Complex`, subtract the real and imaginary parts of the two complex numbers and return the value of `temp` to the caller. Note that the left-hand side operand for the subtraction operator is implicit as in the earlier case of addition operator.

Overloading Assignment Operators

In this section, we will discuss overloading of assignment operators. We will overload += and *= operators.

We define a `Point` class containing two private data members x and y.

```
class Point
{
private:
    int x,y;
```

We write a constructor for `Point` class that takes two default parameters and initializes the x and y variables to the corresponding parameter values.

```
Point(int xx = 0, int yy = 0)
{
    x = xx; y = yy;
}
```

We now write an overload function for the += operator to operate on our `Point` data type.

```
Point operator += (Point point)
```

The function name consists of `operator` keyword followed by the += operator. The function receives a parameter of type `Point` and returns a `Point` object to the caller.

In the function body, we add the x data members of the two objects as follows:

```
x += point.x;
```

The `point.x` refers to the object on the RHS of the operator (+=) and x refers to `this.x`, which is the x attribute of the implicit `Point` object on the LHS of the operator (+=).

Similarly, we add the y members of the two `Point` objects.

```
y += point.y;
```

We now return the object pointed by `this` reference to the caller.

```
return *this;
```

Similarly, we may overload *= operator to perform multiplication between two `Point` objects. The implementation for the *= is as given below:

```
Point operator *= (Point pt1)
{
    x *= pt1.x;
    y *= pt1.y;
    return *this;
}
```

To test our overloaded operator functions, we create two objects of `Point` class A and B in the `main` function.

```
void main()
{
    Point A(10, 20), B(30, 40);
```

We now use the *= operator to add object B to A and assign the result to B.

```
    B += A;
```

We dump the contents of B on the console for user information. Similarly, we test *= operator by using the following method call.

```
    A *= B;
```

We have assigned the result to A. We dump object A for verification.

The complete program that illustrates the overloading of += and *= operators is given in Listing 6.2.

Listing 6.2: Program to demonstrate overloading of assignment operators

```
// Program to demonstrate overloading += and *= // operators
#include "stdafx.h"
#include <iostream>
using namespace std;

class Point
{
private:
    int x,y;

public:
    Point(int xx = 0, int yy = 0)
    {
        x = xx; y = yy;
    }

    Point operator += (Point point)
    {
        x += point.x;
        y += point.y;
        return *this;
    }

    Point operator *= (Point pt1)
    {
        x *= pt1.x;
        y *= pt1.y;
        return *this;
    }
```

```
    void Dump (char *msg)
    {
        cout << msg << " ( " << x << ", " << y << " ) " << endl;
    }
};

void main()
{
    Point A(10, 20), B(30, 40);
    A.Dump ("A: ");
    B.Dump ("B: ");
    B += A;
    B.Dump ("B += A :");

    A *= B;
    A.Dump ("A *= B :");
}
```

The program output is shown below:

```
    A: ( 10, 20 )
    B: ( 30, 40 )
    B += A : ( 40, 60 )
    A *= B : ( 400, 1200 )
```

The output shows the initial values of objects A and B. After the += operator assignment, the modified value of B is displayed to the user. After this, the effect of *= operator is displayed on the console.

Now, we will consider the overloading of some of the more complex operators.

OVERLOADING COMPLEX OPERATORS

When we use arrays in our program, after declaring an array, we use an index in the array to access its elements. We need to keep track of the index value while accessing the various array elements. Also, if we have to access some array element at random, we have to first compute its index value. This makes accessing array elements more difficult. Many a time, it is easier to access an array element using a parameter other than the array index value. We will illustrate this using a program example.

Suppose that we are asked to maintain names and weights of heavy-weight-boxers in a team. We would create two arrays: one will hold the weight and the other would hold the name of the boxer. We will create an AthleteTeam class for encapsulating these two arrays. The class definition would be as shown below:

```
class AthleteTeam
{
    int weight[size];
    string name[size];
public:
    ...;
};
```

The `weight` member refers to an array of integers and the `name` member refers to an array of strings. The `string` is a pre-defined class provided in C++ class libraries.

To look up the weight of an athlete specified by his name, it would be easier to use the following syntax:

```
int weight = AthleteTeam [name];
```

For this, we will need to overload the array index operator (`[ ]`) so that the above syntax returns the weight of the athlete specified in the square brackets.

Overloading Array Index Operator

We declare the function prototype for overloading index operator in the class declaration as follows:

```
int operator[] (string name);
```

Note that in the declaration, we use the `operator` keyword and suffix it with the desired operator (in this case, it is square brackets that denote an array index).

The overloaded function takes one parameter of type `string` and returns an integer to the caller. We define the function as follows:

```
int AthleteTeam::operator [] (string nm)
{
    // implementation
}
```

In the function body, we iterate through all the elements of the array until a match for the specified name is found.

```
int index = 0;
while (index <size && name[index].compare(nm))
    index++;
```

The `string` class defines a function called `compare` that takes an argument of `string` type and compares the `string` referred by the current object and the argument `string`. The function returns `true`, if both strings are equal.

Once a match is found, we return the player's weight from the `weight` array:

```
return weight[index];
```

A call to this overloaded function would look like follows:

```
cout << "Sam's weight: ";
cout << Boxer ["Sam"] << endl << endl;
```

In the above call, `Boxer` is an object of type `AthleteTeam`. The syntax `Boxer[...]` results in calling the overloaded array index operator function defined above.

Overloaded function for array index operator

We will now overload the above index operator function to return the name of the first athlete with the weight specified as the array index. Note that this is another definition for the same function. This feature of creating two functions having different implementations is called function overloading. We will discuss function overloading in detail in Chapter 10.

The function prototype is shown below:

```
string & operator [] (int weight);
```

The compiler resolves between the two implementations with the help of the input parameter. In the earlier case, we passed `string` as an input parameter. In this case, we are inputting an `int` value to the function. The function returns a `string` by reference. The string will hold the first player's name that matches the input weight.

We define the function as follows:

```
// overloading array index operator - overloaded // function
int AthleteTeam::operator [] (string nm)
{
    // implementation
}
```

The function body is similar to the earlier function except for its return value and is shown below:

```
int index = 0;
while (index <size && name[index].compare(nm))
    index++;
return weight[index];
```

A call to the function would be as follows:

```
cout << "Boxer with weight 65: ";
cout << Boxer[65] << endl;
```

We now pass an integer value in the array index in the above statement.

Overloading Function Call Operator

We will now overload another operator, the parentheses used for a method call. Consider the following program code:

```
ClassName   object;
object (arg1, arg2, ...);
```

In the above code, we first create an `object` of type `ClassName`. On the second line, we use this object reference and pass a few parameters to it. Note that we do not call any object method explicitly (as we normally do) as shown by the following statement:

```
object.Method (arg1, arg2, ...);
```

So which object method is called in the above code? The compiler calls the overloaded method for parentheses operator (' (. . .) '). The method receives the enlisted variables as parameters. To define such a function in the current context of our `AthleteTeam`, we declare the following function in the class declaration:

```
void operator() (
    int index,
    string name,
    int weight);
```

The above statement declares that we are overloading the parentheses operator. The function call itself takes three parameters as listed above. We will use this function call to initialize the data members of our `AthleteTeam`. We define the function as follows:

```
// overloading function call (parantheses)
// operator
void AthleteTeam::operator () (int index, string nm, int wt)
{
    ...;
}
```

The first parameter specifies the index in `name` and `weight` arrays. The second parameter specifies the name value and the third parameter specifies the weight. These two parameter values will be stored in the two arrays at the specified index.

In the function body, we set the two array elements using the following program code:

```
name[index] = nm;
weight[index] = wt;
```

This initializes the element of our `AthleteTeam` at the specified index value. A call to this function could be as follows:

```
Boxer (0, "Sachin", 65);
```

The first parameter in the above call specifies the index value for the two arrays. The second parameter specifies the string to be copied in the `name` array and the third parameter specifies the weight value to be copied in the `weight` array. The above call results in setting the `name[0]` element to a value "Sachin" and the `weight[0]` element to value 65.

The program code in Listing 6.3 that defines and uses the above `AthleteTeam` class.

Listing 6.3: Program to demonstrate overloading of some advanced operators

```
// Operator overloading
#include "stdafx.h"

#include <string>
#include <iostream>
```

```
using namespace std;
const size=5;

class AthleteTeam
{
    int weight[size];
    string name[size];
public:
    int operator [] (string name);
    string & operator [] (int weight);
    void operator() (int index, string name, int weight);
};

// overloading function call (parantheses)
// operator
void AthleteTeam::operator () (int index, string nm, int wt)
{
    name[index] = nm;
    weight[index] = wt;
}

// overloading array index operator
string & AthleteTeam::operator [] (int wt)
{
    for (int i=0; i<size; i++)
        if (weight[i] == wt)
            break;
    return name[i];
}

// overloading array index operator - overloaded
// function
int AthleteTeam::operator [] (string nm)
{
    int index = 0;
    while (index <size && name[index].compare (nm))
        index++;
    return weight[index];
}

void main()
{
    AthleteTeam Boxer;
    Boxer (0, "Sachin", 65);
    Boxer (1, "Saurav", 75);
    Boxer (2, "Shashank", 50);
    Boxer (3, "Sam", 80);
    Boxer (4, "Ashok", 55);
```

```
    cout << "Sam's weight: ";
    cout << Boxer ["Sam"] << endl << endl;
    cout << "Comparing two boxers: " << endl;
    if (Boxer ["Saurav"] > Boxer["Ashok"])
    cout << "Saurav weighs more than Ashok" << endl << endl;
    cout << "Boxer with weight 65: ";
    cout << Boxer[65] << endl;
}
```

The program illustrates how to overload the index array operator and the parentheses operator. The program provides two versions for overloaded index array operator method.

The program output is shown below:

```
Sam's weight: 80

Comparing two boxers:
Saurav weighs more than Ashok

Boxer with weight 65: Sachin
```

Overloading Typecast Operator

When you assign an int variable to float type, the compiler does an implicit typecast of an integer number to a floating-point number before assignment. If we assign a float number to an int, we will have to provide an explicit typecast as follows:

```
    float f = 5.4;
    int i = (int) f;
```

What if we have two user-defined data types and we want to assign a variable of one data type to another? We will need to define a typecast from one user-defined data type to another and vice-versa.

We will now develop a program that declares two user-defined data types and provides typecast from one type to another using an overloaded typecast operator method.

We declare FloatNumber class as follows:

```
    class FloatNumber
    {
        float f;
```

The FloatNumber class declares one private data member of type float. The class constructor accepts a default parameter and initializes the value of data member f to the specified parameter value, if one is supplied.

```
    FloatNumber (float x=0)
    {
        f=x;
    }
```

If an object of this `FloatNumber` is to be assigned to an `int` variable, we will need to typecast from `FloatNumber` type to `int` type. We overload the `typecast` operator as follows:

```
operator int()
{
    return (int)f;
}
```

We declare the overloaded function with the `operator` keyword followed by the data type to which conversion is desired.

```
operator int()
```

In this case, we want to convert to `int` data type. Thus, in the above declaration we write `int` following the `operator` keyword. This is followed by opening and closing parentheses indicating that we are defining a function.

The function body is written as usual to any other function. In the function implementation, we read the current value of the data member `f`, typecast it explicitly to `int` and return it to the caller.

Note that though the overloaded function uses a return statement, we have not declared the return type for the function.

When we overload the `typecast` operator, the overloaded function should not declare any return type, including `void` return type.

To call this function on an object variable `fn` of type `FloatNumber`, we will use the following syntax:

```
int n = (int) fn;
```

If we omit (`int`) in the above declaration, it is still valid, as the compiler will implicitly call the overloaded typecast function defined above. Thus, the following statement is valid.

```
int n = fn;
```

We also develop a `Dump` function to dump the object contents on the console for the user information.

Next, we will develop another class that stores an integer number.

```
class IntNumber
{
    int i;
```

The class `IntNumber` declares one private variable of type `int`. We provide a class constructor as follows:

```
IntNumber (int x=0)
{
    i=x;
}
```

Now, we will define an overloaded `typecast` operator to convert `IntNumber` to `FloatNumber`. The function definition is shown below:

```
operator FloatNumber()
{
    return FloatNumber ((float)i);
}
```

Again, we use the `operator` keyword followed by the data type to which conversion is desired. This is followed by parentheses indicating that this is a function call. The function body constructs a `FloatNumber` object and returns it to the caller. Once again, the function declaration does not have any return type specified as in the earlier case.

To understand how to call this overloaded `typecast` function, consider that you have an object fn of type `FloatNumber` and object in of type `IntNumber`. The following statement provides conversion from one data type to another:

```
fn = (FloatNumber) in;
```

Like in the earlier case, if we omit the (`FloatNumber`) typecast, the compiler will implicitly call the above overloaded function. Thus, the following statement is legal and provides the same result as the above statement:

```
fn = in;
```

The full program that employs the above type conversion techniques is given in Listing 6.4.

Listing 6.4:   Program to demonstrate overloading of `typecast` operator

```
#include "stdafx.h"
#include <iostream>
using namespace std;

class FloatNumber
{
    float f;
public:
    FloatNumber (float x=0)
    {
        f=x;
    }
    operator int()
    {
        return (int)f;
    }
    void Dump()
    {
        cout << "FloatNumber = " << fixed << f << endl;
    }
};

class IntNumber
{
    int i;
```

```
public:
    IntNumber (int x=0)
    {
        i=x;
    }
    operator FloatNumber()
    {
        return FloatNumber ((float)i);
    }
    void Dump()
    {
        cout << "IntNumber = " << i << endl;
    }
};

void main()
{
    cout << "Creating FloatNumber with value 5.4" << endl;
    float f = (float)5.4;
    FloatNumber fn(f);
    fn.Dump();
    cout << endl;
    int x = fn;
    cout << "After Implicit typecast of Float Number to int" << endl;
    cout << "int value = " << x << endl;
    cout << endl;

    cout << "Creating IntNumber with value 56" << endl;
    IntNumber in(56);
    in.Dump();
    cout << endl;
    fn = in;
    cout << "After implicit typecast of Int Number to FloatNumber" << endl;
    fn.Dump();
}
```

When we run the above code, we will see the following output:

```
Creating FloatNumber with value 5.4
FloatNumber = 5.400000

After Implicit typecast of FloatNumber to int
int value = 5

Creating IntNumber with value 56
IntNumber = 56

After implicit typecast of IntNumber to FloatNumber
FloatNumber = 56.000000
```

As seen from the output, the program first constructs a `FloatNumber` object. This is assigned to an `int` variable and the result is printed on the console. Next, it creates an `IntNumber` object and assigns it to a `FloatNumber` variable. The initialized `FloatNumber` object is then dumped on the console. In both the cases, we use implicit typecast.

WHAT CANNOT BE OVERLOADED?

As seen from the several examples in this chapter, C++ allows us to overload most of the operators. However, there are some exceptions. The following operators cannot be overloaded.

- The scope resolution operator (' : : ')
- The pointer to member operator (' . * ')
- The ternary operator(' ? : ')
- The dot operator (' . ')
- The `sizeof` operator

SUMMARY

In this chapter, we studied how to create class methods that allow we to override the usual meanings assigned to regular operators. This is called operator overloading. Using operating overloading, one can change the typical meanings assigned to the regular operators (except for some operators). The use of overloaded operators increase the program readability. When you add two complex numbers, the addition involves more operations than adding two real numbers. However, the syntax: complex number1 + complex number2, is more readable to the user than calling an `AddComplex` function that takes two complex operands as parameters.

We studied how to overload binary operators and also some of the complex operators such as array index operator, parentheses operator, typecast operator, etc. C++ allows us to overload most of the operators, except for some. The scope resolution operator (' : : '), pointer to member operator (' . * '), ternary operator(' ? : '), the dot operator (' . ') and the `sizeof` operator cannot be overloaded.

EXERCISES

1. What do you understand by operator overloading? Explain the need for operator overloading.
2. Write a class to represent complex numbers and overload addition and subtraction operators for a created complex data type.
3. Write method signatures for overloading the following operators: +, −, and * operators.
4. Write method signatures for overloading following operators: [], (), and `typecast` operators.
5. Write a `Distance` class that contains a data member representing the distance between two points. Overload +, == and > operators to add, equate and verify the two objects of `Distance` class.

6. Create a class to represent an integer. Overload the unary operators ++, -- to perform increment and decrement operations on the objects of this class.

7. Write a class to represent a character string. Overload the == operator to compare two objects of this class for equality.

8. Use the character string class from the above example and write an overloaded function for += operator to concatenate two string objects of the above type.

9. For the string class of Exercise 7, overload the ++ operator to change a string from lower case to upper case.

10. Write a program to store a player's name and the runs scored by him in a match. These two data members must be stored in an array. Overload the [] operator to access the runs scored by a player by having name as the input type.

11. Write a TollCollector class. The class keeps track of the total toll collected. Implement prefix increment operator (overloaded function) for this class that increments the toll count when a toll is collected from a truck driver.

12. Write a Car class that implements the prefix and post-fix increment and decrement operators to change its gears.

13. State whether the following statements are true or false:
    (a) An operator is overloaded by declaring a function using the overload keyword.
    (b) For an overloaded addition operator method, the method parameter represents the operand on the right hand side of the addition operator.
    (c) For an overloaded multiplication operator method, the operand on the left hand side of multiplication side is implicitly passed to the method.
    (d) When we overload the typecast operator, the overloaded function should not declare any return type, including void return type.
    (e) Operator overloading is defined as a concept to create new C++ operators.
    (f) We need to define only one argument while overloading binary operators.
    (g) We will get a compilation error when we overload the * operator to perform addition operation.
    (h) The output of the overloaded += operator is assigned to the left-hand side object.

7

Constructors and Destructors

In Chapter 4, we studied how to declare and define a class. In Chapter 5, we learned various types of methods that may be defined for a class and in Chapter 6, we learned a different kind of class methods which are used for overloading operators. In this chapter, we will look at another type of class methods that are called during class instantiation and object destruction.

A class acts as a template based on which the objects are created. We learned how to instantiate the class and create objects for the use of an application program. Each object receives its own memory allocation and all the objects are stored in locations independent of other objects. The objects may be created at compile time or at runtime.

Whenever an object is created, the runtime calls a certain method in the class definition. This method is called class `Constructor`. Similarly, when the object is destroyed, the runtime calls the `Destructor` defined in the class. In this chapter, we will learn the following:

- Defining a class constructor
- Defining multiple constructors for a class
- Calling a desired parameterized constructor during instantiation
- Defining constructors with default parameter values
- Understanding ambiguities in calling constructors with default parameter values
- Proper ordering of default parameter list
- Understanding default constructor provided by compiler
- Creating a copy constructor
- Understanding class destructors.

We will begin by defining a simple constructor for a class.

DEFINING CONSTRUCTOR

A class method having the name same as the class name is called the *class constructor*.

The class constructor is invoked during the object creation process. Thus, when we use the `new` keyword for creating an instance of the class, the class constructor is called. But as seen in the examples in the previous chapters, we did not declare any constructor in those class definitions. If we do not provide a constructor, the compiler provides a constructor of its own. This is called the *default constructor*. The default constructor is a no-argument constructor.

We provide a constructor of our own by writing a class method with the name same as the class name. We may pass zero or any number of parameters to this constructor. The only restriction that applies to the constructor definition is that the constructor will have no return type.

The general syntax for constructor is as follows:

```
class classname
{
public:
    classname(); // constructor
    classname(argument list); //another constructor
    ...
}
```

Here are some of the key points to remember while defining a class constructor.

- The constructor has the same name as that of the class.
- A constructor does not have a return type, not even a void return type.
- A constructor may or may not take arguments.
- You may declare more than one constructor in a class definition.
- If we do not provide a constructor of our own, the compiler provides a no-argument default constructor.
- If we write any constructor (with zero or more arguments), the compiler does not provide the default no-argument constructor.

The runtime calls the constructor during the object creation process. The constructor is typically used for initializing the class variables at the time of object creation. However, it may be used additionally for allocating the resources required by the objects of the class during their lifespan.

The program code in Listing 7.1 shows the declaration for a class `Point` containing a user-defined constructor.

Listing 7.1:   Class constructors

```
#include "stdafx.h"
#include <iostream>

using namespace std;

class Point
{
public:
    int x, y;
```

```
public:
    Point()
    {
        x=0;
        y=0;
        cout << "Constructor called\n";
    };
};
void main()
{
    Point p1;
    cout << "Point p1(" << p1.x << "," << p1.y << ")" << endl;
    Point *p2 = new Point();
    cout << "Point p2(" << p2->x <<"," << p2->y << ")" << endl;
}
```

The Point class declares two data members, x and y. We will initialize these variables during object creation time. Thus, we write a constructor for the class.

The following statement declares a class constructor:

```
    Point()
```

Note that the above method declaration does not return anything, not even the void type. The constructor does not take any arguments. The body of the class constructor initializes the two data members to zero.

```
    x=0;
    y=0;
```

We also print a message on the user console so that we will know whenever the runtime calls the constructor.

```
    cout << "Constructor called\n";
```

To test the above class definition, we write a main method. In the main method, we first create an object of Point class by declaring a variable of type Point.

```
    Point p1;
```

During the object creation process, the runtime calls our constructor. The constructor initializes the two variables x and y and prints a message on the user console. The output statement retrieves the values of x and y variables of Point object p1 and prints them on the user console.

```
    cout << "Point p1(" << p1.x <<", "<< p1.y << ")"  << endl;
```

Next, the program creates another Point object using the new keyword:

```
    Point *p2 = new Point();
```

Once again during the object creation process, the runtime calls our constructor. This initializes the two data members of the Point class and prints a message on the user console. The reference to the created object is assigned to the variable p2 of type pointer to Point class. The member initialization is verified by executing the following program statement:

```
    cout << "Point p2(" << p2->x << "," << p2->y << ")" << endl;
```

This prints the values of x and y variables of Point object p2 on the user console. When we run the above code, we will see the following messages on the console.

```
Constructor called
Point p1(0,0)
Constructor called
Point p2(0,0)
```

Note that each time the object is created, the message: Constructor called is printed on the console. The constructor initializes both members of the class to zero. The member values for each constructed object are printed on the user console as shown above.

Having seen how to write a single constructor, we will now proceed with writing multiple constructors for the same class. Why do we need multiple constructors for a class? Whenever we create objects of a given class, we may like to provide different initialization for each created object. The initialization values are passed as parameters to the constructor. This necessitates the declaration of multiple constructors having different parameters list.

MULTIPLE CONSTRUCTORS

As mentioned above, we may declare multiple constructors for a class. While creating an object, we may decide to use any one of these constructors. More than one constructor facilitates the customization of the created object. A constructor provides a way of controlling the object initialization process. Each constructor follows the rules defined earlier for constructor declaration. Multiple constructors will vary in their argument lists. This is equivalent to function overloading (function overloading is discussed in detail in Chapter 10). Thus, when we have multiple constructors declared within a class, we say that we have overloaded constructors for the class. None of the constructor declarations should have a return type.

The program code in Listing 7.2 illustrates how to define multiple constructors for a class and how to call the desired constructor while instantiating the class.

Listing 7.2: Multiple constructors in a class

```
#include "stdafx.h"
#include <iostream>

using namespace std;

class Point
{
public:
    int x, y;
public:
    Point()
    {
        x=0;
        y=0;
        cout << "Constructor with zero arguments called\n";
    };
```

```
    Point (int x1)
    {
        x = x1;
        y = 0;
        cout << "Constuctor with one argument called\n";
    };
    Point (int x1, int y1)
    {
        x = x1;
        y = y1;
        cout << "Constuctor with two arguments called\n";
    };
};

void main()
{
    Point p1;
    cout << "Point p1(" << p1.x << "," << p1.y << ")" << endl;

    Point p2(5);
    cout << "Point p2(" << p2.x << "," << p2.y << ")" << endl;

    Point p3(10,10);
    cout << "Point p3(" << p3.x << "," << p3.y << ")" << endl;
}
```

The above class definition for `Point` class declares two data members and three constructors. The first constructor, as in the case of our earlier example does not take any arguments, and initializes both data members to zero. The constructor prints an appropriate message on the user console.

```
        Point()
        {
            x=0;
            y=0;
            cout << "Constructor with zero arguments called\n";
        };
```

The second constructor takes a parameter of integer type.

```
        Point (int x1)
```

In the constructor body, we use this parameter to initialize the x data member of the class.

```
        x = x1;
```

The y data member of the class is initialized to zero as in the earlier case.

```
        y = 0;
```

A message is printed on the user console to indicate that a constructor with a single argument is called.

```
        cout << "Constuctor with one argument called\n";
```

The last constructor in our example takes two arguments:

```
Point (int x1, int y1)
```

The two parameters x1, y1 are used for initializing the x and y data members respectively of the Point class:

```
x = x1;
y = y1;
```

A message is printed on the user console to indicate that a two-parameter constructor is being called:

```
cout << "Constuctor with two arguments called\n";
```

Our next task is to invoke an appropriate constructor during object creation time. How do we decide which constructor to call? This is simple; we simply pass appropriate arguments to a call to a constructor. This is illustrated in the main method of the above program example. In the main method, first we declare a variable p1 of type Point.

```
Point p1;
```

As no parameters are specified after p1 variable declaration, this results in calling the no-argument constructor initializing both x, y variables to value zero.

The second declaration in the main method passes an integer value of 5 to the variable declaration as shown below:

```
Point p2(5);
```

Note the syntax used. We enclose the parameter list in parentheses drawn after the variable name as if a method is being called. As only one parameter is passed, this calls the constructor that takes a single argument. The single argument constructor initializes the x data member to the value of the received parameter and y to the value, zero. The constructor also prints an appropriate message on the console indicating the type of constructor being called.

The third variable declaration in the main method passes two parameters.

```
Point p3(10,10);
```

During the creation of p3 object, the third constructor in our class that takes two parameters will be called. This constructor initializes the x and y members of the class to the two respective parameters received via variable declaration in the program. Thus, in this case, both the data members will be initialized to the value 10. As in the earlier case, the constructor prints an appropriate message on the user console.

When we compile and run the above code, we will see the following output on the console.

```
Constructor with zero arguments called
Point p1(0,0)
Constuctor with one argument called
Point p2(5,0)
Constuctor with two arguments called
Point p3(10,10)
```

Note the messages printed on the console as different constructors are being called. After constructing the object, the object values are immediately printed on the console to verify that each object is indeed initialized as per our expectations.

USING PARAMETERIZED CONSTRUCTORS IN DYNAMIC OBJECTS

Calling a desired parameterized constructor while constructing an object dynamically is as simple as calling the appropriate constructor at the time of static object creation. The desired list of parameters is enclosed in parentheses following the `Point` declaration. For example, the following statement calls the no-argument constructor of the `Point` class and prints the values of data members on the user console for verification.

```
Point *p1 = new Point();
cout << "Point p1(" << p1->x << "," << p1->y << ")" << endl;
```

The following program statement calls a single argument constructor thereby initializing x to 5 and y to 0.

```
Point *p2 = new Point(5);
```

The following statement calls the two argument constructor initializing both x and y to 10.

```
Point *p3 = new Point(10,10);
```

CONSTRUCTORS WITH DEFAULT ARGUMENTS

As seen in Chapter 5, C++ allows us to set default values to the function parameters. We may use such default arguments while defining our class constructor. The example below defines a two-argument constructor that uses a default value for the second parameter if it is not supplied in the constructor call.

The full program that demonstrates the use of default argument constructors is given in Listing 7.3.

Listing 7.3: Default argument constructors

```
#include "stdafx.h"
#include <iostream>

using namespace std;

class Point
{
public:
    int x, y;
public:
    Point (int x1, int y1=0)
    {
        x = x1;
```

```
        y = y1;
        cout << "Constuctor with two arguments called\n";
    };
};

void main()
{
    cout << "Calling Point Constructor" << endl;
    cout << "Overriding default parameter" << endl;
    Point *p1 = new Point(10,10);
    cout << "Point p1(" << p1->x << "," << p1->y << ")"
        << endl << endl;

    // Calling constructor by using default argument value
    cout << "Calling Point Constructor" << endl;
    cout << "Using default parameter" << endl;
    Point *p2 = new Point(10);
    cout << "Point p2(" << p2->x << "," << p2->y << ")" << endl;
}
```

The preceding program defines a constructor with two parameters; the second parameter being a default parameter.

The following statement of the program defines a two-argument constructor that uses a default value for its second argument.

```
        Point (int x1, int y1=0)
```

If the call to this constructor supplies values for both the parameters, these will be used in the constructor body for initializing the appropriate class variables. The following call to the constructor supplies both the values.

```
        Point *p1 = new Point(10,10);
```

If a call to the constructor does not supply the second argument, the program will use a default value of zero for the second argument. The following call uses a default value for the second parameter. Thus, x data member is initialized to 10 and the y data member is initialized to zero.

```
        Point *p2 = new Point(10);
```

When we compile and run the above program, we will see the following output:

```
        Calling Point Constructor
        Overriding default parameter
        Constuctor with two arguments called
        Point p1(10,10)

        Calling Point Constructor
        Using default parameter
        Constuctor with two arguments called
        Point p2(10,0)
```

Default Argument Ambiguities

When we define overloaded methods in our program code, a call to such method may be ambiguous under certain situations. Consider a case where we define the following constructors for the `Point` class:

```
Point (int x1)
{
    x = x1;
    cout << "Single Argument Constructor called\ n";
};
Point (int x1, int y1=0)
{
    x = x1;
    y = y1;
    cout << "Constructor with two arguments called\n";
};
```

The definition of both these constructors is technically and syntactically valid. However, consider the following call for instantiating the `Point` class:

```
Point *p = new Point(10);
```

In this case, which constructor would the compiler use: a single argument or a two-argument constructor? As the method call specifies a single parameter, the compiler could use the first constructor, that is, a single-argument constructor. However, the compiler could also use the second constructor in this case by taking the default value for the second parameter as 0. Obviously, this call is ambiguous and the compiler will flag an error during compilation as shown below:

```
C:\TC\BIN>cl test.cpp
Microsoft (R) 32-bit C/C++ Optimizing Compiler Version 12.00.8168 for
80x86
Copyright (C) Microsoft Corp 1984-1998. All rights reserved.

test.cpp
test.cpp(28) : error C2668: 'Point::Point' : ambiguous call to overloaded
function
```

Thus, if we decide to declare constructors having default parameters, we will have to ensure that we do not create ambiguous calls while instantiating the class.

Ordering Default Parameter List

When we create default parameters for our constructor, the parameter order is important, as discussed under the heading "Default Parameter Order" in Chapter 5. Just as in the case of a normal method that takes the default parameters, the default parameters must always appear at the end of the parameter list. For example, the following declaration would result in a compile time error:

```
Point (int x1=0, int y1)
```

The error reported by the compiler is shown below:

```
C:\TC\BIN>cl test.cpp
Microsoft (R) 32-bit C/C++ Optimizing Compiler Version 12.00.8168 for
80x86
Copyright (C) Microsoft Corp 1984-1998. All rights reserved.

test.cpp
test.cpp(8) : error C2548: 'Point::Point' : missing default parameter for
parameter 2
```

All the parameters that take default values must appear towards the end of the parameter list.

DEFAULT CONSTRUCTOR

As mentioned earlier, the compiler supplies a default no-argument constructor. However, this is not the case if we declare any constructor in our class definition. Let us look at the following class declaration:

```
class Point
{
public:
    int x, y;
public:
    Point (int x1, int y1)
    {
        x = x1;
        y = y1;
        cout << "Constructor with two arguments called\n";
    };

};
```

The class declares a single constructor that takes two arguments. If we make the following call in our program code assuming that the compiler would supply a no-argument constructor of its own, it results in a compile time error.

```
Point p = new Point();
```

The error reported by the compiler is shown below:

```
test.cpp
test.cpp(20) : error C2512: 'Point' : no appropriate default constructor
available
```

Though we have not defined a no-argument constructor in the program code, the compiler does not supply its own no-argument constructor since we have defined at least one constructor ourself. Thus, if we write our own constructor, whether no-argument or the one that takes arguments, the compiler will not supply its own default constructor.

COPY CONSTRUCTOR

At certain times, we may wish to create a copy of an existing object. For this purpose, we may create a constructor in our class definition that takes the object to be copied as an argument. The definition of such a *copy constructor* is shown below:

```
Point (Point &p)
{
    x = p.x;
    y = p.y;
    cout << "Copy Constructor called\n";
};
```

The constructor takes a single argument, that is, a reference to the object of Point class. The data members of the passed object are explicitly copied in the respective data members of the new Point object.

The program code in Listing 7.4 illustrates how to define and use a copy constructor.

Listing 7.4: Copy constructor demonstration program

```
#include "stdafx.h"
#include <iostream>

using namespace std;

class Point
{
public:
    int x, y;
public:
    Point (int x1, int y1)
    {
        x = x1;
        y = y1;
        cout << "Constructor called\n";
    };
    Point (Point &p)
    {
        x = p.x;
        y = p.y;
        cout << "Copy Constructor called\n";
    };
};

void main()
{
    Point p1(5,5);
    cout << "Point p1(" << p1.x << "," << p1.y << ")" << endl;
    Point p2(p1);
    cout << "Point p2(" << p2.x << "," << p2.y << ")" << endl;
```

```
        // Testing for two objects
        cout << "Setting data members of two objects\n";
        p1.x = 10; p1.y = 10;
        p2.x = 20; p2.y = 20;
        cout << "Point p1(" << p1.x << "," << p1.y << ")" << endl;
        cout << "Point p2(" << p2.x << "," << p2.y << ")" << endl;
}
```

The Point class declares two constructors, a two-argument constructor as in the earlier example and a copy constructor discussed in Listing 7.4. In the main method, we first create an object p1 that sets both the data members of the Point object to the value 5. The program prints these values on the user console for verifications.

```
        Point p1(5,5);
        cout << "Point p1(" << p1.x << "," << p1.y << ")" << endl;
```

The following statement uses a copy constructor to construct object p2 of type Point.

```
        Point p2(p1);
```

The newly created object p2 will have its data members aligned to the data members of the p1 object that is passed as an argument to the copy constructor. We verify this by printing the data member values on the console.

```
        cout << "Point p2(" << p2.x << "," << p2.y << ")" << endl;
```

Next, we will like to verify that the program has created two independent objects. For this, we set the individual data members of the two objects to different values and dump the two objects on the console. This is done using the following code fragment.

```
        cout << "Setting data members of two objects\n";
        p1.x = 10; p1.y = 10;
        p2.x = 20; p2.y = 20;
        cout << "Point p1(" << p1.x << "," << p1.y << ")" << endl;
        cout << "Point p2(" << p2.x << "," << p2.y << ")" << endl;
```

When we compile and run the above program, we will see the following output:

```
        Constructor called
        Point p1(5,5)
        Copy Constructor called
        Point p2(5,5)
        Setting data members of two objects
        Point p1(10,10)
        Point p2(20,20)
```

The output clearly shows the calls made to two different constructors. After setting data members of the two objects, the two objects are dumped on the console. The values held by the two objects are clearly seen to be different, confirming the presence of two independent objects.

Beware of object references

In the earlier example, the two objects were created and the references to these objects were stored in variables p1 and p2. Now, consider using pointer type variables for storing object references. Look at the following declarations:

```
Point *p1 = new Point(5,5);
Point *p2 = p1;
```

The first statement creates an object of Point class with both its data members initialized to 5. The object reference is assigned to pointer variable p1. The next statement may be mistakenly seen to create another object of Point class using copy constructor and assign it to pointer variable p2. However, what really happens in this case is that, the newly declared pointer variable p2 receives the contents of pointer variable p1. It means, the reference to the object that p1 is pointing to is copied into p2. Thus, both variables p1 and p2 refer to the same object and the second statement creates no new object. This may be easily verified by assigning different values to the data members by using reference p1 first and then reference p2. This is shown in the code fragment below:

```
// Testing for two objects
cout << "Setting data members of two objects\n";
p1->x = 10; p1->y = 10;
p2->x = 20; p2->y = 20;
cout << "Point p1(" << p1->x << "," << p1->y << ")" << endl;
cout << "Point p2(" << p2->x << "," << p2->y << ")" << endl;
```

If we execute the above code fragment by inserting it into the earlier program code, we will get the following output:

```
Setting data members of two objects
Point p1(20,20)
Point p2(20,20)
```

This clearly indicates that both variables p1 and p2 refer to the same object. The modifications made using p2 variable affect our original Point object.

Having considered the various aspects of defining and invoking constructors, we will now study the class destructor.

CLASS DESTRUCTOR

As mentioned earlier, a class constructor is typically used for initializing the object state during its creation. Additionally, it may be used for allocating the resources required by the object during its life span. Such resources should be cleaned up before the object is destroyed and removed from the system. C++ provides a method called Destructor for this purpose.

Destructor Syntax

A class destructor is defined as follows:

```
~classname( )
{
    // implementation
}
```

The following rules apply while defining a class destructor:

- A destructor is a class method having the same name as the class name and is prefixed with a tilde (~) character.
- Destructor does not take any arguments.
- Destructor does not return anything, not even the `void` data type.
- We cannot write more than one destructor for a class.

Whenever an object is destroyed, the runtime calls the destructor if one is defined.

The program code in Listing 7.5 illustrates how to define a class destructor and how the runtime calls destructor at object deletion time.

Listing 7.5:   Class destructors

```
#include "stdafx.h"
#include <iostream>

using namespace std;

class Point
{
public:
    int x, y;
public:
    Point (int x1, int y1)
    {
        x = x1;
        y = y1;
        cout << "Constructor called\n";
    };
    ~Point()
    {
        cout << "Destructor called\n";
    }
};

void main()
{
    Point p1(5,5);
    cout << "Point p1(" << p1.x << "," << p1.y << ")" << endl;
}
```

The class `Point` defines two data members `x` and `y` as in the case of earlier examples. The class defines a constructor that takes two arguments and uses them to initialize the two data members.

```
Point (int x1, int y1)
```

The constructor prints an appropriate message on the console whenever it is called.
The class defines a destructor as follows:

```
~Point()
```

In the destructor implementation, we simply print a message on the user console indicating that it is being called.

```
cout << "Destructor called\n";
```

In the `main` method, we create an instance of `Point` class.

```
Point p1(5,5);
```

This results in calling our class constructor and printing an appropriate message on the console indicating that the constructor has been called. We dump the object contents on the console for the user's information.

```
cout << "Point p1(" << p1.x << "," << p1.y << ")" << endl;
```

After this, we close the body of the `main` method. This causes the variable `p1` to go out-of-scope, resulting in the destruction of object `p1`. The object destruction results in calling our destructor. When the destructor is called, it should print an appropriate message on the console indicating to the user that it is being called.

If we compile and run the above program, we will see the following output:

```
Constructor called
Point p1(5,5)
Destructor called
```

Note that we do not call the destructor explicitly anywhere in our program code. The runtime calls our destructor whenever it destroys the object of that type. The runtime calls our destructor before it destroys the object.

Cleaning Up Resources

The destructor is typically used for cleaning up the resources allocated during the object creation. The program code in Listing 7.6 illustrates how to free the resources allocated in the class constructor, during the object destruction.

Listing 7.6:   Freeing object resources

```
#include "stdafx.h"
#include <iostream>

using namespace std;
```

```
class Point
{
public:
      int x, y;
      char *ptr;
public:
      Point (int x1, int y1)
      {
          x = x1;
          y = y1;
          cout << "Constructor called" << endl;
          cout << "Allocating 100 bytes ..." << endl;
          ptr = new char[100];
      };
      ~Point()
      {
          cout << "Destructor called" << endl;
          cout << "Freeing resources ..." << endl;
          delete ptr;
      }
};

void main()
{
      Point p1(5,5);
      cout << "Point p1(" << p1.x << "," << p1.y << ")" << endl;
}
```

Listing 7.6 is similar to the one discussed in the previous section. In this example, we allocate a byte array in the class constructor.

```
cout << "Allocating 100 bytes ..." << endl;
ptr = new char[100];
```

As the array is created dynamically, the runtime will not free this resource whenever our `Point` object is destroyed. We need to de-allocate the memory explicitly in our destructor. We do so by calling the `delete` operator in our class destructor as follows:

```
cout << "Freeing resources ..." << endl;
delete ptr;
```

This results in freeing the memory allocated for the byte array. When we compile and run the above code, we will see the following output:

```
Constructor called
Allocating 100 bytes ...
Point p1(5,5)
Destructor called
Freeing resources ...
```

Note that we do not call the destructor explicitly. The runtime calls our destructor during object destruction.

If we do not delete the resources dynamically allocated in the class constructor, it results in memory leaks (refer to 0 for a description of memory leaks).

SUMMARY

In this chapter, we studied another important type of class methods, called constructors and destructors.

A class constructor is a class method having the name same as the class name. The constructor does not have a return type. A constructor may take zero or more parameters. If we do not supply a constructor, the compiler provides a no-argument default constructor. It is important to note that if we write our own constructor, the compiler does not provide the default constructor. A class may define more than one constructor. We decide which constructor to call during object creation by passing an appropriate parameter list to the constructor. We may set the default values for the constructor parameters. If we set the default parameter values, the ambiguities in constructor call should be resolved. All the default parameters should appear at the end of the parameter list.

A class destructor is a class method having the same name as the class name and prefixed with tilde (~) character. The destructor does not return anything and does not accept any arguments. A class definition may contain one and only one destructor. The runtime calls the destructor, if available, during the object destruction. A destructor is typically used for freeing the resources allocated in the class constructor.

EXERCISES

1. Describe a constructor and its use.
2. Describe a destructor and its use.
3. What is the difference between a constructor and a destructor?
4. What do you understand by overloaded constructors? Give an example.
5. What do you understand by copy constructor?
6. Write the syntax for constructor and destructor of a class.
7. What do you understand by the statement "defining constructor with default parameter values"?
8. Write the correct syntax for defining constructor with default parameter values.
9. What are the ambiguities involved in calling constructors with default parameter values?
10. What do you understand by defining multiple constructors? What is the use of defining multiple constructors?
11. Assume a class `Vehicle`. Define the class constructor and destructor. The parameters for the constructor should be `VehicleNo(int)`, `VehicleColor(string)`, `VehicleType(int)`.
12. Write an `Employee` class with overloaded constructors that take different input parameters. The parameters can be `EmployeeNo`, `Name`, `Designation`, and `Department`.

13. Write a class and a main function to show the order in which the constructor and destructors are invoked.

14. Write a `Base` class with one parameterized constructor and a `Derive` class constructor that passes a parameter to the `Base` class constructor.

15. Write a base class `Location` with members (`int x`, `int y`, `int getX()`, `int getY()`). Write the constructor for `Location` to initialize the two data members.

16. A class may define more than one constructor. How do you make a call to each of the constructors? Write the suitable class and the constructors and also write the appropriate code to call the different constructors.

17. Choose the correct answer(s):
    (a) When you instantiate an object, the runtime calls a particular method in the class definition—this is called:
        (i) A constructor   (ii) A method
        (iii) Inheritance   (iv) Destructor
    (b) Which of the following is invoked during the object creation process?
        (i) Constructor   (ii) Method
        (iii) Virtual Method   (iv) Overloaded function
    (c) If you do not provide a constructor, the compiler provides a:
        (i) Default constructor with appropriate number of parameters
        (ii) Constructor with default arguments
        (iii) Overloaded constructor
        (iv) Default constructor with no-arguments
    (d) Which of the following statements are true in case of constructors?
        (i) Constructor name is the same as the class name
        (ii) Constructor does have a `void` return type.
        (iii) Constructor may or may not take arguments
        (iv) It is not valid to declare more than one constructor in a class definition.

18. State whether the following statements are true or false:
    (a) When an object goes out of scope, its destructor gets called automatically.
    (b) Constructor and the destructor must be invoked explicitly.
    (c) In a class, we can define more than one constructor with same name.
    (d) We can define a return type for a class constructor.
    (e) A copy constructor is executed when one object is assigned to another.

8

Inheritance

After covering the basic C++ syntax in Chapter 2 we were introduced to object-oriented programming in Chapter 4, where we talked about defining classes. We covered one of the important features, namely encapsulation of object oriented-programming in Chapter 4. Another important feature of object-oriented programming is inheritance. In this chapter, we will discuss inheritance.

We will learn the following in this chapter:

- What is inheritance?
- Single inheritance
- The protected access modifier.
- Creating multiple level inheritance
- The use of protected, public, and private access modifiers in case of multiple level inheritance.
- Constructor/destructor calling sequence during sub-class object creation.
- How to pass parameters to a superclass constructor?

WHAT IS INHERITANCE?

One of the main characteristics of an object-oriented language is *inheritance*. In nature, we observe that children inherit several characteristics from their parents. Similarly, in object-oriented programming, if we wish to inherit the functionality of an existing class, we define a new class based on an existing class. The existing class whose functionality is inherited is called the *base class* and the new class that inherits the functionality is called a *derived class*. The base class acts like a *parent* and the derived class becomes its *child*.

To illustrate inheritance with an example, consider that we need to represent several types of vehicles in our software. To define a family of four-wheel vehicles, we may create a class called Automobile. In this class we would define the functionality for a four-wheel vehicle that is common to all. We may now derive additional classes from the Automobile class such as Car, Truck or a Van. These additional classes would inherit the common functionality defined in Automobile car. In addition, these classes would define functionality that is unique to each one of them.

The important advantage of inheritance is the reusability of the code. Once a base class is defined and fully tested its functionality can be reused in a derived class.

We will now learn about the various aspects of the inheritance.

SINGLE INHERITANCE

Consider the following definition for a Point class.

```
class Point
{
    int x, y;
public:
    void setx (int x1)
    {
        x = x1;
    }
    int getx ()
    {
        return x;
    }
    void sety (int y1)
    {
        y = y1;
    }
    int gety ()
    {
        return y;
    }
};
```

The Point class defines two private data members x and y representing the x, y coordinates of a point. We also define get/set public methods to modify/access these data members. Suppose, we wish to add some more functionality to this Point class by adding a color value to this point object. To do so, we will need to modify the class definition and add one more data member to the class that represents the color value for the given point. We will also need to add get/set methods to access this member. It is generally recommended not to touch a tested code as the code modifications may result in the introduction of bugs. Now, how do we extend the functionality of our tested robust `Point` class to add the color attribute to the point? We use inheritance to achieve this. We define a new class called `ColorPoint` that inherits from `Point` class.

The scheme of (single) inheritance is illustrated in Figure 8.1.

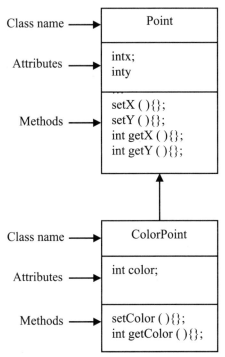

Figure 8.1 Single inheritance.

The definition of `ColorPoint` class is given below:

```
class ColorPoint:public Point
{
    int color;
public:
    void setColor (int clr)
    {
        color = clr;
    }
    int getColor ()
    {
        return color;
    }
};
```

Note the declaration statement for the `ColorPoint` class:

```
Class ColorPoint:public Point
```

The colon (`':'`) indicates that our new class `ColorPoint` will inherit from the class specified on the right-hand side of the colon. When a class inherits from some other class, it will derive the functionality of the base class as if it were its own functionality. Thus, the `ColorPoint` class will exhibit the `get`/`set` methods for access/modification of x, y attributes as if those are defined for the `ColorPoint` class itself. The general syntax for inheritance is discussed later.

In addition to the inherited functionality, we will add more functionality of its own to `ColorPoint` class. In the body of the `ColorPoint` class, we declare a variable called `color` to represent the color attribute for our point object. We define `get`/`set` methods to access this color attribute.

We will now write a `main` function to test our classes. (The complete program listing follows this discussion.)

```
void main ()
{
    Point p;
```

In the `main` function, first we create an object of `Point` class. We call set methods of the `Point` class to set the values of x and y members.

```
p.setx(10);
p.sety(10);
```

We print the current values of x, y on the user console by calling the `get` methods of the `Point` class:

```
cout << "Point p:(" << p.getx() << "," << p.gety () <<")" << endl;
```

We now declare a variable of class `ColorPoint`:

```
ColorPoint clrPt;
```

As the `ColorPoint` class inherits from `Point` class, it will have access to the public methods of the `Point` class. (We are using public modifier here; we will study different access modifiers later.) We now use the inherited methods to set the x, y coordinates of the `ColorPoint` object.

```
clrPt.setx(20);
clrPt.sety(20);
```

Note that we have not defined `setx`, `sety` methods in the `ColorPoint` class. These are the methods of the `Point` class that the `ColorPoint` class has inherited. We now set the color value for our point by calling the `setColor` method of the `ColorPoint` class.

```
clrPt.setColor(0);
```

We will print the x, y coordinates by calling the inherited get methods:

```
cout << "ColorPoint p:(" << clrPt.getx() << ","
        << clrPt.gety() << ")" << endl;
```

The get methods are not defined in the ColorPoint class and are inherited from the base class Point. To print the color value, we call the getColor method of the ColorPoint class.

```
cout << "ColorPoint color: " << clrPt.getColor() << endl;
```

The complete program that implements the above-discussed single inheritance is given in Listing 8.1:

Listing 8.1:   Program to illustrate single inheritance

```
#include "stdafx.h"
#include <iostream>

using namespace std;

class Point
{
    int x, y;
public:
    void setx (int x1)
    {
        x = x1;
    }
    int getx ()
    {
        return x;
    }
    void sety (int y1)
    {
        y = y1;
    }
    int gety ()
    {
        return y;
    }
};

class ColorPoint:public Point
{
    int color;
public:
    void setColor (int clr)
    {
        color = clr;
    }
```

```cpp
        int getColor ()
        {
            return color;
        }
};

void main ()
{
    cout << "Creating Base Class object ..." << endl;
    Point p;
    cout << "Calling class methods ..." << endl;
    p.setx(10);
    p.sety(10);
    cout << "Point p:(" << p.getx() << "," << p.gety() <<")" << endl << endl;
    cout << "Creating sub-class object ..." << endl;
    ColorPoint clrPt;
    cout << "Calling base class methods ..." << endl;
    clrPt.setx(20);
    clrPt.sety(20);
    cout << "Calling class method ..." << endl;
    clrPt.setColor(255);
    cout << "Calling base class methods ..." << endl;
    cout << "ColorPoint p:(" << clrPt.getx() << ","   << clrPt.gety() <<")" << endl;
    cout << "Calling class method ..." << endl;
    cout << "ColorPoint color: " << clrPt .getColor() << endl;
}
```

The program output is shown below:

```
Creating Base Class object ...
Calling class methods ...
Point p:(10,10)

Creating sub-class object ...
Calling base class methods ...
Calling class method ...
Calling base class methods ...
ColorPoint p:(20,20)
Calling class method ...
ColorPoint color: 255
```

Note how the sub-class object of type `ColorPoint` calls the base class methods.

ACCESS MODIFIERS

So far, we have seen two types of access modifiers—`public` and `private`. The public and private access modifiers control the visibility of the class members. Now, we will study one more access modifier called `protected`. The `protected` modifier also controls the visibility of the class members, however, it becomes meaningful only when we use inheritance.

If a class member is declared using `public` access modifier, it is accessible to any program code defined inside the class, defined in an inherited class or defined outside the class. In case of `private` access modifiers, such members will be visible only within the current class definition. When we create a class hierarchy by inheritance, we will like to make certain members of the base class accessible to all its children, yet make them inaccessible to any code that is defined outside this hierarchy of classes. This is achieved by using the `protected` keyword.

The above discussion is summarized in Table 8.1.

Table 8.1   Variable visibility for different access specifiers

Access specifiers	Same class	Derived class	Outside code
Public	✓	✓	✓
Private	✓	✗	✗
Protected	✓	✓	✗

Protected Modifier

Consider the following class declaration:

```
class A
{
private:
    int x, y;
protected:
    void setx (int x1);
    int getx ();
public:
    void sety (int y1);
    int gety ();
};
```

The preceding class definition contains three sections—`private`, `protected` and `public`. The two data members x, y are declared in the `private` section and thus will be accessible only to the code within the class definition. The `setx` and `getx` methods are defined with `protected` scope and `sety`, `gety` are defined with `public` scope. We will derive a class from this base class A to understand the `protected` scope. Let us create a class B that inherits from class A using following declaration:

```
class B:public A
```

The object of class B will have access to public methods of class A. Thus, the following method calls are valid:

```
B ObjectB;
ObjectB.sety (20);
int y = ObjectB.gety();
```

What if we call the protected method using the above object reference? The following calls would be illegal:

```
ObjectB.setx (20); // illegal call
int x = ObjectB.getx();// illegal call
```

As both methods `setx`, `getx` are declared using `protected` access modifier in the base class, these are not visible outside the class hierarchy, i.e. outside the base class and its subclasses. So, how does the outside code use this method? For this, we will write a public method in the subclass B that internally calls the protected method of class A. The method definition is shown below:

```
class B:public A
{
// rest of the class code
public:
    int getXCoordinate()
    {
        return getx();
    }
// rest of the class code
};
```

We define a new method called `getXCoordinate` in our subclass B. The implementation of this method calls the protected `getx` method of the base class A. The method `getx` is surely visible in class B as class B publicly inherits from class A. The outside program code can now obtain the value of x-coordinate by using the following program code:

```
B ObjectB;
int x = ObjectB.getXCoordinate();
cout << x << endl;
```

A protected class member is visible to the defining class and its immediate subclasses.

The functionality of the protected modifier is shown in Figure 8.2. The figure shows the valid and the invalid calls made from class B on the members of class A.

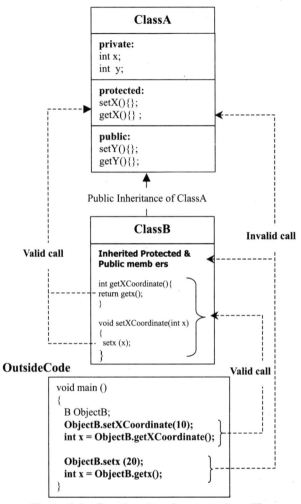

Figure 8.2 Functionality of protected modifier.

The complete program for the above-discussed code is given in Listing 8.2:

Listing 8.2: Demonstration on the use of protected access modifier

```
#include "stdafx.h"
#include <iostream>

using namespace std;

class A
{
     int x, y;
protected:
     void setx (int x1)
```

```
    {
        x = x1;
    }
    int getx ()
    {
        return x;
    }
public:
    void sety (int y1);
    int gety ();
};

class B:public A
{
public:
    int getXCoordinate()
    {
        return getx();
    }
    void setXCoordinate(int x)
    {
        setx (x);
    }
};

void main ()
{
    cout << "Creating subclass object" << endl;
    B ObjectB;
    cout << "Calling protected setx method indirectly" << endl;
    ObjectB.setXCoordinate(10);
    cout << "Calling protected getx method indirectly" << endl;
    int x = ObjectB.getXCoordinate();
    cout << "x = " << x << endl;
}
```

The class Point declares two protected methods getx and setx. These methods will be visible within class B that publicly inherits from class A. However, these methods are not visible to the objects of class B. Thus, in class B, we have added two more public methods getXCoordinate and setXCoordinate that indirectly access the protected methods of class A.

When we compile and run the above code, we will see the following output:

```
Creating subclass object
Calling protected setx method indirectly
Calling protected getx method indirectly
x = 10
```

We will now study the general syntax of class inheritance and the visibility of the base class members to the subclasses under various situations.

MULTIPLE LEVEL INHERITANCE

It is possible to extend the functionality of a derived class by deriving further classes from it. This is known as *multiple level inheritance*. Consider the class declaration as follows:

```
class A
{
private:
    int x, y;
public:
    void setx (int x1);
    int getx ();
    void sety (int y1);
    int gety ();
};
```

We now derive class B from class A using the following declaration:

```
class B:public A
{
    // class implementation code
};
```

We further derive class C from class B as follows:

```
class C:public B
{
    // class implementation code
};
```

In the above examples we have multiple levels of inheritance. Now, let us study the effect of base class member visibility to its subclasses.

Class A defines two `private` data members x and y. As discussed earlier, these will be visible only to the code defined in class A and not to the subclasses of class A. Thus, these variables cannot be accessed directly by the code defined in class B or class C. The members are also obviously invisible to any code outside the class A definition.

Class A defines four `public` methods, getx, setx, gety and sety. All these methods will be visible to the code defined in class B or class C. Also, these methods will be visible to the code defined outside any of the above classes.

Figure 8.3 depicts multiple level of inheritance.

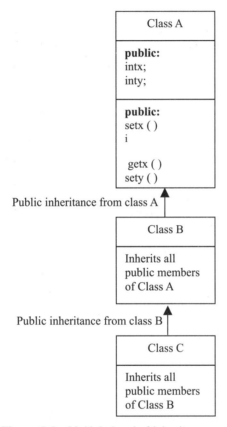

Figure 8.3   Multiple level of inheritance.

Protected Access

Now, what happens if we define some of the members of class A as `protected`? Let us consider that we declare getx method as `protected` rather than `public`. We will study the visibility of getx method to the code defined outside class A.

```
protected:
      int getx ();
```

The method is visible to any code in class B or class C. Thus, if class B contains a method definition as follows, it can use getx method of class A.

```
class B:public A
{
// rest of the class implementation
public:
    void ClassBMethod (int x1)
    {
        int x = getx();
    }
// rest of the class implementation
};
```

Similarly, a method implementation in class C too can use getx method of class A.

```
class C:public B
{
// rest of the class implementation
public:
    void ClassCMethod (int x1)
    {
        int x = getx();
    }
// rest of the class implementation
};
```

Now, what if we declare a main method that creates an object of class B or class C and uses this object reference to invoke getx method of class A. As the method is declared protected, the method would not be accessible to an object of subclass. The following code fragment illustrates this:

```
void main ()
{
    C ObjectC;
    ObjectC.setx(20);        // this is legal as setx
                             // is public
    int x = ObjectC.getx();  // this will not compile as
                             // getx is protected
}
```

The preceding discussion is summarily represented in Figure 8.4.

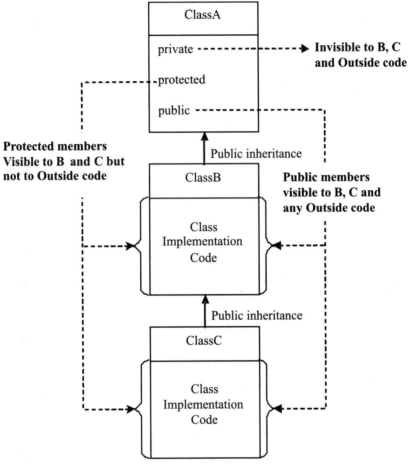

Figure 8.4 Protected access.

The complete program for the above-discussed code is given in Listing 8.3.

Listing 8.3:   Further demonstration on protected access modifier

```
#include "stdafx.h"
#include <iostream>

using namespace std;

class A
{
private:
    int x, y;
protected:
    int getx ()
```

```
        {
            return x;
        }
public:
        void setx (int x1)
        {
            x = x1;
        }
};

class B:public A
{
public:
        void ClassBMethod (int x1)
        {
            int x = getx();
        }
};

class C:public B
{
public:
        void ClassCMethod (int x1)
        {
            int x = getx();
        }
};

void main ()
{
        C ObjectC;
        ObjectC.setx(20);
        // this will not compile
        // int x = ObjectC.getx();
        // cout << x << endl;
}
```

Note that ObjectC of type class C has access to inherited setx method as this is declared public in the base class. However, ObjectC does not have an access to getx method that is declared protected in the base class.

If we un-comment the following program statement,

```
    //  int x = ObjectC.getx(); // this will not compile
```

and try to compile the program, we will get a compilation error as follows:

```
    error C2248: 'getx' : cannot access protected member declared in class 'A'
```

PUBLIC/NON-PUBLIC DERIVATIONS

So far, all our class derivations were public. We will first study the general syntax of inheritance and then look up the effect of non-public derivations.

General Syntax of Class Inheritance

The general syntax of class inheritance is shown below:

```
class classname: AccessModifier baseclassname
```

The `classname` specifies the name for the derived class. The `baseclassname` specifies the name of the base class and the `AccessModifier` defines the mode of access for the base class members by the derived class.

We will now study different types of inheritance.

TYPES OF INHERITANCE

When we inherit from an existing class, we derive the functionality of the class from which we inherit. However, we may decide not to pass on the privileges we have gained to our subclasses. Accordingly, we may decide on the type of inheritance while inheriting from an existing class. The three types of inheritance are:

- Public
- Private
- Protected

In the following sections, we will study these three types of inheritance.

Public Inheritance

Consider the following class definition:

```
class A
{
private:
    int x, y;
public:
    void setx (int x1);
    int getx ();
    void sety (int y1);
    int gety ();
};
```

The class A defines two data members `x` and `y`. These two data members have `private` scope by default. However, to make it explicit, these have been defined under the `private` section of the class. Thus, these two members would be accessible only to methods of the current class.

We now derive a class based on the above class A as follows:

```
class B:public A
```

The class B above inherits from class A using `public` access modifier. Now, let us study what is inherited. The class B would inherit all the `public` methods of class A. If we create an object of class B, we would be able to apply the `setx`, `getx`, `sety` and `gety` methods on this object. The following statements are valid:

```
B ObjectB;
ObjectB.getx();
ObjectB.sety();
```

However, the following statement would be invalid:

```
ObjectB.x = 10; // invalid
```

This is invalid because the object of a derived class is trying to access the `private` member of the base class. Similarly, trying to access the data member y of the `Point` class through the reference of a derived class object would be invalid. Thus, the following statement is invalid too:

```
int y = ObjectB.y; // invalid
```

Whatever applies to the `private` data members also applies to the `private` methods of the base class. In the `Point` class, if we define say `getx` method as `private` to the `Point` class by declaring it in `private` section, the method would not be accessible to the derived class object.

The scheme of public inheritance is shown in Figure 8.5.

In public inheritance, the derived class has access to all the public methods and the data members of the base class. The derived class cannot access the private methods and data members of the base class.

Private Inheritance

Considering the class definition for class A as given in the previous section, we will now derive class B from class A as follows:

```
class B:private A
```

Note that we have used `private` access modifier in place of `public` modifier in our class derivation. When we inherit using `private` keyword, all the `protected` and `public` members of the base class will become `private` to the derived class. Thus, the code in derived class will be able to access these members. The following method definition is valid:

```
class B:private A
{
// rest of the class implementation
```

```
public:
    void ClassBMethod ()
    {
        int x = getx();
    }
// rest of the class implementation
};
```

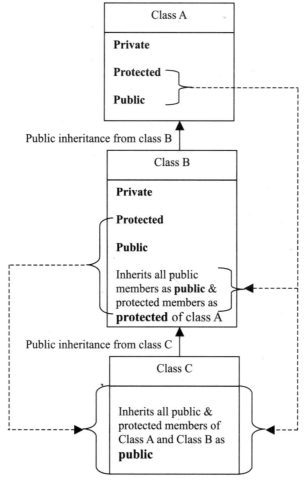

Figure 8.5   Public inheritance.

Figure 8.6 schematically represents private inheritance.

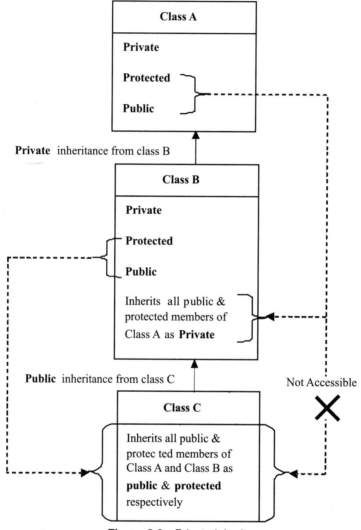

Figure 8.6 Private inheritance.

Note that the derived class cannot pass these inherited members to further derived classes. Let us consider the following derivation:

```
class C:public B
```

Here class C publicly inherits from class B as shown in Figure 8.6.

Thus, all the protected and public members of class B would be visible in class C and private members of class B will not be accessible to class C. If we now define a method in class C that tries to use getx method, it would be illegal access as shown in the code further:

```
class C:public B
{
public:
    void ClassCMethod ()
    {
        int x = getx(); // illegal access
    }
};
```

If we try to compile the above class definition, the compiler will throw an error similar to the one shown below:

```
error C2247: 'getx' not accessible because 'B' uses 'private' to inherit from 'A'
```

Note that the actual error message may vary depending on the compiler we use.

Protected Inheritance

In the above derivation of class B, what would happen if we use `protected` modifier in case of `private` modifier? The declaration is given below:

```
class B:protected A
```

The class B inherits all the `public` and `protected` methods of class A and treats them as `protected` within its own definition. This is represented in Figure 8.7.

The public `getx` method defined in class A now becomes `protected` in class B. This has significance while accessing the `getx` method from a code that is defined outside the subclasses of class B. If we define `main` method as follows, the call to `getx` method would be illegal.

```
void main ()
{
    B ObjectB;
    int x = ObjectB.getx(); // does not compile
}
```

However, if we derive another class from class B as shown in the above diagram, the `getx` method would be visible within the definition of the newly derived class. The following class derivation is valid:

```
class C:public B
{
public:
    void ClassCMethod ()
    {
        int x = getx(); // this is valid
    }
};
```

Having studied multiple level inheritance`and the effect of different access modifiers, we may now study how the class constructors and destructors are called during the creation and destruction of a subclass object.

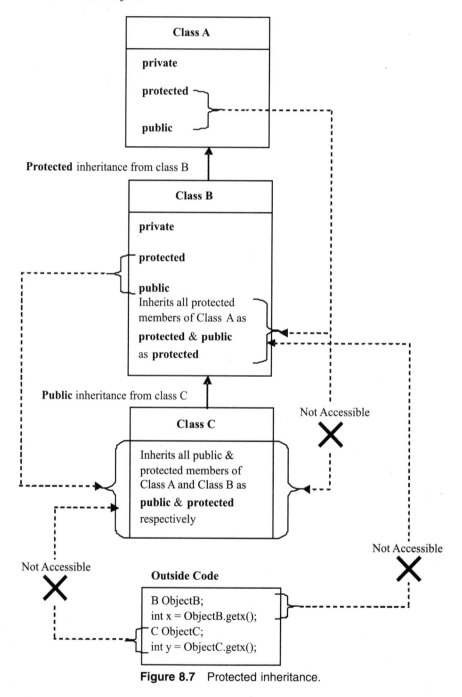

Figure 8.7 Protected inheritance.

CALLING SEQUENCE FOR CONSTRUCTORS AND DESTRUCTORS

Whenever we create an object of a derived class, the runtime creates an object of its immediate super class and all its super classes up the hierarchy up to the object of the base class. Thus, if class A is the base class and class B derives from A, class C derives from B, and class D derives from C, whenever we create an object of class D, the program will create objects of class C, class B and class A. During the object creation process, the respective class constructors are called. We will study the order of calling the class constructors and destructors during object creation.

Consider the following definition for our base class:

```
class BaseClass
{
public:
    BaseClass()
    {
        cout << "BaseClass constructor called " << endl;
    }
    ~BaseClass()
    {
        cout << "BaseClass destructor called " << endl;
    }
};
```

The `BaseClass` defines a no-argument constructor and a destructor. Both methods print a message on the user console whenever they are called.

We now derive a class from this base class and write constructor and destructor as follows:

```
class FirstChild : public BaseClass
{
public:
    FirstChild()
    {
        cout << "FirstChild constructor called " << endl;
    }
    ~FirstChild()
    {
        cout << "FirstChild destructor called " << endl;
    }
};
```

The child class constructor and destructor both print a message on the user console whenever they are called.

As the child class inherits from the base class, whenever we create an object of child class, the runtime first creates an object of base class. Similarly, whenever the object of child class is destroyed, the runtime destroys the child object first and then the base class object. To test this, we write a main method and create an object of child class as follows:

```
void main()
{
    FirstChild firstChild;
}
```

If we run this program, we will get the following output on the console:

```
BaseClass constructor called
FirstChild constructor called
FirstChild destructor called
BaseClass destructor called
```

Note that the base class constructor is called first followed by the subclass constructor. Thus, the runtime creates an object of base class first and then creates an object of child class on top of it. Similarly, during the subclass object destruction process, the destructor for the child class gets called before the destructor for the base class.

The class hierarchy may now be extended further by deriving another class from class B. Such a declaration is shown below:

```
class SecondChild : public FirstChild
{
    public:
    SecondChild()
    {
        cout << "SecondChild constructor called " << endl;
    }
    ~SecondChild()
    {
        cout << "SecondChild destructor called " << endl;
    }
};
```

Now, if we create an object of SecondChild class, the runtime will first construct the object of the base class, followed by the object of the FirstChild class and finally the object of the SecondChild class.

Similarly, whenever the program destroys the object of SecondChild class, the destructor for SecondChild class is called first, followed by the destructor of the FirstChild class and finally the destructor for base class. This is easily verified using the following main function.

```
void main()
{
    SecondChild secondChild;
}
```

When we run the above main program, we will see the following output on the console:

```
BaseClass constructor called
FirstChild constructor called
SecondChild constructor called
SecondChild destructor called
FirstChild destructor called
BaseClass destructor called
```

The complete program for the above-discussed code is given in Listing 8.4 for ease of quick reference.

Listing 8.4:   Constructor and destructor calling sequence demonstration

```
#include "stdafx.h"
#include <iostream>

using namespace std;

class BaseClass
{
public:
    BaseClass()
    {
        cout << "BaseClass constructor called " << endl;
    }
    ~BaseClass()
    {
        cout << "BaseClass destructor called " << endl;
    }
};

class FirstChild : public BaseClass
{
public:
    FirstChild()
    {
        cout << "FirstChild constructor called " << endl;
    }
    ~FirstChild()
    {
        cout << "FirstChild destructor called " << endl;
    }
};

class SecondChild : public FirstChild
{
    public:
    SecondChild()
```

```
    {
        cout << "SecondChild constructor called " << endl;
    }
    ~SecondChild()
    {
        cout << "SecondChild destructor called " << endl;
    }
};

void main()
{
    cout << "Creating First Child ..." << endl << endl;
    {
        FirstChild firstChild;
    }
    cout << endl << "Creating Second child ..." << endl << endl;
    {
        SecondChild secondChild;
    }
}
```

Note that we create the `FirstChild` object within the braces to define the lifespan for the object.

```
    {
        FirstChild firstChild;
    }
```

At the closing brace, the `FirstChild` object goes out-of-scope resulting in its destruction by the runtime. During the destruction process, the various destructors are called as seen in the program output below. Also, the `SecondChild` object is created within the braces to control its lifespan.

The program output is shown below:

```
Creating First Child ...

BaseClass constructor called
FirstChild constructor called
FirstChild destructor called
BaseClass destructor called

Creating Second child ...

BaseClass constructor called
FirstChild constructor called
SecondChild constructor called
SecondChild destructor called
FirstChild destructor called
BaseClass destructor called
```

Parameter Passing to Superclass Constructors

We have seen the order in which constructors and destructors are called during the creation of a subclass object. We will now study how to pass the parameters to the superclass constructors during the object creation process. Consider the following class definition:

```
class A
{
    int a;
public:
    A(int a1)
    {
        a = a1;
    }
    void dumpA ()
    {
        cout << "A: " << a << endl;
    }
};
```

Class A defines one `private` member of type integer. This class defines a constructor that takes a single parameter of type integer and initializes the data member a using the received parameter. The utility method `dumpA` prints the value of the data member on the user console.

We will now derive a class from class A as follows:

```
class B :   public A
{
    int b;
```

We have also declared a `private` data member called b of type integer in the class definition. We will now write the class constructor. Note that the class constructor will automatically call the constructor of its superclass, that is, of class A. The class A constructor requires a parameter of type integer. Now, how do we declare a constructor for class B? The declaration should be as follows:

```
    B(int a1):A(a1)
```

The class constructor receives one parameter of type integer and passes its value to its super class constructor. If class B requires another parameter to initialize its data member, we will modify the constructor declaration as follows:

```
    B(int b1, int a1):A(a1)
```

Here, the first parameter b1 may be used for initializing the data member of class B and the second parameter, as before, is passed on to the constructor of class A.

The complete constructor for class B may now take the following form:

```
    B(int b1, int a1):A(a1)
    {
        b = b1;
    }
```

The parameter b1 is used for initializing the data member b. The parameter a1 is passed to the constructor of class A.

The complete program illustrating the parameter passing to the superclass constructors is given in Listing 8.5.

Listing 8.5:   Passing parameters to superclass constructor

```cpp
#include "stdafx.h"
#include <iostream>

using namespace std;

class A
{
    int a;
public:
    A(int a1)
    {
        a = a1;
    }
    void dumpA ()
    {
        cout << "Dumping object A" << endl;
        cout << "a = " << a << endl;
    }
};

class B : public A
{
    int b;
public:
    B(int b1, int a1):A(a1)
    {
        b = b1;
    }
    void dumpB()
    {
        dumpA();
        cout << "Dumping object B" << endl;
        cout << "b = " << b << endl;
    }
};

void main()
{
    cout << "Creating subclass object B" << endl;
    B ObjectB (5, 3);
    ObjectB.dumpB();
}
```

Note that we pass two parameters to the constructor of class B.

```
B ObjectB (5, 3);
```

The first parameter initializes the data member of class B to 5. The above call implicitly calls constructor for class A by passing the parameter value 3 to its constructor. The data member of class A is initialized to this parameter value of 3.

When we run the program, we will see the following output:

```
Creating subclass object B
Dumping object A
a = 3
Dumping object B
b = 5
```

SUMMARY

In this chapter we studied an important feature of object-oriented programming, namely, inheritance. Inheritance helps in preserving our investment in code. We extend the functionality of an existing class by deriving a new class that inherits from the existing class. We looked at single inheritance whereby we derive a class from a base class. The derived class had an access to all the public members of the base class, while the access to the private members of the base class was not permitted.

In addition to the `public` and `private` access modifiers, we discussed another access modifier called `protected` modifier. The `protected` modifier restricts the visibility of class members to its subclasses and the code defined outside the class hierarchy cannot access protected members.

We can create a class hierarchy by further subclassing down the line of subclasses. This is called multiple level inheritance. We create multiple levels of class hierarchy. A protected member of a base class will be visible across the entire class hierarchy making it accessible to the lowest subclass in the hierarchy.

When we derive a class from an existing base class, we can further control the base class member visibility within the derived class and the further derived classes by using an appropriate access modifier during class derivation. A class may derive using any one of the three access modifiers—`public`, `private` or `protected`. In case of public modifiers, all the inherited members of the base class will be treated as public members of the inherited class. In case of private derivation, all the inherited members of the base class will be treated as private members of the inherited class, preventing the access to such members by further derived classes. In a class of protected derivation, the inherited base class members are treated as protected members of the derived class, thereby allowing only the further subclasses to access these members while not allowing the objects of further subclasses to access these members.

When a subclass object is created, all its superclass objects are created. During the construction process, the runtime first creates an object of base class, and then its immediate subclass, followed by its immediate subclass and so on till the desired subclass object in the hierarchy is created. During the construction of the subclass object, the runtime calls the constructors for all the created objects in the order starting from the base class to the desired subclass in the order specified in the class hierarchy. Similarly, when the derived class object is destroyed, the runtime calls the destructors starting from the current object that is being destroyed, up the class hierarchy up to the base class.

A superclass constructor may require few parameters. Such parameters should be listed in the constructor definition of the subclass and the subclass should pass such parameters to its superclass in its class derivation statement.

In the next chapter, we will further deal with inheritance. We will discuss *multiple inheritance*. This is different from multiple level inheritance discussed in this chapter.

EXERCISES

1. What do you understand by class inheritance?
2. Describe the different types of inheritance.
3. Describe multiple level inheritance.
4. Define and describe the inheritance syntax.
5. Explain the use of `public`, `private`, `protected` access modifiers in inheritance.
6. Explain the calling sequence for constructor and destructor when we instantitate a subclass.
7. Design an application for a publication company. Create a class called `Publication` that stores the `Book_Title(string)`, `Book_Price(float)`. From this class, derive two classes `Book` that stores `page_count (int)` and `Tape` that stores `playing_duration (int)` in minutes. Each of these classes have `getData()` method to get the data from the user and `displayData()` to display data to the user. Write a main function to test the `Book` and `Tape` classes by creating instances of them. Ask the user to enter data using the `getData` method and then display the same back to the user.
8. Write a derived class constructor that takes one argument and passes this argument along to the constructor in the base class.
9. When we derive a class from a single base class, the phenomenon is called:
   (a) Hierarchical inheritance
   (b) Single inheritance
   (c) Multiple inheritance
   (d) Multiple level inheritance
10. "A protected member of a base class will be visible across the entire class hierarchy making it accessible to the lowest subclass in the hierarchy". Under what category of inheritance will this condition be applicable? Write the appropriate classes depicting the point described in the given statement.
11. Write a base class `Location` with members (`int x, int y, int getX(), int getY()`). Derive a class called `Point` from `Location` with members (`boolean Visible, void Show(), void Hide(), boolean isVisible(), void MoveTo (int newX, int newY)`).

12. Using the `Point` class above, derive a new class `Circle` with members (`int radius,` `void Expand (int ExpandBy)`). Write the appropriate constructor for `Circle` to initialize the derived members and the radius. Make a call to the base class constructor to initialize its variables.

13. Design and develop a Railway Traffic control system where `Train` is the base class for `PassengerTrain` and `GoodsTrain`. `ControlTower` notifies each train when to stop at a signal or start its journey.

14. Try to structure `Furniture`, `Chair` and `Table` classes in an inheritance hierarchy.

15. Modify the code in Exercise 14 to include constructors and verify the calling sequence of the constructors when we create objects of these classes.

16. State whether the following statements are true or false:

    (a) A class must inherit from only one base class.

    (b) A derived class inherits all the members of the base class.

    (c) A derived class can access `private` data members of its base class.

    (d) Base class members may be overridden by declaring a member in the derived class with the same name.

    (e) The derived classes do not inherit base class constructors and destructors.

    (f) During the subclass object creation, the base class constructor is invoked before the derived class constructor.

    (g) When a class uses `public` inheritance to derive from another class, the `protected` members of the base class become `public` in the derived class.

    (h) In case of `public` inheritance, the `private` members of a base class are inherited as `private` members in a subclass.

    (i) When we subclass, we must recompile the base class.

9

Multiple Inheritance

In Chapter 8, we studied single inheritance. Inheritance is a very important feature of object-oriented programming and helps us preserve our investments in code. We also covered the various aspects of single inheritance. In this chapter, we will continue our study of inheritance by discussing multiple inheritance. More specifically, we will learn the following in the context of multiple inheritance:

- What is multiple inheritance?
- How different class constructors are called during subclass object creation.
- The sequence of calling destructors during the destruction of subclass object.
- Passing parameters to superclass constructors.
- Effect of access modifiers.

MULTIPLE INHERITANCE—AN ILLUSTRATION

After few years of code development, we may possess a good collection of classes that we will like to use in our current projects. Obviously, we will create new classes, which will inherit the functionality of existing classes. We have seen single inheritance, which involves creating classes derived from one base class. What if we have two well-developed, well-tested classes from which we will like to derive a new class? Our new class should inherit the functionality of two existing classes. This is achieved with the help of the C++ feature called *multiple inheritance*.

Consider the following declarations for the two base classes:

```
class RootA
{
    //implementation
};

class RootB
{
    //implementation
};
```

To create a new class that derives from the above two base classes, we use the following declaration:

```
class Child : public RootA, public RootB
{
    //implementation
};
```

The Child class will inherit from both the base classes RootA and RootB as shown in Figure 9.1.

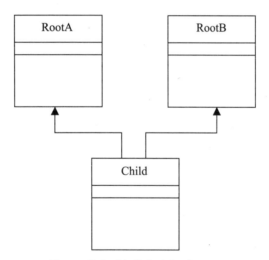

Figure 9.1 Multiple inheritance.

The inheritance rules and the use of access modifier in subclass derivations as discussed in Chapter 8 apply in this case. The Child class inherits publicly from both RootA and RootB. We may use any other access modifiers here to control the visibility of the members of the superclass in the derived class.

When we create an object of Child class, it will exhibit the functionality of both the base classes. To illustrate this, we will discuss a simple program example.

The complete program that illustrates multiple inheritance of classes is given in Listing 9.1

Listing 9.1:   Program to demonstrate multiple inheritance

```cpp
#include "stdafx.h"
#include <iostream>

using namespace std;

class RootA
{
public:
    void ClassMethodA()
    {
        cout << "Class A method called" << endl;
    }
};

class RootB
{
public:
    void ClassMethodB()
    {
        cout << "Class B method called" << endl;
    }
};

class Child : public RootA, public RootB
{
public:
    void ClassMethodChild()
    {
        cout << "Child class method called" << endl;
    }
};

void main()
{
    cout <<
    "Creating subclass object based on RootA and RootB classes ..." << endl;
    Child child;
    cout << "Invoking child class method ..." << endl;
    child.ClassMethodChild();
    cout << "Invoking RootA base class method ..." << endl;
    child.ClassMethodA();
    cout << "Invoking RootB base class method ..." << endl;
    child.ClassMethodB();
}
```

The RootA class in the above program defines a public method called ClassMethodA. The method prints appropriate message on the user console whenever it is called. Similarly, the RootB class defines a public method called ClassMethodB; this too prints appropriate message on the user console whenever it is called. The Child class derives from both RootA and RootB classes and defines a public method called ClassMethodChild.

The main function creates an object of Child class and calls its ClassMethodChild. The method prints a message on the user console indicating that it is being called. The child object then calls the inherited method of Root A, i.e. method ClassMethodA. Next, it calls the inherited method of Root B, i.e. method ClassMethodB. The methods print appropriate messages on the user console as they are being called. The program output is shown below:

```
Creating subclass object based on RootA and RootB classes ...
Invoking child class method ...
Child class method called
Invoking RootA base class method ...
Class A method called
Invoking RootB base class method ...
Class B method called
```

When we inherit from multiple classes, the derived class will inherit the functionality of all its base classes.

CONSTRUCTOR CALLING SEQUENCE

In the case of multiple inheritance, when we create an object of a derived class, the constructors for all its base classes are called. In this section, we will study the order in which these constructors are called.

Consider the following declaration for a derived class that inherits from two classes RootA and RootB.

```
class Child : public RootA, public RootB
```

In the class derivation, we have listed RootA before RootB. During the creation of Child class object, the base class constructors will be called in the same order as defined in the child class declaration. Thus, in the above case, when we create a Child class object, the RootA constructor will be called before RootB constructor. This can be easily verified using the complete program listing given in Listing 9.2.

The following program in Listing 9.2 illustrates the constructor calling sequence in case of multiple inheritance.

Listing 9.2:   Constructor calling sequence in case of multiple inheritance

```
// Multiple Inheritance
// Constructor calling sequence
#include "stdafx.h"
#include <iostream>
```

```
using namespace std;

class RootA
{
public:
    RootA ()
    {
        cout << "RootA constructor called"<< endl;
    }
};

class RootB
{
public:
    RootB ()
    {
        cout << "RootB constructor called"<< endl;
    }
};

class Child : public RootA, public RootB
{
public:
    Child ()
    {
        cout << "Child class constructor called"<< endl;
    }
};

void main()
{
    cout << "Child class inherits RootA, RootB" << endl;
    cout << "Creating Child class object ..." << endl;
    Child child;
}
```

Each constructor prints an appropriate message on the user console indicating whenever it is called. The `main` function simply constructs a `Child` class object to show the entire object creation process. The program output is shown below:

```
Child class inherits RootA, RootB
Creating Child class object ...
RootA constructor called
RootB constructor called
Child class constructor called
```

To confirm that the sequence for the base class constructor calling depends on the order in which the base classes are specified in the declaration of the child class, try modifying the definition for the child class as follows:

```
class Child : public RootB, public RootA
```

Now, run the program. The program output is shown below:

```
Child class inherits RootA, RootB
Creating Child class object ...
RootB constructor called
RootA constructor called
Child class constructor called
```

Note that now the `RootB` constructor is called before the `RootA` constructor.

In the case of multiple inheritance, all base class constructors are called during the derived class object creation. The order in which the base class constructors are called is dictated by the order in which the base classes are listed in the derived class declaration.

DESTRUCTOR CALLING SEQUENCE

We will now study the order in which the base class destructors are called whenever a derived class object is destroyed in case of multiple inheritance.

We use the class declaration from the previous section:

```
class Child : public RootA, public RootB
```

Whenever a `child` class object is destroyed, the destructor for the child class will be called first, followed by the destructor for `RootB`, followed by the destructor for `RootA`. The sequence is exactly opposite to the sequence of calling constructors during the object creation process. This can be verified by running the code below:

The program code in Listing 9.3 illustrates the order in which the base class destructors are called during the destruction of `child` class object that inherits from multiple base classes:

Listing 9.3: Destructor calling sequence in case of multiple inheritance

```
// Multiple Inheritance
// Destructor calling sequence

#include "stdafx.h"
#include <iostream>

using namespace std;

class RootA
{
public:
    ~RootA ()
```

```
    {
        cout << "RootA destructor called"<< endl;
    }
};

class RootB
{
public:
    ~RootB ()
    {
        cout << "RootB destructor called"<< endl;
    }
};

class Child : public RootA, public RootB
{
public:
    ~Child ()
    {
        cout << "Child class destructor called"<< endl;
    }
};

void main()
{
    cout << "Creating Child object ..." << endl;
    Child child;
    cout << "Destroying Child object ..." << endl;
}
```

We define destructors for RootA and RootB classes that print a message on the user console whenever the corresponding objects are destroyed. The Child class inherits from RootA and RootB classes. The destructor for Child class prints a message on the console whenever the Child class object is destroyed. The main function simply constructs a Child class object and destroys it.

Each destructor prints an appropriate message on the user console whenever it is called. The program output is shown below:

```
    Creating Child object ...
    Destroying Child object ...
    Child class destructor called
    RootB destructor called
    RootA destructor called
```

If we change the order in which the base classes are specified in the derived class declaration, the sequence of calling the base class destructors will vary accordingly. Note that the destructor calling sequence is exactly opposite to the constructor calling sequence. The object that is constructed first is destroyed last and the object that is constructed last is destroyed first.

PARAMETER PASSING TO BASE CLASS CONSTRUCTORS

In this section, we will study how to pass parameters to the base class constructors in the case of multiple inheritance. Let us define a constructor for our base class RootA as follows:

```
RootA (int a1)
```

This constructor takes an argument of type int. Similarly, let us define the constructor for the second base class as follows:

```
RootB (float b1)
```

This constructor takes a parameter of type float.

Now, we will derive another class that inherits from both RootA and RootB. The class declaration would be as follows:

```
class Child : public RootA, public RootB
```

We derive our Child class by publicly inheriting from both RootA and RootB classes. Whenever you construct an object of Child class, the objects of both base classes will be created. The runtime automatically calls the base class constructors during the child creation process. As we have defined a constructor for each of our base classes, there is no default no-argument constructor provided by the compiler for our base classes. Thus, we will be required to write a constructor for our child class that would pass parameters to the two child class constructors. As we do not explicitly call these constructors through the child class constructor, we must define a constructor that takes appropriate number of parameters and passes them to the base class constructors. The declaration for the child class constructor is shown here:

```
Child (int a1, float b1):RootA(a1), RootB(b1)
```

We write our child class constructor as taking two parameters, one of type int and the other of type float. Following the constructor declaration, we write a colon followed by the constructor for our first base class, followed by the constructor for the second base class. We pass appropriate parameters to these constructors. The RootA constructor takes an integer parameter as required by its definition. The RootB constructor takes a float parameter as required by the definition of RootB class. The above declaration instructs the compiler to generate code so as to call the appropriate constructors with the desired parameters whenever a child class object is created. The body of the child class constructor would be defined as in the earlier cases and does not require an explicit call to the base class constructors.

How do you create a child object? To create a child object, you would write a statement similar to the following one:

```
Child child (2, 5.0);
```

We create an object that is referred by the variable child. During the construction, we pass two parameters to the constructor. The two parameters are passed on to the appropriate base class constructors. Note that the parameters which are passed to the child class constructor are visible in the constructor body and may be used by the constructor to do any child class initializations, if desired.

The complete program that illustrates how to pass parameters to the base class constructors during multiple inheritance is given in Listing 9.4.

Listing 9.4: Parameter passing to superclass constructors

```
// Multiple Inheritance
// Parameter passing to base class constructors
#include "stdafx.h"
#include <iostream>

using namespace std;

class RootA
{
public:
    RootA (int a1)
    {
        cout << "RootA constructor called, parameter: "
            << a1 << endl;
    }
};

class RootB
{
public:
    RootB (float b1)
    {
        cout << "RootB constructor called, parameter: "
        << b1 << endl;
    }
};

class Child : public RootA, public RootB
{
public:
    Child (int a1, float b1):RootA(a1), RootB(b1)
    {
        cout << "Child class constructor called, parameters: "
            << a1 << ", " << b1 << endl;
    }
};
```

```
void main()
{
    cout << "Creating Child class object ... " << endl;
    Child child (2, 5.0);
}
```

Each constructor prints an appropriate message on the user console indicating the type of parameter it has received during the construction. The program output is shown below:

```
Creating Child class object ...
RootA constructor called, parameter: 2
RootB constructor called, parameter: 5
Child class constructor called, parameters: 2, 5
```

ACCESS MODIFIERS

When we inherit from multiple base classes, the same rules for base class member visibility apply as those discussed earlier in case of single inheritance (Chapter 8). The access to the members of each base class is independent of the access to the members of other base classes from which we derive your class.

Consider the following declaration for a derived class that inherits from two base classes:

```
class Child : public RootA, public RootB
```

As the Child class publicly inherits from both RootA and RootB classes, the objects of Child class will have access to all the public members of both base classes. This is represented in Figure 9.2.

The privileges obtained by the Child class will be passed to further derived classes of Child class. Now, let us modify the above declaration as follows:

```
class Child : private RootA, public RootB
```

We now inherit from RootA using private modifier. Thus, the inherited members of RootA will become private to Child class. It implies that objects of Child class will not be able to use an inherited member of RootA. Similarly, RootA members will not be visible to further children of Child class. This inheritance is displayed in Figure 9.3.

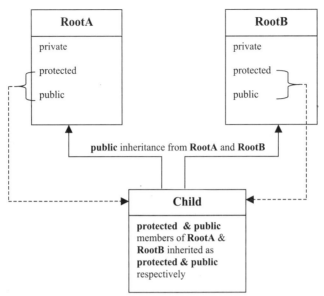

Figure 9.2 Access of derived class objects to base classes' objects.

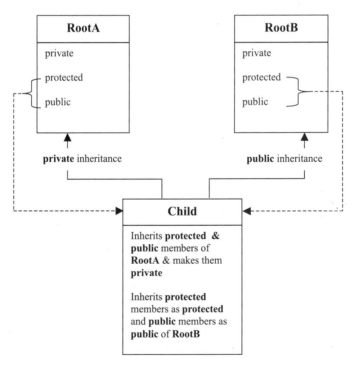

Figure 9.3 Inheritance with private modifier.

Let us consider that the RootA class defines a public method called RootAMethod. When Child class inherits from RootA using private modifier, the following code would be illegal:

```
Child child;
child.RootAMethod(); // this will not compile
```

Let us derive further from Child class as follows:

```
class SecondChild: public Child
```

As the Child class inherits publicly from RootB, all public members of RootB will be visible within SecondChild class, to the classes derived further from SecondChild and also to objects of SecondChild class. However, since Child class privately inherits from RootA, members of Child A will not be visible within SecondChild class implementation, to the further derived classes and also to the objects of SecondChild class.

Thus, the following call to RootA method would be illegal:

```
SecondChild child;
child.RootAMethod(); // this will not compile
```

However, the following call is legal:

```
SecondChild child;
child.RootBMethod();
```

This is illustrated in the example given in Listing 9.5.

Listing 9.5: The private, public inheritance

```
// Multiple Inheritance
#include "stdafx.h"
#include <iostream>

using namespace std;

class RootA
{
public:
    void RootAMethod ()
    {
        cout << "RootA Method called"<< endl;
    }
};

class RootB
{
public:
    void RootBMethod ()
```

```cpp
        {
            cout << "RootB Method called"<< endl;
        }
};

class Child : private RootA, public RootB
{
public:
    void ChildMethod()
    {
        cout << "Child class method called" << endl;
        RootAMethod();
    }
};

class SecondChild: public Child
{
public:
    void SecondChildMethod()
    {
        cout << "Second child class method called" << endl;
        ChildMethod();
    }
};

void main()
{
    Child child;
    cout << "Using Child class object: " << endl;
    // this will not compile
    //   child.RootAMethod();
    child.RootBMethod();
    cout << endl;

    SecondChild secondchild;
    cout << "Using Second Child class object: " << endl;
    // this will not compile
    // secondchild.RootAMethod();
    secondchild.RootBMethod();
    cout << endl;

    cout <<
    "Calling RootA method indirectly through Second Child class method: "
    << endl;
    secondchild.SecondChildMethod();
  }
```

The program output is given below:

```
Using Child class object:
RootB Method called

Using Second Child class object:
RootB Method called

Calling RootA method indirectly through Second Child class method:
Second child class method called
Child class method called
RootA Method called
```

Note that both `Child` and `SecondChild` objects cannot call the `public` method of `RootA` as `Child` derives from `RootA` using `private` modifier. However, both the objects can call the `public` method of `RootB` as `Child` derives publicly from `RootB`. The method of `RootA` may be called indirectly by calling a `public` method of `SecondChild` class. This is illustrated by the last statement of the `main` function:

```
secondchild.SecondChildMethod();
```

Here, the object of the second child calls its own public method–`SecondChildMethod`. This method calls the inherited public `ChildMethod` of `Child` class. This, in turn, calls the privately inherited `RootAMethod` of `RootA` class.

PROTECTED INHERITANCE

In the above example, we studied the member visibility for private and public inheritance. In case of protected inheritance, the members of the base class will be visible to further subclasses of the derived class as it was seen for single inheritance. In the above program, we will modify the `Child` class declaration as follows:

```
class Child : protected RootA, public RootB
```

The `Child` class now inherits from `RootA` using protected modifier as shown in Figure 9.4.

Thus, the public members of `RootA` will now become protected members of `Child` class. These members will be visible to the subclasses of `Child`, but not to the objects of `Child` class. Therefore, if we call `RootAMethod` through the method of `SecondChild` class, it will be a valid call.

```
SecondChildMethod()
{
    cout << "Second child class method called" << endl;
    RootAMethod(); // this is valid
}
```

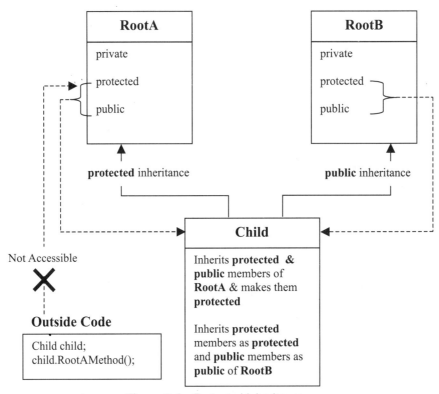

Figure 9.4 Protected inheritance.

However, if we use an object of `SecondChild` class as a reference while calling the `RootAMethod`, it will be illegal:

```
SecondChild secondchild;
cout << "Using Second Child class object: " << endl;
// secondchild.RootAMethod(); // this will not
// compile
```

This is illustrated in the program code in Listing 9.6.

Listing 9.6:   Protected inheritance

```
// Multiple Inheritance
#include "stdafx.h"
#include <iostream>

using namespace std;

class RootA
{
public:
    void RootAMethod ()
    {
        cout << "RootA Method called"<< endl;
    }
};
```

```cpp
class RootB
{
public:
    void RootBMethod ()
    {
        cout << "RootB Method called"<< endl;
    }
};

class Child : protected RootA, public RootB
{
public:
    void ChildMethod()
    {
        cout << "Child class method called" << endl;
        RootAMethod();
    }
};

class SecondChild: public Child
{
public:
    void SecondChildMethod()
    {
        cout << "Second child class method called" << endl;
        cout << "Calling RootA method" << endl;
        RootAMethod();
    }
};

void main()
{
    Child child;
    cout << "Using Child class object: " << endl;
    //  child.RootAMethod(); // this will not
    //  compile
    child.RootBMethod();
    cout << endl;

    SecondChild secondchild;
    cout << "Using Second Child class object: " << endl;
    //  secondchild.RootAMethod(); // this will not
    //  compile
    secondchild.RootBMethod();
    cout << endl;

    cout << "Calling indirectly through Second Child class method: " << endl;
    secondchild.SecondChildMethod();
}
```

Note that the `public` method of `RootA` is not accessible to either `Child` or `SecondChild` class objects as shown in the following statements:

```
//  child.RootAMethod(); // this will not
//  compile
//  secondchild.RootAMethod(); // this will not
//  compile
```

This is because `Child` class inherits from `RootA` using `protected` access modifier. However, when an object of `SecondChild` class calls its own `public` method, it in turn, can call the inherited `protected` method of `RootA`. This is shown using the following call:

```
secondchild.SecondChildMethod();
```

The `SecondChildMethod` which is the `public` method of `SecondChild` class calls `RootAMethod` directly.

The program output is shown below:

```
Using Child class object:
RootB Method called

Using Second Child class object:
RootB Method called

Calling indirectly through Second Child class method:
Second child class method called
Calling RootA method
RootA Method called
```

VIRTUAL CLASSES

Multiple inheritance though useful comes with its own set of problems. A typical problem encountered in multiple inheritance and its solution is discussed in this section.

Consider the following class definition for the base class:

```
class GrandParent
{
    int Age;
public:
    SetAge (int age)
    {
        Age = age;
    }
    int GetAge ()
    {
        return Age;
    }
};
```

The GrandParent class declares a private data member called Age. The class also defines appropriate get/set methods to access this data member. We will now derive a class called Parent1 from this as follows:

```
class Parent1: public GrandParent
{
};
```

Class Parent1 does not declare any members. Likewise, we derive another class called Parent2 from GrandParent as follows:

```
class Parent2: public GrandParent
{
};
```

We will now use multiple inheritance to create a new class called Child class that inherits from both Parent1 and Parent2. (In real life situations, this kind of inheritance may seem absurd.) The class definition for Child class is shown below:

```
class Child: public Parent1, public Parent2
{
};
```

The class hierarchy for the above classes would be as shown in Figure 9.5.

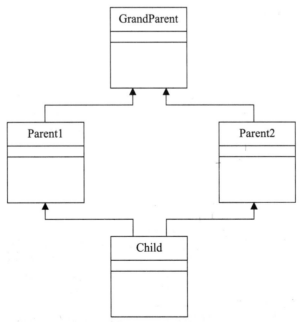

Figure 9.5 Class hierarchy in multiple inheritance.

Now, we will write a `main` method that creates an object of `Child` class. When we construct a `Child` class object, it contains the copy of both `Parent1` and `Parent2` objects. As each parent object is derived from `GrandParent` class, both `Parent1` and `Parent2` objects contain an independent copy of `GrandParent` object. This is depicted in Figure 9.6.

After creating an object of `Child` class, we will call the `SetAge` method of `GrandParent` class that our `Child` class has inherited through its two parents. A call to this method would be as follows:

```
child.SetAge (100); // ambiguous call, does not
// compile
```

However, the above call to `SetAge` method would be ambiguous. Note that, the `SetAge` method is inherited by `Child` class through two different paths, one through `Parent1` class and another through `Parent2` class. To resolve this ambiguity, we need to specify which version of `SetAge` is to be called. We do this using a scope resolution operator as follows:

```
child.Parent1::SetAge (100);
```

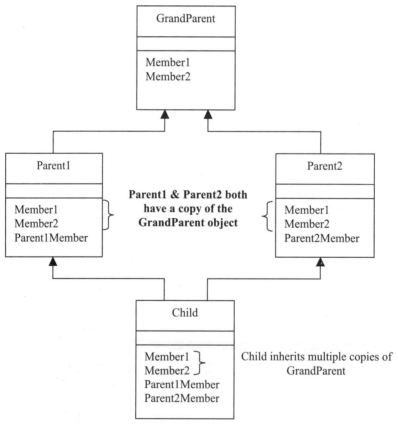

Figure 9.6 Derived classes with copies of parent class objects.

We will now be using the copy of `Parent1` to set the age of the `GrandParent`. What if we use `Parent2` class in the above statement instead of `Parent1`? This is still valid and the program would compile. However, we will be using the `SetAge` method inherited by `Parent2`. Since both `Parent1` and `Parent2` objects possess their own copy of `GrandParent` object, each of the above calls will set the `Age` value for the `GrandParent` object in its own independent copy. However, since there is only one `GrandParent` as observed from the class hierarchy diagram, we would expect the same data member to be modified in either case. Let us look at the full example to see what happens when you try to access the common data member of the `GrandParent` class. The complete program listing for the above case is given below:

The program code in Listing 9.7 creates a `Child` object that inherits from two classes `Parent1` and `Parent2`. Both these classes, in turn, inherit from `GrandParent` class. The `main` method creates an object of `Child` class and calls the `SetAge` method of `GrandParent` through two different paths. Later, it prints the `Age` value by calling the `GetAge` method, again through two different paths.

Listing 9.7:   Program to illustrate diamond-shape problem in multiple inheritance

```cpp
// Multiple Inheritance
#include "stdafx.h"
#include <iostream>

using namespace std;

class GrandParent
{
    int Age;
public:
    void SetAge (int age)
    {
        Age = age;
    }
    int GetAge ()
    {
        return Age;
    }
};

class Parent1: public GrandParent
{
};

class Parent2: public GrandParent
{
};

class Child: public Parent1, public Parent2
{
};
```

```
void main()
{
    cout << "Creating Child class object ..." << endl;
    Child child;
    cout << "Setting GrandParent age to 150 through Parent1 path ..."<< endl;
    child.Parent1::SetAge(150);
    cout << "Setting GrandParent age to 100 through Parent2 path ..."<< endl;
    child.Parent2::SetAge(100);

    cout << "Retrieving GrandParent age through Parent1 path ..."<< endl;
    cout << "Age = " << child.Parent1::GetAge() << endl;
    cout << "Retrieving GrandParent age through Parent2 path ..."<< endl;
    cout << "Age = " << child.Parent2::GetAge() << endl;
}
```

When we run the above program, we will get the output as follows:

```
Creating Child class object ...
Setting GrandParent age to 150 through
Parent1 path ...
Setting GrandParent age to 100 through
Parent2 path ...
Retrieving GrandParent age through
Parent1 path ...
Age = 150
Retrieving GrandParent age through
Parent2 path ...
Age = 100
```

Obviously, something has gone wrong here. Since we have only one GrandParent class in our class hierarchy, we would expect the same value for Age in both the cases. The problem has arisen due to the fact that two independent copies of GrandParent object are maintained by the system. To resolve this problem, we use virtual keyword during inheritance.

Virtual Inheritance

Modify the definitions of the Parent1 and Parent2 classes in the above code as follows:

```
class Parent1: public virtual GrandParent
{
};

class Parent2: public virtual GrandParent
{
};
```

We use `virtual` keyword in the class declarations as also depicted in Figure 9.7.

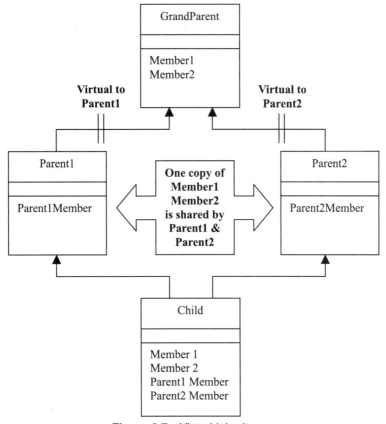

Figure 9.7 Virtual inheritance.

This tells the compiler to maintain a single copy of the object of the inherited class. Now, if we call the inherited `SetAge` method as shown in the following code fragment, both the calls would operate on a single copy of `GrandParent`. As a result, the last modification would prevail.

```
child.Parent1::SetAge(150);
child.Parent2::SetAge(100);
```

To verify that only a single copy is operated upon, we would execute the following statements:

```
cout << "Age: " << child.Parent1::GetAge() << endl;
cout << "Age: " << child.Parent2::GetAge() << endl;
```

In both the cases, it should print the same value for the age of `GrandParent`. As a matter of fact, since only one copy is maintained by the system, there is no ambiguity while calling get/set methods on the `Age` member. Thus, the scope resolution used in the above statements is not required and we could modify the above statements to the following:

```
    child.SetAge(200);
    cout << "Age: " << child.GetAge() << endl;
```

The full program listing containing the above code changes is given in Listing 9.8. It demonstrates the use of `virtual` keyword during multiple inheritance.

Listing 9.8: Demonstration on the use of virtual keyword

```
// Multiple Inheritance
#include "stdafx.h"
#include <iostream>

using namespace std;

class GrandParent
{
    int Age;
public:
    void SetAge (int age)
    {
        Age = age;
    }
    int GetAge ()
    {
        return Age;
    }
};

class Parent1: public virtual GrandParent
{
};

class Parent2: public virtual GrandParent
{
};

class Child: public Parent1, public Parent2
{
};

void main()
{
    cout << "Creating Child class object ..." << endl;
    Child child;
    cout << "Setting GrandParent age to 150 through Parent1 path ..."<< endl;
    child.Parent1::SetAge(150);
    cout << "Setting GrandParent age to 100 through Parent2 path ..."<< endl;
    child.Parent2::SetAge(100);
```

```
cout << "Retrieving GrandParent age through Parent1 path ..."<< endl;
cout << "Age = " << child.Parent1::GetAge() << endl;
cout << "Retrieving GrandParent age through Parent2 path ..."<< endl;
cout << "Age = " << child.Parent2::GetAge() << endl << endl;

// scope resolution is not required as illustrated below
cout <<
    "Setting GrandParent age to 200 without using scope resolution"<< endl;
child.SetAge(200);
cout <<
    "Retrieving GrandParent age without using scope resolution"<< endl;
cout << "Age: " << child.GetAge() << endl;
}
```

When we run the above program, we would get the following output:

```
Creating Child class object ...
Setting GrandParent age to 150
through Parent1 path ...
Setting GrandParent age to 100
through Parent2 path ...
Retrieving GrandParent age through
Parent1 path ...
Age = 100
Retrieving GrandParent age through
Parent2 path ...
Age = 100

Setting GrandParent age to 200 without
using scope resolution
Retrieving GrandParent age without
using scope resolution
Age: 200
```

Note that irrespective of the path followed to access the Age member of GrandParent object, we operate on a single copy of GrandParent object in all the cases.

SUMMARY

In this chapter, we discussed multiple inheritance. A class may be derived from more than one base class. This phenomenon is called *multiple inheritance*. Such derived class inherits the characteristics of all its base classes.

When a derived class object is created, the constructors for all its bases are called. The base class constructors are called in the same sequence as they are listed in the declaration of derived class. When a child class object is destroyed, the destructors for all its base classes are called. The destructors are called in exactly the opposite sequence as that of the constructors. An object that is constructed first is destroyed last and the object that is constructed last is destroyed first.

A base class constructor may take some arguments. Such arguments are listed in the constructor declaration of the child class and passed to the respective child class constructors.

A derived class may inherit from a child class using any of the three access modifiers: public, protected or private. Each derivation from a base class is independent of others and we may use different access modifiers for each of the base classes. Depending on the access modifier used, the derived class gains the privileges on the base class methods. In case of public derivations, all the base class methods are treated public in derived class, in case of protected these are treated protected and in case of private derivation, those are treated private to the derived class.

Multiple inheritance may give rise to the diamond-shape problem, when we derive a class from two base classes that, in turn, derive from a common base class. We should use `virtual` keyword while deriving the base classes from a superbase class. This instructs the compiler to maintain a single copy of the superbase class, when a derived class object is created, thereby solving the multiple copies problem present in diamond-shape.

EXERCISES

1. What is multiple inheritance?
2. Describe the syntax of multiple inheritance.
3. Explain the use of `public`, `private`, `protected` access specifiers in multiple inheritance.
4. Explain when constructors and destructors are called in multiple inheritance.
5. Describe `virtual` base class.
6. In case of multiple inheritance, explain the syntax for passing the parameters to the base class constructors.
7. For multiple inheritance, write a program to show the invocation of the destructors.
8. We have the following classes: `BaseProcessor`, `ProcessorI`, `ProcessorII`, `SuperProcessor`. The `SuperProcessor` inherits from `ProcessorI` and `ProcessorII`. Write the appropriate classes and structure them into multiple inheritance.
9. Modify the above classes to define constructors and destructors. Compile and run the program and observe the calling sequence of the constructor and destructor.
10. In Exercise 9, the inheritance structure has a diamond-shape problem. How will you solve the problem? Make the suitable changes required in the classes.
11. State whether the following statements are true or false
    (a) We may multiple inherit from more than 2 base classes.
    (b) In case of multiple inheritance, all the base class constructors are invoked before the derived class constructor.

(c) When we derive a class from more than one base class, the phenomenon is called:
   (i) Hierarchical inheritance
   (ii) Single inheritance
   (iii) Multiple inheritance
   (iv) Multiple level inheritance
(d) You may use different access modifiers while inheriting simultaneously from different base classes.
(e) The duplication of inherited members due to multiple paths can be avoided by making the common base class as:
   (i) Public
   (ii) Abstract
   (iii) Virtual
   (iv) Protected
(f) While writing a virtual base class, the keywords virtual and public must be used in the order of virtual public *<class_name>*.

10

Polymorphism

In Chapter 1, when we discussed the important features of object-oriented languages, we talked about three important points, namely, encapsulation, inheritance and polymorphism. We discussed encapsulation in Chapter 4 and inheritance in Chapter 8 and Chapter 9. In this chapter, we will cover the third important feature, that is, polymorphism. More specifically, we will learn the following in this chapter:

- What is polymorphism?
- Types of polymorphism
- Static polymorphism using function overloading and operator overloading
- Dynamic polymorphism
- Virtual functions
- Pure virtual functions
- Abstract classes.

THE MEANING OF POLYMORPHISM

Polymorphism is an important feature of any object-oriented languages. Polymorphism means 'one name, many forms' (polymorph in Greek means 'many forms', where *poly* stands for many and *morph* stands for form). Polymorphism helps in creating more readable program code. Consider that we need to write a function for printing different data types on the user console or on a printer. In C language or any other language that does not support polymorphism, we will land up writing several functions each responsible for printing a specific data type. Each of these functions will have a unique name. Though the functionality of each method is same from the user point of view, the user will be required to remember the names of all such functions while using these in the application. The C++ polymorphism feature allows we to use only one function name for all such functions. Each function will have its own independent implementation. When we call this function with a common name, the runtime decides which implementation to call depending on the current program context.

TYPES OF POLYMORPHISM

There are two types of polymorphism:
- Static polymorphism
- Dynamic (runtime) polymorphism.

Static polymorphism is also called *early binding* and dynamic (runtime) polymorphism is called *late binding*. In the case of static polymorphism, the compiler resolves at the compile time which implementation to call a method having a common name. That is why this is known as *early binding*.

In the case of runtime polymorphism, the runtime environment decides which implementation to call for during the program execution. That is why it is called *late binding*.

The static polymorphism, which is also known as *compile time polymorphism* is implemented using function overloading techniques.

Function overloading is implemented for:
- Normal functions
- Operator overloaded functions.

We will first discuss static polymorphism.

Static Polymorphism

As stated above, static polymorphism is implemented in C++ by way of function and operator overloading. Of these, we have already discussed operator overloading in Chapter 6. We will now discuss function overloading.

Function overloading

As discussed earlier, many a time, it is advisable to use the same function name for several logically related functions. If there are several functions having the same name, how does the compiler differentiate between them when the program calls such a function? The compiler differentiates them by looking up the parameters specified in the current call to the function. If these parameters differ in number or in their data types or in the order in which they appear, the compiler would be able to decide which implementation to use in the current context.

Let us suppose that we want to format and display different data types on the user console. We would write a function called Show for this purpose. The function will receive an argument of a specific data type that is to be displayed on the console. The function declarations would be as follows:

```
void Show (int i);
void Show (float f)
void Show (char *ptr);
```

As each function declaration varies in its input parameter data type, the compiler would be able to easily differentiate between the implementations during a call to the function. The calls to the above functions would be as:

```
Show (5);
Show ((float)5.0);
char *ptr = "Test";
Show (ptr);
```

Note that in the second Show statement above, we use an explicit typecast for the input parameter, as the default data type for a floating point number is double. If we do not use a typecast in this case, the compiler flags an error, as it is unable to find a matching function that takes double as an input parameter.

Rules for function overloading

In overloading a function, the following rules apply:

- All the overloaded functions have the same name.
- The number of arguments may differ.
- The data type of arguments may differ.
- The order of arguments may differ.
- The return type may differ.

We will now discuss these rules. As stated earlier, all the implementations must obviously have the same name.

Rule 1. The number of arguments may differ: The number of arguments specified in a function declaration may vary. Thus, the following declarations would be considered as overloaded functions.

```
void Show (int i);
void Show (int i, float f);
void Show (int i, float f, double d);
```

Rule 2. The data type of arguments may differ: For functions having equal number of arguments but differing in their data types, the functions would be considered as overloaded functions as in the following case:

```
void Show (int i);
void Show (float i);
```

Rule 3. The order of arguments may differ: In the case of multiple parameters, we come across another interesting case. If the order in which the parameters are specified differs, the functions would be treated as overloaded functions, as shown here:

```
void Show (int i, float f);
void Show (float f, int i);
```

The two declarations above use the same number of parameters and also their respective data types are same. However, the order in which these parameters are specified differs and thus the compiler would be able to differentiate between the two implementations in a call to this function.

Function overloading example

We will now discuss a concrete example of function overloading. We will develop a class called `Calculator`. We will implement the addition operation in our calculator. Our calculator would implement both real and complex number additions. For this, we will need to create a class for representing `Complex` numbers. In the `Complex` number class, we declare two attributes for representing the real and the imaginary portions of a complex number.

```
class Complex
{
public:
    int real, imag;
```

The class constructor initializes these two variables. We will also provide a `dump` method that prints the values of real and imaginary portions on the user console.

We add a method to our `Calculator` class for adding two real numbers as follows:

```
class Calculator
{
    public:
        int Add(int a, int b)
        {
            return (a + b);
        }
```

The `Add` method takes two integers as arguments. The function adds the two input numbers and returns an integer containing the result of addition to the caller. This takes care of adding two real numbers. Next, we will write an `Add` method for adding complex numbers.

```
Complex Add(Complex a, Complex b)
{
    ...
}
```

We use the same name `Add` as in the case of real number addition. This is an overloaded method. The method receives two parameters as in the earlier `Add` method; however, the data types for this method differ from those for the earlier one. The method receives `Complex` data types. The method performs the addition of two complex numbers, generates a new complex number as a result and returns it to the caller.

```
return (Complex (a.real + b.real, a.imag + b.imag));
```

Having defined `Complex` and `Calculator` classes, we will write a `main` method that uses the above `Add` methods to add real and complex numbers. In the `main` method, we will first create an instance of `Calculator` class.

```
Calculator calc;
```

We will do the real number addition by using the following method call:

```
calc.Add(50, 70)
```

The compiler differentiates this call from the other `Add` method by examining the parameters passed in the above call. Thus, it calls our first implementation of `Add` method that adds two real numbers.

To add complex numbers, we use the following call:

```
Complex c1 (10, 5);
Complex c2 (2, 4);
Complex c3 = calc.Add (c1, c2);
```

We first create two complex numbers and then pass them as parameters to the `Add` method. The return result is copied to a new complex number. Once again, the compiler uses the proper method implementation in the above statement.

The complete program that illustrates the use of function overloading is given in Listing 10.1.

Listing 10.1: Program to demonstrate function overloading

```cpp
#include "stdafx.h"
#include <iostream>

using namespace std;

class Complex
{
public:
    int real, imag;
public:
    Complex (int r, int i)
    {
        real = r;
        imag = i;
    }
    void dump()
    {
        cout << "Real = " << real << " Imag = " << imag << endl;
    }
};
```

```
class Calculator
{
    public:
        int Add(int a, int b)
        {
            return (a + b);
        }
        Complex Add(Complex a, Complex b)
        {
            return (Complex (a.real + b.real, a.imag + b.imag));
        }
};

void main()
{
    Calculator calc;
    cout << "Real Number Addition: " << endl;
    cout << "50 + 70 = " << calc.Add(50, 70) << endl;
    cout << endl;

    cout << "Complex Number Addition: " << endl;
    Complex c1 (10, 5);
    Complex c2 (2, 4);
    Complex c3 = calc.Add (c1, c2);

    cout << "C1: ";
    c1.dump();
    cout << "C2: ";
    c2.dump();
    cout << "C3 = C1 + C2 : " ;
    c3.dump();
}
```

The program output is shown below:

```
Real Number Addition:
50 + 70 = 120

Complex Number Addition:
C1: Real = 10 Imag = 5
C2: Real = 2 Imag = 4
C3 = C1 + C2 : Real = 12 Imag = 9
```

Note that the proper implementation of Add method is called depending on the input parameters.

Operator overloading

The other type of static polymorphism is implemented for operator overloading. In the case of operator overloading, we change the meaning of the existing C++ operators by providing a different implementation than the one provided by the compiler. For example, we may change the meaning assigned to a usual addition operator ('+') depending on the operands on which it is operating. The same addition operator may be used to add two complex numbers or two strings. The function name for an overloaded operator remains the same for the same operator while the parameter types differ. This is for the case of static polymorphism. Operator overloading was fully discussed in Chapter 6 and the reader may refer to this chapter for an in-depth coverage of operator overloading.

Merits/demerits of static polymorphism

In the case of static polymorphism, the calls to the overloaded methods are resolved at the compile time. This helps in creating faster programs. However, since all such calls must be resolved at compile time, it deprives us of the flexibility of plugging the new code at the runtime. This flexibility is provided in dynamic polymorphism that is discussed in the next section.

Dynamic Polymorphism

In the last section, we studied static polymorphism. In the case of static polymorphism, for the overloaded functions, the compiler resolves which function to call at the compile time. In the case of *dynamic polymorphism*, this decision is delayed until the runtime. To understand dynamic polymorphism, consider a base class containing a public method called `MyMethod`. We derive a class from it and implement a method with the same name in the derived class. We say that we override the base class method in the derived class. This feature is called *method overriding*. This is schematically depicted in Figure 10.1.

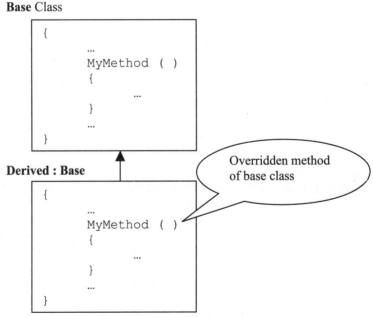

Figure 10.1 Method overriding.

We will now create objects of both base and derived classes. We also create a pointer to the base class object and use it to invoke `MyMethod`. This should invoke the method in the base class. We now set this pointer pointing to the derived class object and invoke `MyMethod` again. Which implementation should the runtime call? One would expect that since the pointer is pointing to the derived class object, it should invoke the derived class implementation of `MyMethod`. A similar situation arises when you create a pointer to derived class and typecast it to base class. Using this pointer, we invoke `MyMethod` in both, base and derived classes. The runtime has to resolve and call the proper implementation in both the cases. As the method binding is deferred to runtime, this is called late binding. In this section, we will study how the late binding affects overridden method calling.

Using Pointers for Calling Overridden Methods

Consider the `Base` class definition as follows:

```
class Base
{
public:
    void Show ()
    {
        cout << "In Base class Show method" << endl;
    }
};
```

The `Base` class defines one `public` method called `Show`. The method prints a message on the user console whenever it is called. We now derive a class from `Base` class.

```
class Derived:public Base
{
public:
    void Show ()
    {
        cout << "In Derived class Show method" << endl;
    }
};
```

The `Derived` class overrides the `Show` method of `Base` class and prints a message on the user console whenever it is called.

Now, to test method calling, we will write a `main` method. In the `main` method, we create objects of both `Base` and `Derived` classes.

```
Base base;
Derived derived;
```

We declare a pointer variable to `Base` class and initialize it to point to the `Base` class object created in the above statement.

```
Base *baseptr = &base;
```

We use this pointer to call the base class Show method.

```
baseptr->Show();
```

This should print a message on the user console indicating which implementation of Show is being called. We will actually compile and run the code to see which method is called.

We now set the above pointer to point to the derived class object and call the Show method again.

```
baseptr = &derived;
baseptr->Show();
```

We expect that this would call the Show method of the derived class. We will discuss the result after running the program and studying the program output.

Likewise, we could create a pointer to the derived class, set it to point to the derived class object and invoke Show method. Later, we will typecast this pointer to the base class and again invoke Show method. We will study the program output for this case too. The complete program for this discussion is given in Listing 10.2.

Listing 10.2:   Calling overridden methods using pointers

```
#include "stdafx.h"
#include <iostream>

using namespace std;

class Base
{
public:
    void Show ()
    {
        cout << "In Base class Show method" << endl;
    }
};

class Derived:public Base
{
public:
    void Show ()
    {
        cout << "In Derived class Show method" << endl;
    }
};

void main()
{
    Base base;
    Derived derived;
    cout << "Using pointer to base class" << endl;
```

```
Base *baseptr = &base;
baseptr->Show();
baseptr = &derived;
baseptr->Show();

cout << endl;

cout << "Using pointer to derived class" << endl;
Derived *derivedptr = &derived;
derivedptr->Show();
derivedptr = (Derived *) &base;
derivedptr->Show();
}
```

When we run the above program, we will get the following output on the console.

```
Using pointer to base class
In Base class Show method
In Base class Show method

Using pointer to derived class
In Derived class Show method
In Derived class Show method
```

Discussion: If we study the above program output, it is not quite as per our expectations. Let us analyze the output. The first call to the Show method invokes the base class implementation. This is understandable, as we have used the pointer to a base class that points to a base class object. What about the second call to Show method?

```
baseptr = &derived;
baseptr->Show();
```

The pointer is now pointing to the derived class object. From the output, we see that this has invoked the base class implementation, which is unexpected. During the second call, the pointer was pointing to derived class object and thus we would expect that the runtime would invoke the derived class implementation of the Show method. However, the runtime has invoked the base class implementation. This is because the runtime looks up the variable type that is used for accessing the method. In both the above situations, we have used a variable of type pointer to Base class. Thus, the runtime invokes the base class implementation of the Show method in both cases, ignoring the type of object the pointer points to.

A similar situation arises in case of pointer to a derived class, as seen in the latter part of the main function. Here, we use a variable of type pointer to the derived class, initialize it to point to derived class object and invoke Show method. Later, we set the pointer pointing to the base class object and invoke the Show method. In both the cases, the runtime invokes the derived class implementation of the Show method. This is because the runtime only checks the pointer variable type and ignores the object it is pointing to.

How do we remedy the above situation so that the runtime can call the desired function that depends on the current program context? C++ solves this problem with the help of `virtual` keyword. This is discussed in the next section.

VIRTUAL FUNCTIONS

The solution to the problem presented in the previous section is very simple. Just modify the base class function declaration as follows:

```
virtual void Show ()
```

We prefix the function declaration with the `virtual` keyword. The rest of the program code remains unmodified. Now, run the program one more time after doing the above modification. The program output is shown here:

```
Using pointer to base class
In Base class Show method
In Derived class Show method

Using pointer to derived class
In Derived class Show method
In Base class Show method
```

It is observed that the runtime now calls the implementation of the Show method as expected. The runtime now looks up the object reference to which the pointer points to and invokes the method implemented in the current object rather than using the pointer type as reference for deciding which implementation to call.

Pure Virtual Functions

When you create a class hierarchy by way of subclassing, many a times, the base classes are too general to have any method implementations. The methods declared in the base class are overridden in the derived classes. The derived classes provide the implementations for these methods. In such situations, rather than providing an empty implementation for the base class methods, we declare them as pure virtual functions. A pure virtual function does not provide the implementation and is declared as follows:

```
virtual void Show() = 0;
```

All classes that derive from this base class must now override and implement all the virtual functions. The use of pure virtual functions is illustrated with a program example in the following section.

We declare a Base class containing a pure virtual function as follows:

```
class Base
{
public:
    virtual void Show () = 0;
};
```

We derive a class from the above Base class and override its Show method. Note that the declaration of Show method in the derived class does not use virtual keyword.

```
class Derived1:public Base
{
public:
    void Show ()
    {
        cout << "In Derived1 Show method" << endl;
    }
};
```

We further derive from the above Derived1 class as follows:

```
class Derived2:public Base
{
public:
    void Show ()
    {
        cout << "In Derived2 Show method" << endl;
    }
};
```

Again, we override the inherited Show method and provide a new implementation in the derived class.

To test the effect of calling Show method in this class hierarchy, we create two objects of type Derived1 and Derived2 in our main function.

```
Derived1 derived1;
Derived2 derived2;
```

Next, we declare a pointer to the Base class and initialize it to point to Derived1 object.

```
Base *baseptr = &derived1;
```

We call the Show method using this pointer. This should call the implementation provided in the Derived1 class.

```
baseptr->Show();
```

Next, we set the pointer pointing to object of Derived2 class and call the Show method once again. This time, it should run the implementation provided in Derived2 class.

```
baseptr = &derived2;
baseptr->Show();
```

The full program for the above-discussed code is given in Listing 10.3.

Listing 10.3:   Using virtual functions

```cpp
#include "stdafx.h"
#include <iostream>

using namespace std;

class Base
{
public:
    virtual void Show () = 0;
};

class Derived1:public Base
{
public:
    void Show ()
    {
        cout << "In Derived1 Show method" << endl;
    }
};

class Derived2:public Base
{
public:
    void Show ()
    {
    cout << "In Derived2 Show method" << endl;
    }
};

void main()
{
    Derived1 derived1;
    Derived2 derived2;

    Base *baseptr = &derived1;
    cout << "Using pointer to Base class" << endl;
    cout << "Calling Show method in Derived1 class" << endl;
    baseptr->Show();
    cout << "Calling Show method in Derived2 class" << endl;
    baseptr = &derived2;
    baseptr->Show();
}
```

When we run the program, we will see the following output:

```
Using pointer to Base class
Calling Show method in Derived1 class
In Derived1 Show method
Calling Show method in Derived2 class
In Derived2 Show method
```

As expected, each invocation of Show method executes the appropriate implementation depending on the current object reference.

Merits/Demerits of Dynamic Polymorphism

In dynamic polymorphism the call to a particular form of function is determined at runtime, this process is called late binding. The late binding specifies that the call to the function is resolved at runtime depending on the current program context. Late binding helps in the development of large applications where code flexibility is desired. By using late binding, code changes can be easily accomplished without major modifications.

ABSTRACT CLASSES

In the earlier section, we discussed the use of pure virtual functions. If a class contains one or more pure virtual functions, it cannot be instantiated. As there is no implementation provided for a pure virtual function, the compiler does not allow we to create an instant of class containing such functions. Such a class is called an Abstract class. We cannot create an instance of an abstract class, so why should we have abstract classes? An abstract class is used as a template on which the class hierarchy may be created. Generally, our base level classes would be abstract. These base level classes are typically too generalized to have any implementations and that is why they are created as abstract classes.

All classes that derive from an abstract class must provide the implementation for each of the virtual functions declared in the base class. If not, the derived class itself would become abstract. Consider the following declaration for the abstract class.

```
class Base
{
public:
    virtual void Show () = 0;
};
```

The Base class is abstract as it has at least one function that is a pure virtual function. We now derive a class from this Base class as follows:

```
class Derived:public Base
{
};
```

Now, try creating an object of `Derived` class using the following statement:

```
Derived derived; // does not compile
```

The compiler flags the error indicating that `Derived` class is abstract as it does not provide the implementation for the inherited `Show` method. For the program to compile, we must either provide the implementation for the `Show` method in the `Derived` class or not attempt to instantiate the `Derived` class in our program code.

SUMMARY

In this chapter we studied an important feature of object-oriented languages, namely, polymorphism. Polymorphism means having same name and many faces. There are two types of polymorphism supported in C++. These are static and dynamic polymorphism.

Static polymorphism is implemented using function overloading or operator overloading. In polymorphism, we use the same function name for different implementations. Each implementation differs from the other by the number of arguments, the type of arguments or the order of appearance of the arguments. The compiler determines which implementation to use by looking up the parameters in the function call. The function binding is done at the compile time and thus this type of polymorphism is called static polymorphism. When we overload the functions to achieve static polymorphism, the compiler ignores the return types for such functions and the return types for each may differ from other implementations. In the case of static polymorphism, as the function calls are resolved at the compilation time, there is no time wasted in binding the function at the runtime, resulting in faster execution of the code. However, we loose the flexibility of plugging-in a function at the runtime.

Dynamic polymorphism defers the function binding to the runtime giving us the desired flexibility of plugging-in the desired function while running the application code. We implement dynamic polymorphism by creating functions with the same name across a class hierarchy; it means that the base class and its derived class and its further derived classes may declare a function with the same name. As these functions are defined in different classes, they need not differ in their argument list as in the case of static polymorphism.

When we define a function in a derived class having the name same as a function in a base class, we say that we override the function definition in a derived class. To execute such overridden functions, we create a pointer type variable of either the base or the derived class type. However, the compiler always calls the implementation of the function depending on the type of pointer irrespective of the object type to which it may be currently pointing. This problem is resolved with the help of `virtual` keyword.

In declaration of the base class function, we prefix the function name with `virtual` keyword. A derived class overrides such a function without using `virtual` keyword. The compiler now calls the appropriate implementation depending on the object type to which the pointer currently points to. This is independent of the pointer type, the pointer may be of base class pointer or a derived class pointer.

Sometimes, the base class function declarations are too generic to have any implementation. In such cases, we declare such functions as pure virtual functions. A pure virtual function is created by assigning zero in the function declaration. A class containing a pure virtual function is treated as an abstract class, as it cannot be instantiated. All classes derived from an abstract class must implement all the pure virtual functions of the base class; otherwise, these derived classes become abstract themselves, it means they cannot be instantiated.

Having discussed the major features of object-oriented languages in detail, the next chapter will cover another important topic, i.e. how to handle errors or to be more precise, exceptions, in our program code.

EXERCISES

1. What do you understand by polymorphism?
2. Describe compile time and runtime polymorphism.
3. Describe `virtual` functions and their need.
4. What are abstract classes? When do we define an abstract class?
5. Write the valid structure of an abstract class.
6. Write three classes `Location`, `Point` and `Circle`. Class `Point` derives from class `Location` and the class `Circle` derives from class `Point`. The individual class details are: class `Location` with a constructor initializing two data members (`int x, int y`), the methods (`int getX(), int getY()`), class `Point` with a constructor initializing data members (`int InitX, int InitY`) data member (`int visible`), the methods (`void Show(), void Hide(), void Drag(int drag), int isVisible(), void MoveTo(int a, int b)`), and class `Circle` with constructor (`int InitX, int InitY, int initRadius`), methods (`void Show(), void Hide(), void Expand (int ExpandBy), void Contract(int ContractBy)`. Study the class inheritance and determine which methods must be declared as `virtual`.
7. Find errors in the following class declarations:

```
public class Location
{

protected:
    int X; int Y;
    Location(int InitX, int InitY)
    {
        X = InitX;
        Y = InitY;
    }
public:
    int GetX(){return X;}
    int GetY(){return Y;}
};

class Point : public Location
{
protected:
    int visible;

public:
    Point(int InitX, int InitY);
    virtual void Show();
```

```
    void Hide();
    virtual void Drag(int drag);
    int IsVisible(){return visible;}
    void MoveTo(int NewX, int NewY);
};

class Circle : private Point
{
protected:
    void Show();
    virtual void Hide();
    virtual void Expand(int expand);
    void Contract(int ContractBy);
};
```

8. Write four classes Shape, Circle, Square, and Triangle. Shape is the base class for the other classes. Implement the appropriate DrawShape() method in the Shape class that is overloaded in the derived classes. Compile and run the program to check the calls to the overloaded methods.

9. Modify the above classes to implement the virtual keyword and then using the base class pointer try executing the respective class method. Compile and run the program to check the output.

10. "A pure virtual function is created by assigning zero in the function declaration". Modify the Shape, Circle, Square and Triangle classes of Exercise 8 on the basis of the given statement. Compile and run the program to check the output.

11. "A class containing a pure virtual function is treated as an abstract class, as it cannot be instantiated". Modify the Shape, Circle, Square and Triangle classes of Exercise 8 on the basis of the given statement. Compile and run the program to check the output.

12. "When you overload the functions to achieve static polymorphism, the compiler ignores the return types for such functions and the return types for each may differ from other implementations". Write appropriate classes to verify the given statement.

13. Write three classes Vehicle, Car and Bus. Vehicle is the base class for the Car and the Bus classes. Write the class implementations where Vehicle will have only pure virtual functions.

14. State whether the following statements are true or false:
    (a) Polymorphism is supported by C++ only at compile time.
    (b) Compile time polymorphism is achieved by overloading functions and operators.
    (c) A virtual function is a member function that is declared within a base class and redefined by a derived class.
    (d) When a virtual function is not redefined by a derived class, the version defined in the base class will be used.
    (e) A class containing a virtual function is said to be an abstract class.
    (f) An abstract class may be instantiated.
    (g) An abstract class only acts as a base class for other classes.
    (h) Version of a virtual function that is executed is determined by the type of the object pointed to at the time of the call.
    (i) A virtual function equated to zero is called as the standard virtual function.

11

Handling Exceptions

We have discussed several program examples in the previous chapters. We assumed these to be totally idealistic, without errors. Thus, we did not make any provisions for handling exceptional conditions at runtime in these program examples. Practically, every program may come across some exceptional conditions at runtime that are beyond its control. Like any other language, C++ provides a mechanism for handling such exceptional conditions. In this chapter, we will learn how to incorporate the exception handling code in our program. We will learn the following:

- What is meant by an exception?
- The `try/catch` construct for catching and processing exceptions.
- Throwing exceptions explicitly through your program code.
- Multiple exception handlers.
- Rethrowing an exception up the call hierarchy.
- Creating user-defined exception classes.
- Exception class hierarchy.
- Exception processing order.
- Catching all uncaught exceptions.

EXCEPTIONAL CONDITIONS

A program may terminate abnormally under exceptional conditions. A programmer is often required to handle such situations where an exceptional condition is created in a program code. One of the simplest examples for such a situation would be the simple arithmetic division of two numbers in your program code. What if the denominator of the division operation is zero? If we have an arithmetic expression that attempts to divide by zero, our program code will terminate abnormally. C++ allows us to implement a mechanism to catch such exceptional conditions in our program code and return control to the program after appropriately handling such situations. In this chapter, we will learn these techniques of exception handling. C++ provides three constructs `try`, `catch` and `throw` for this purpose. We will learn the use of these constructs and their full syntax in the following section.

THE TRY/CATCH/THROW CONSTRUCTS

If we want to catch exceptions in our program code, we need to create a `try...catch` block and use `throw` statement to invoke an exception handler, if one is available. We will first discuss the general syntax for defining a `try...catch` block and using `throw` statement.

Syntax:
The general syntax for `try...catch` block is as follows:

```
try
{
    // code to be tested
    throw exception
}
catch (datatype arg)
{
    // exception handler code
}
```

We create a `try` block—a block of code that is enclosed in curly braces and starts with the `try` keyword. The code written in the `try` block is the one that we suspect may generate an exception during runtime. At runtime, if an exceptional condition, such as division by zero occurs, we call `throw` in the `try` block. The `throw` statement takes an argument that contains the exception code.

The `try` block is immediately followed by a `catch` block. The `catch` block is a block of code enclosed in curly braces and starts with the `catch` keyword. The `catch` statement receives a parameter. The data type of the parameter is indicated in the parentheses that follow the `catch` keyword.

The above syntax would be best explained with a program example. We will write a program that accepts two integers from the user and performs an arithmetic division on the two numbers. If the denominator of the division is zero, we will throw an exception and gracefully quit the program.

The program code in Listing 11.1 illustrates the use of `try...catch` block and `throw` statement.

Listing 11.1:   Exception handling

```
#include "stdafx.h"
#include <iostream>

using namespace std;

int main()
{
    int a, b;
    cout << "Enter Numerator: ";
    cin >> a;
    cout << "Enter Denominator: ";
    cin >> b;
    try
    {
        if (b==0)
            throw 0;
        cout << "a/b = " << a/b << endl;
    }
    catch (int i)
    {
        cout << "Exception: Attempting to divide by zero" << endl;
    }
    return 0;
}
```

In the `main` function, we accept two integers by prompting the user to input `Numerator` and `Denominator` values. We then define a `try` block. In the `try` block, we test the value of the denominator. If it is zero, we call `throw` with a value of 0. Instead of 0, we could use any other integer value as explained in the next paragraph.

A `catch` block follows the `try` block. The `catch` block receives an integer parameter. If the connected `try` block throws an integer value, the code in the `catch` block would be executed. In the `catch` block, we print an appropriate message to the user and gracefully quit the program. A typical program output for denominator having value 0 is shown here:

```
Enter Numerator: 10
Enter Denominator: 0
Exception: Attempting to divide by zero
```

Argument Types for `catch` Statement

In the previous section, we wrote a program to catch an arithmetic overflow due to division by zero. The `try` block used the `throw` statement to generate an exception that was handled by the `catch` block. The `throw` statement took an integer argument. What will happen if, by mistake, we used the number `0.0f` as an argument to the `throw` statement instead of 0? The value of the argument in either case is zero. However, in the earlier case, it was `int` zero and now it is a float zero. The catch block expects an integer argument. Thus, when the throw statement uses a floating point number as an argument, the catch block will fail to catch this exception. If we modify the above program to change 0 to 0.0f in the throw statement and re-run the program, we will get an output as follows:

```
Enter Numerator: 10
Enter Denominator: 0
abnormal program termination
```

The program now quits by printing the abnormal termination message on the user console leaving no clue to the user as to what went wrong in the running code.

When we write the exception handlers using catch block, it is important to understand that the argument type to the catch block is very significant. If we are throwing a float number in the exception, the argument data type in the catch block should be accepting a float number to catch this exception. The following code syntax shows how to write a catch block that processes the exception with double data type.

```
try
{
    // program statement;
    throw 0.0;
}
catch (double d)
{
    // exception handler;
}
```

The argument to throw statement is 0.0, which is a double data type by default.

Likewise, if we wish to use a char data type in the throw statement, we will need to write a corresponding catch statement that takes a char data type as its input. This is shown below:

```
try
{
    // program statement;
    throw 'a';
}
catch (char c)
{
    // exception handler;
}
```

Now, what if our program throws more than one exception and each exception type differs from the other? In this case, we will need multiple catch statements associated with a single try block.

Multiple `catch` Blocks

C++ allows us to have multiple `catch` blocks associated with a single `try` block. Thus, if the `try` block throws more than one type of exception, it will be caught by an appropriate `catch` block. The general syntax for multiple `catch` blocks is as follows.

```
try
{
    // code to be tested
    throw exception1;
    // code to be tested
    throw exception2;
    // code to be tested
    throw exception3;
}
catch (datatype1 arg1)
{
    // exception handler code
}
catch (datatype2 arg2)
{
    // exception handler code
}
catch (datatype3 arg3)
{
    // exception handler code
}
```

In the above code, exception1 may be a variable of datatype1, exception2 may be a variable of datatype2 and exception3 may be a variable of datatype3. It is important that each of the exception variables should match at least one of the data types listed in several `catch` blocks. If not, the exception that is thrown will not be processed by any of the provided exception handlers resulting in abnormal program termination.

We now define multiple `catch` blocks each taking a different data type as argument. All such `catch` blocks are associated with a single `try` block. The `try` block itself throws more than one type of exception depending on the program context. At runtime, the exception type is matched to the corresponding data types in the `catch` block and the error handler code defined in the matching `catch` block is executed. Once a matching block is found, rest of the error handlers are ignored and the program continues with the next statement following the last `catch` block after processing the error handler in the invoked `catch` block.

We will now modify our divisor program discussed in the earlier section so as to include multiple `catch` blocks.

We assume that our divisor program is capable of handling only 32 bit numbers. Thus, if the user inputs a number larger than $0xffff$, the program should flag an error, prompt the user with an appropriate message and quit gracefully. Our program will now be required to throw two different types of exceptions.

The complete program is given in Listing 11.2.

Listing 11.2:   Defining multiple exception handlers

```cpp
#include "stdafx.h"
#include <iostream>

using namespace std;

int main()
{
    int a, b;
    cout << "Enter Numerator: ";
    cin >> a;
    cout << "Enter Denominator: ";
    cin >> b;
    try
    {
        if (a>0xffff || b >0xffff)
            throw 'E';
        if (b==0)
            throw 0;
        cout << "a/b = " << a/b << endl;
    }
    catch (char)
    {
        cout << "Exception: Input Number too large" << endl;
    }
    catch (int)
    {
        cout << "Exception: Attempting to divide by zero" << endl;
    }
    return 0;
}
```

In the `try` block, we test for the value of input numbers a and b. If any of these numbers have a value larger than 0xffff, we throw an exception with a `char` argument having value 'E'.

```cpp
if (a>0xffff || b >0xffff)
    throw 'E';
```

Next, we test the denominator value for zero; if it is zero, we throw an exception with integer argument having value 0.

```
if (b==0)
    throw 0;
```

The program contains two `catch` blocks, one for exception of type `char`,

```
catch (char)
```

And the other for exception of type `int`,

```
catch (int)
```

Note that both the `catch` statements use only the data type and not the variable name as in the earlier case. For example, we may declare the above `catch` statement as follows:

```
catch (int n)
```

In this case, the exception code value thrown by the `try` block will be available as the parameter value. The variable n will hold this value. If we are not interested in the exception code, we may avoid the use of the variable as we do in our current program example.

Depending on the program context, the appropriate exception handler is invoked. Let us try running the program with different input types. A typical output where the input number is larger than 0xffff is shown below:

```
Enter Numerator: 100000
Enter Denominator: 10
Exception: Input Number too large
```

Note that in the above case, the exception handler that handles `char` exception type is invoked. Now, let us try running the program with `denominator` value equal to zero. The typical output is shown below:

```
Enter Numerator: 1000
Enter Denominator: 0
Exception: Attempting to divide by zero
```

In the above case, the exception handler that handles integer exception types is invoked.

Finally, we will now run the program with valid inputs so that the program does not encounter any exceptions.

The typical output is as shown:

```
Enter Numerator: 1000
Enter Denominator: 100
a/b = 10
```

As expected, there are no exceptions generated in the above case and the program runs successfully printing the result of the division of two numbers.

THROWING EXCEPTIONS

We may include the exception handling code anywhere in our program. Our program may contain several functions. Each function may implement its own exception handler. The following code segment illustrates this.

```
void Method1 ()
{
    try
    {
        // function code
        throw 0;
    }
    catch (int i)
    {
    }
}

void Method2 ()
{
    try
    {
        // function code
        throw 'E';
    }
    catch (char c)
    {
    }
}

int main()
{
    Method1();
    Method2();
    try
    {
        // program code
        throw 0;
    }
    catch (int i)
    {
    }
}
```

Here, we have defined three methods, Method1, Method2 and our regular main method. Each method does error checking using its own try...catch block and provides an exception handler independent of one another.

We may desire to provide a centralized error handling for several functions within the program, especially if the error processing is the same for several situations. To achieve this, C++ allows we to throw an exception from a function so that it will be handled by the calling function. We can then put the entire error handling code in the calling function and not bother about exception handling in the function that generates the exception in the first case.

The general syntax for declaring a method that throws an exception to its caller is as follows:

```
returntype MethodName (arg-list) throw (arg-list);
```

After the argument list for a method, we use the keyword `throw` and list the data types of all the exceptions that the method may throw to the calling program.

We will now modify the above code segment so as to provide a centralized error handling. The modified code is shown below:

```
void Method1 () throw (int)
{
    // function code
    throw 0;
}

void Method2 () throw (char)
{
    // function code
    throw 'E';
}

int main()
{
    try
    {
        Method1();
        Method2();
        // program code
        throw 0;
    }
    catch (int i)
    {
    }
    catch (char c)
    {
    }
}
```

`Method1` throws an `int` type of exception and `Method2` throws a `char` type of exception. Both methods do not employ any `try...catch` blocks. Thus, no error handling is done in these methods. The `main` method encapsulates calls to `Method1` and `Method2` in a `try...catch` block and provides error handling for processing both `int` and `char` type of exceptions. As we can see it clearly from the above example, this makes our program more readable and simplifies the coding by providing a centralized exception handler and eliminating the need for a distributed error checking in each function of your application.

We will now take a concrete program example to illustrate this concept further. We will use our earlier example of dividing two integers. We write a method called `Divisor` that takes two `int` type input parameters, divides the first number by the second and returns an `int` result to the caller. We will not provide any error handling within the body of the method. We will throw exceptions, if any, to the caller. Thus, we define our `Divisor` method as follows:

```
int Divisor (int a, int b) throw (int, char)
```

The `Divisor` method throws two types of exceptions. The caller is responsible for catching these exceptions and providing appropriate exception handlers for them. The `Divisor` method tests for the exceptions as in the earlier case and throws an appropriate exception type.

```
if (a>0xffff || b >0xffff)
    throw 'E';
if (b==0)
    throw 0;
```

The `Divisor` method does not use a `try...catch` block. The calling method employs `try...catch` block to process any exceptions thrown by the `Divisor` method.

```
try
{
    int result = Divisor (a, b);
    cout << "a/b = " << result << endl;
}
```

The `try` block contains two associated `catch` blocks to catch `char` and `int` types of exceptions.

```
catch (char c)
{
    cout << "Exception: Input Number too large" << endl;
}
catch (int i)
{
    cout << "Exception: Attempting to divide by zero" << endl;
}
```

The program code in Listing 11.3 illustrates how to throw an exception to the caller from a method.

Listing 11.3:   Throwing exceptions

```
#include "stdafx.h"
#include <iostream>

using namespace std;
```

```
int Divisor (int, int);
int main()
{
    int a, b;
    cout << "Enter Numerator: ";
    cin >> a;
    cout << "Enter Denominator: ";
    cin >> b;
    try
    {
        int result = Divisor (a, b);
        cout << "a/b = " << result << endl;
    }
    catch (char)
    {
        cout << "Exception: Input Number too large" << endl;
    }
    catch (int)
    {
        cout << "Exception: Attempting to divide by zero"
            << endl;
    }
    return 0;
}

int Divisor (int a, int b) throw (int, char)
{
    if (a>0xffff || b >0xffff)
        throw 'E';
    if (b==0)
        throw 0;
    return a/b;
}
```

By providing a centralized exception handling, the function code is simplified.

RETHROWING EXCEPTIONS

Sometimes, after processing an exception a method may like to pass on the exception to its caller for further processing or simply for the knowledge of the caller. This is achieved by using a throw statement without any arguments in the exception handler. This is illustrated in the following program given in Listing 11.4.

Listing 11.4:   Exception passing

```
#include "stdafx.h"
#include <iostream>

using namespace std;
```

```
void Method1 () throw (int)
{
    try
    {
        // program code
        throw -1;
    }
    catch (int)
    {
        cout << "In the.exception handler of Method1" << endl;
        throw;
    }
}

void main()
{
    try
    {
        Method1();
    }
    catch (int)
    {
        cout << "In the exception handler of main method" << endl;
    }
}
```

Here, Method1 is declared to throw an exception of type integer. The method also implements a try...catch block for processing internal errors. In the try block, when an exception occurs, the method throws -1. This will be caught by the attached catch block. In the catch block, we process the exception as desired. We will now rethrow the same exception to the caller of Method1 by executing throw statement without any parameters as

```
throw;
```

The caller of Method1, that is the main method in the above program employs try...catch block to capture exceptions thrown by Method1. It provides its own exception handler to handle the exceptions thrown by Method1. When we run the program, we will see the following output indicating that both the exception handlers are called.

```
In the exception handler of Method1
In the exception handler of main method
```

Thus, it is possible to process an exception using an exception handler provided within the method generating the exception and later on throwing it to its caller for further processing.

So far, we have used catch blocks accepting primitive data types as parameters. We will now write our own exception classes and learn how to define catch blocks for processing such exceptions.

USER-DEFINED EXCEPTION CLASSES

Instead of using pre-defined data types in C++ as exception types, we can create our own exception classes and use them as exception types in our exception handling code. By defining our exception classes, we will gain further control on exception processing. This is best illustrated with an example.

Consider that your program requires the user to input a number in the range of 0 to 100. Instead of using the built-in data types of C++, we will now write our own exception classes to validate the input. If the user inputs a number greater than 100, we will throw an out of range exception and if the input number is less than zero, we will throw a negative number exception. For this, we will need to create two exception classes of our own.

First, we create an exception for out of range condition. We define a class called `OutOfRangeException` as follows:

```
class OutOfRangeException
{
public:
        OutOfRangeException ()
        {
            cout << "Exception: Out of Range" << endl;
        }
};
```

The class defines a constructor that prints a message to the user whenever an object of this type is constructed. Similarly, we will create another class for negative number input. The class definition is shown below:

```
class NegativeNumberException
{
public:
        NegativeNumberException ()
        {
            cout << "Exception: Negative input" << endl;
        }
};
```

Again, the class constructor prints an appropriate message on the user console. Once the two user-defined classes for exceptions are created, we need to use these as data types in the `catch` block of our error handler code. To catch `OutOfRangeException`, we will create a `catch` block as follows:

```
catch (OutOfRangeException)
{
    // error handler code
}
```

Similarly, to catch negative number exception, we will write a `catch` block as follows:

```
catch (NegativeNumberException)
{
    // error handler code
}
```

Next, we will need to throw exceptions of these types in your `try` block. For this, we would first construct an object of the user-defined exception type and then use it as a parameter in the `throw` statement. For example, to throw `OutOfRangeException`, we will use the following code fragment:

```
OutOfRangeException e;
throw e;
```

The program code in Listing 11.5 creates two user-defined exception types, defines a `main` program that employs a `try...catch` block to throw and process these exception types.

Listing 11.5:   User defined exceptions

```cpp
#include "stdafx.h"
#include <iostream>

using namespace std;

class OutOfRangeException
{
public:
    OutOfRangeException ()
    {
        cout << "Exception: Out of Range" << endl;
    }
};

class NegativeNumberException
{
public:
    NegativeNumberException ()
    {
        cout << "Exception: Negative input" << endl;
    }
};

void main()
{
    int number;
    cout << "Enter a positive integer in the range 0 to 100: ";
    cin >> number;
```

```
    try
    {
        if (number > 100)
        {
            OutOfRangeException e;
            throw e;
        }
        if (number < 0)
        {
            NegativeNumberException e;
            throw e;
        }
    }
    catch (OutOfRangeException)
    {
        cout << "Valid range for input is 0 to 100" << endl;
    }
    catch (NegativeNumberException)
    {
        cout << "Enter number greater than 0" << endl;
    }
}
```

Compile and run the above code. A typical output when the user inputs a number greater than 100 is shown below:

```
        Enter a positive integer in the range 0 to 100: 200
        Exception: Out of Range
        Valid range for input is 0 to 100
```

Note that the message 'Out of Range' is printed by the constructor of OutOfRangeException class. The next message for valid range is printed in the error handler of the main program.

For a negative number input, the typical output is shown below:

```
        Enter a positive integer in the range 0 to 100: -1
        Exception: Negative input
        Enter number greater than 0
```

In this case, the NegativeNumberException is generated. The first exception message is printed by the class constructor for NegativeNumberException class and the second one by the error handler defined in the main function.

DERIVING FURTHER FROM EXCEPTION CLASSES

In the previous section, we saw how to create user-defined exception classes. In this section, we will study how to derive further from such user-defined exception classes.

Consider the following definition for a user-defined exception class:

```
class MyException
{
public:
    MyException ()
    {
        cout << "MyException constructor called" << endl;
    }
};
```

We derive another class from the above class using the statement:

```
class DerivedMyException: public MyException
```

The `DerviedMyExcpetion` class publicly inherits from `MyException` class.
We will now write a `main` function that takes command-line arguments.

```
void main(int argc, char **argv)
```

If the user invokes the above program without any arguments, we will throw an exception of type `MyException` and if the user invokes the program with any argument, we will throw the `DerivedMyException` type of exception.

In the `main` method, we create a `try` block for checking the number of command-line arguments. If the `argc` equals 1, we create an object of `MyException` class and throw it.

```
if (argc == 1)
{
    MyException e;
    throw e;
}
```

Else, we will create an object of `DerivedMyException` type and throw it.

```
else
{
    DerivedMyException e1;
    throw e1;
}
```

For the `try` block we now associate two `catch` blocks:

```
catch (DerivedMyException)
{
    cout << "Invalid argument" << endl;
}
catch (MyException)
{
    cout << "No arguments passed" << endl;
}
```

We first test the derived class for exception and then its base class.

The full program for this example is given in Listing 11.6.

Listing 11.6:   Subclassing user-defined exceptions

```cpp
#include "stdafx.h"
#include <iostream>
using namespace std;

class MyException
{
public:
    MyException ()
    {
        cout << "MyException constructor called" << endl;
    }
};

class DerivedMyException: public MyException
{
public:
    DerivedMyException ()
    {
        cout << "DerivedMyException constructor called"
            << endl;
    }
};

void main(int argc, char **argv)
{
    try
    {
        if (argc == 1)
        {
            MyException e;
            throw e;
        }
        else
        {
            DerivedMyException e1;
            throw e1;
        }
    }
    catch (DerivedMyException)
    {
        cout << "Invalid argument" << endl;
    }
    catch (MyException)
```

```
    {
        cout << "No arguments passed" << endl;
    }
}
```

The program output when no command-line arguments are supplied is as follows:

```
        MyException constructor called
        No arguments passed
```

Note that the program throws an exception of type `MyException`, which is caught by the corresponding `catch` block.

We will now run the program with some argument passed on the command line. We will see the following output:

```
        MyException constructor called
        DerivedMyException constructor called
        Invalid argument
```

Note that in this case, the program throws an exception of type `DerivedMyException`. As `DerivedMyException` class derives from `MyException` class, the objects of both derived and base classes are constructed as seen from the above output.

EXCEPTION PROCESSING ORDER

When we derive classes from existing exception catches, the order in which they are listed in the `catch` blocks becomes important for their proper processing. In program Listing 11.6, we catch the derived class exception before its base class exception. What will happen if we change this order? This change is shown the following code snippet:

```
        catch (MyException)
        {
            cout << "No arguments passed" << endl;
        }
        catch (DerivedMyException)
        {
            cout << "Invalid argument" << endl;
        }
```

Try making the above change in the program and run the program with and without arguments. After making the above change, if we run the program without any command-line argument, the following output would be generated:

```
        MyException constructor called
        No arguments passed
```

The program generates an exception of type `MyException` that is caught by the corresponding `catch` block.

Now, try running the program with some command-line argument. The output is shown below:

```
MyException constructor called
DerivedMyException constructor called
No arguments passed
```

As expected, the program constructs an object of type `DerivedMyException`. During this construction, the objects of both, base class and subclass, are created as seen from the above output. However, when we look at the message printed by the exception handler, it is unexpected. We should have got the message 'Invalid argument' in this case. The printed message indicates that the program has invoked the exception handler for the `MyException` class rather than for `DerivedMyException` class. This is because, if we list the catch block for a base class before a catch block for a derived class, all exceptions of derived class types will be called by base class catch block and the derived class exception handlers will never be called. Thus, the order in which the catch blocks are listed is important for the proper processing of the generated exceptions.

The standard C++ library provides several exception classes (Table 11.1) from which we may derive our exception classes. The class hierarchy for built-in exception classes is discussed in the following section.

Exception Class Hierarchy

The C++ standard library provides several built-in classes for exception handling. The class hierarchy for these various exception classes is illustration in Figure 11.1.

CATCHING UNCAUGHT EXCEPTIONS

So far, we have seen how to use primitive and user-defined data types in exception processing. We use multiple `catch` blocks to capture different types of exceptions. What if we still miss to catch a certain type of exception that may occur at runtime? In this case, the program will terminate with an abnormal termination. We can avoid this situation by catching all unhandled exceptions in another exception handler. To do this, we provide a `catch` block that takes three dots as input parameter, as shown below:

```
catch (...)
{
    // exception handler code
}
```

This should be the last block amongst all the `catch` blocks. If an exception is not handled by any of the `catch` blocks, this last `catch` block will be executed. If we list this `catch` block before any of the other `catch` blocks, any exception would be caught by this block and the rest of the exception handlers will never be invoked.

Table 11.1 Exception class descriptions

Class	Description
The exception class	This class plays the role of the base class for all exceptions thrown by any expression and by the standard C++ library.
The bad_alloc class	This class provides information of an exception thrown to indicate that an allocation request did not succeed.
The bad_cast class	The bad_cast exception is thrown when a casting of a reference type fails. Normally it is thrown when the dynamic_cast operator is used.
The bad_exception class	This class provides information of an exception that can be thrown from an unexpected handler. For example, if an unexpected handler is invoked as a result of an exception in your program code and your handler does not know how to handle this type of exception, you may throw a bad_exception to the caller.
The bad_typeid class	The bad_typeid exception is thrown by the typeid operator when the operand for typeid is a NULL pointer.
The logic_error class	This class performs the role of a base class for all exceptions thrown to report errors. These errors are normally activated before the program executes. For example, in case of violations of logical preconditions, the program may throw this kind of exception.
The domain_error class	This class performs the role of a base class for all exceptions thrown to report a domain error.
The invalid_argument class	This class performs the role of a base class for all exceptions thrown to report an invalid argument.
The length_error class	This class performs the role of a base class for all exceptions thrown to report an attempt to generate an object too long to be specified.
The out_of_range class	This class performs the role of a base class for all exceptions thrown to report an argument that is out of its valid range.
The runtime_error class	This class performs the role of a base class for all exceptions thrown to report errors detected only when the program executes.
The overflow_error class	This class performs the role of a base class for all exceptions thrown to report an arithmetic overflow.
The range_error class	This class performs the role of a base class for all exceptions thrown to report a range error.
The underflow_error class	This class performs the role of a base class for all exceptions thrown to report an arithmetic underflow.
The ios_base::failure class	This member class of ios_base performs the role of a base class for all exceptions thrown by the member function called clear that is defined in template class basic_ios.

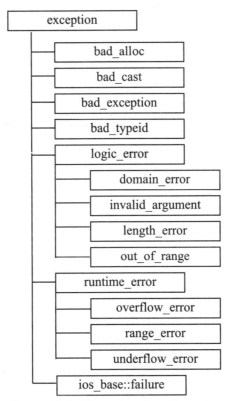

Figure 11.1 Exception class hierarchy.

Consider our earlier example, where we expect the user to input a number in the range of 0 to 100. We will now rewrite this program such that if the input number is greater than 100, we will throw 1.0 — a double number. We will provide the corresponding catch statement that takes double parameter. If the input number is less than 0, we will throw 0 — an integer. We catch this by providing a catch block that takes int parameter. What if the user inputs a character instead of number? Our program does not take care of this and will result in abnormal termination. To take care of such unforeseen exceptions, we use the above syntax of three dots in the last catch block. The complete program listing that illustrates the above concept is discussed below.

The program code in Listing 11.7 illustrates to requests the user to input a number in the range 0 to 100. If the user inputs a number greater than 100, the program throws a double number as an exception. If the user inputs a negative number, the program throws an int value as an exception. For any other invalid input, the exception is handled by the last catch block.

Listing 11.7: Uncaught exceptions

```
#include "stdafx.h"
#include <iostream.h>
```

```
void main()
{
    int number;
    cout << "Enter a positive integer in the range 0 to 100: ";
    cin >> number;
    try
    {
        if (number > 100)
            throw 1.0;
        else if (number < 0)
            throw 0;
        else
            throw 'E';
    }
    catch (double)
    {
        cout << "Number too large" << endl;
    }
    catch (int)
    {
        cout << "Negative numbers not allowed" << endl;
    }
    catch (...)
    {
        cout << "Invalid input" << endl;
    }
}
```

When we run the above program, the typical output when the input number is greater than 100 is shown below:

```
Enter a positive integer in the range 0 to 100: 200
Number too large
```

Note that the exception is handled by the catch block that takes double as input parameter. If the input number were negative, the typical program output would be as follows:

```
Enter a positive integer in the range 0 to 100: -1
Negative numbers not allowed
```

In this case, the exception is handled by the catch block that takes int parameter.

Finally, we will input a character instead of a number in the above program. The typical program output for this case is shown below:

```
Enter a positive integer in the range 0 to 100: c
Invalid input
```

In the above case, the exception is handled by the last `catch` block that takes three dots as input parameter.

SUMMARY

Any running program may encounter unexpected exceptional conditions that may result in application crash if such exceptions are not properly handled by your application code. To handle the exceptions in your program, C++ defines `try...catch` blocks. The code that we suspect may generate an exception at runtime is enclosed in a `try` block. If an exception occurs, we use `throw` statement along with an appropriate parameter in the `try` block to generate an exception code for the `catch` block. Every `try` block has one or more associated `catch` blocks. Each `catch` block takes a parameter of primitive data type. The runtime matches the data type of thrown error code with the data types used by the associated `catch` blocks. When a match is found, the runtime executes the code defined in the matching `catch` block.

An application may consist of several methods and each method may provide its own exception processing code. To avoid the wide distribution of exception handling code, C++ allows a method to throw an exception to its caller. For this, we declare our method as throwing an exception of a desired type. The caller provides an exception handler for the called methods. Thus, the entire exception handling code may be centralized with careful planning and using the `throw` feature of exception processing by methods.

Sometimes, a method may process an exception and yet it will like to pass on the exception to its caller for further processing or simply for its knowledge. C++ uses `throw` statement without any parameters in the `catch` block to re-throw the exception to its caller. The method must be declared as throwing an exception of a proper data type.

In addition to the primitive data types, we may create our exception data types by defining our own exception classes. We create an exception class just the way we create any other C++ class. To throw an exception of this exception class type, we create an object of this class and use it as a parameter in the `throw` statement. The associated `catch` statement will declare a parameter of this exception class type.

We may derive further classes based on the existing exception classes. In the `catch` block hierarchy, a subclass should be listed before its base class.

If the exception is not caught by any of the `catch` blocks, C++ provides an unconditional `catch` block that can handle any uncaught exceptions. This is done by writing three dots in the `catch` block. This should be the last catch block in the `catch` blocks hierarchy.

EXERCISES

1. What is meant by handling exceptions?
2. Explain `try...catch` and `throw` constructs.
3. What does throwing and rethrowing exceptions mean?
4. When should we use multiple `catch` blocks?
5. What are user-defined exception classes? Give an appropriate example.

6. Write a program that validates user input for entering values less than 0. Write a suitable exception class to handle invalid number exception.

7. Write a suitable program to show how an exception is rethrown and then caught in a `try...catch` block of the caller.

8. Write a program to demonstrate how multiple exceptions can be thrown.

9. Write a user defined exception class called `illegalAgeGroup`. Implement the class by throwing the exception when the user enters an invalid age group.

10. "An application may consist of several methods and each method may provide its own exception processing code". Provide the appropriate implementation of the `try...catch` block according to the given statement.

11. Modify the code developed in exercise 10 to have a generalized `try...catch` block.

12. 'If the exception is not caught by any of the `catch` blocks, how can we catch such uncaught exceptions'? Provide the appropriate implementations of the `try catch` block in view of this point.

13. "A method may process an exception and yet it will like to pass on the exception to its caller for further processing or simply for its knowledge". Provide the appropriate implementation of `try...catch` block for the methods considering the given statement.

14. We are supposed to throw an exception of `InvalidPassword` class type. Write the `try...catch` implementation to catch the thrown exception.

15. A `catch` statement catches a derived exception if it is looking for the base class. Write the `try...catch` block to verify the given statement.

16. State whether the following statements are true or false:
    (a) C++ exception handling is implemented using `try`, `catch` and `rethrow` keywords.
    (b) C++ exception handling supports nested `try...catch` blocks.
    (c) More than one exception handler cannot be associated with a single `try` block.
    (d) The `bad_alloc` exception is thrown if an error occurs when attempting to allocate memory with `new` keyword.
    (e) Exception class constructor is called when an exception is thrown.
    (f) The code that we suspect may generate an exception at runtime is enclosed in a `try` block.
    (g) A program aborts abnormally if an exception is not caught.
    (h) A `catch` block must take a parameter of only primitive data type.
    (i) C++ uses `throw` statement without any parameters in the `try` block to rethrow the exception to its caller.
    (j) If the exception is not caught by any of the `catch` blocks, C++ provides an unconditional `catch` block that can handle any uncaught exceptions. This is done by writing three dots in the `catch` block. This should be the last `catch` block in the `catch` block hierarchy.

12

Templates

In Chapter 1, we studied function overloading. In the case of function overloading, we use the same name for different implementations of the function. Each function takes a different set of parameters. We assume that the implementation code within each such function is different from the implementations provided in the other overloaded functions. What if the implementation code remains the same except for the data types of objects on which the function operates? We will encounter such situations in real life where the implementation across several functions remains the same except for the type of data they operate upon. We discuss such cases in this chapter. This is where we use the *template* feature of C++. Template was not part of the original C++ specifications and was added later. Most of the current day compilers support templates. In this chapter, we will learn the need for templates and how to create and use them in our program code.

We will learn the following in this chapter:

- Need for templates
- Types of templates
- Function templates
- Templates with single arguments
- Templates with multiple arguments
- Instantiating templates
- Overriding pre-defined templates

- Class templates
- Creating classes based on templates
- Using user-defined data types as parameters to templates

NEED FOR TEMPLATES

Now that we have briefly described the need for templates, let us take an example to illustrate why we need templates. Consider a function that finds the minimum of two integers. We could write the function declaration as follows:

```
int min (int a, int b);
```

The function `min` takes two arguments of type `int` and returns an `int` to the caller that is a minimum of two input numbers. We may overload this function for finding the minimum of two `float` numbers. In this case, the function declaration may look like follows:

```
float min (float a, float b);
```

Both `min` functions will have identical implementations except for the data type they operate upon. We may further extend this for finding the minimum of two `double` numbers or even two characters. In each such case, the implementation would be identical to our original function that operates on integers, except for the fact that each function operates on a different data type. Thus, we land up writing code for several such functions for which the implementation is identical. This not only increases the code size but also results in maintenance problem. If there is a logical bug in the implementation of the algorithm used by the function, it is likely that the same bug exists in every version of the overloaded function. In such a situation, we will need to modify all the definitions.

To resolve this problem, C++ provides the feature called `template`. Template is a sort of footprint on the basis of which functions are created by the compiler. Most likely, we would have seen the use of templates in word processing and page formatting software. We create standard templates for our use and format the documents by applying the correct template depending on the current context. Similarly, in C++, we create a template that takes a `generic` data type. The compiler generates the code based on this template depending on the current context that is the desired input data type.

TYPES OF TEMPLATES

C++ defines two types of templates

- Function templates
- Class templates

The templates that we have been discussing so far are *function templates*. A function template acts like a prototype for a function. We base our actual implementation of the function on this template.

The class templates are discussed later in this chapter under a separate section. We will now study an example to understand how to define and use function templates.

Function Templates

Consider the definition of a min function as shown here:

```
int min (int a, int b)
{
    return (a < b) ? a:b;
};
```

The function takes two arguments of type int, finds the minimum of the two, (i.e. the lesser) by using a conditional operator and returns an integer result to the caller. As seen in the above definition, the function operates on integer arguments. A function that finds the minimum of two float numbers would have an identical implementation except for its return type and the input parameters. The function definition that finds minimum of two given float numbers is shown here:

```
float min (float a, float b)
{
    return (a < b) ? a:b;
};
```

In the definition of the second function, what we have done is to essentially replace each occurrence of data type int with the float data type. We could replace the int data type with a generic data type to create a template. For example, we could simply use some label such as T to replace int in the above definition to create a template. Such a definition is shown below:

```
T min (T a, T b)
{
    return (a < b) ? a:b;
};
```

We could now replace T with a double to create another version of min function that operates on double data types and returns us a minimum of two input double numbers. The same template maybe used even for finding the lesser of two characters by replacing T with a char data type. The full syntax for function templates is discussed in the following section.

Templates with single argument types

The syntax for a function template that takes arguments of a single data type is as follows:

```
template <class T>
T FunctionName (T arg1, T arg2, T arg3, ...)
{
    // function body
}
```

Here, T specifies the generic data type that is replaced by the compiler during a call to the specified function. We assume only one data type in the above declaration, which is represented by the generic data type T. The compiler replaces each occurrence of T with the data type specified in the actual function call.

The first statement marks the beginning of the template definition:

```
template <class T>
```

The template and class are reserved words. This is followed by the function declaration:

```
T FunctionName (T arg1, T arg2, T arg3, ...)
```

The FunctionName specifies the name of the function. The generic data type T is used for both return type and the arguments to the function. In practice, a function may take more than one type of data as input parameter. We will discuss how to create templates that take multiple types of data as parameters in the section "Templates with Multiple Argument Types" later in this chapter.

Following the function declaration, we write the function body in braces. The function body contains the implementation code and will use the generic parameter T wherever required. The compiler will replace this generic parameter with the actual parameter passed on to the function during a method call.

Creating functions based on template

To create a function based on the above template we would write program statements as follows:

```
int a = 10, b = 20;
int c = min (a, b);
```

Note that the call to the min function is identical to a call to any of the usual functions. It is the compiler that generates an appropriate code based on the template for this function call. To call a function that operates on float arguments, we would include code similar to the one shown below:

```
float a = 10, b = 20;
float c = min (a, b);
```

Once again, the compiler generates an appropriate code for the above call that is based on the template for min function.

We will now develop a full program listing that illustrates the use of a function template.

We write the template for a function that finds the minimum of two numbers. The template definition is shown here:

```
template <class T>
T min (T a, T b)
{
    return (a < b) ? a:b;
};
```

To create and call a function that operates on integer data type, we use the following program statements:

```
int i=10, j=20;
cout << "Minimum of" << i << "and" << j << ":"
    << min (i, j) << endl;
```

To call a function that compares two characters, we use the following code:

```
char c1='a', c2='A';
cout << "Minimum of" << c1 << "and" << c2 << ":"
    << min (c1, c2) << endl;
```

The compiler generates an appropriate implementation for each of the above calls.

The complete program that creates functions for operating on int, float and char data types based on a template is given in Listing 12.1.

Listing 12.1: Using templates

```
#include "stdafx.h"
#include <iostream>

using namespace std;

template <class T>
T min (T a, T b)
{
    return (a < b) ? a:b;
};

void main()
{
    int i=10, j=20;
    cout << "Minimum of " << i << " and " << j << " = " << min (i, j)<< endl;
    float f1=10.0, f2=5.0;
    cout << "Minimum of " << fixed << f1 << " and " << f2 << " = "<< min (f1, f2) << endl;
    char c1='a', c2='A';
    cout << "Minimum of " << c1 << " and " << c2 << " = "<< min (c1, c2) << endl;
}
```

When we run the program Listing 12.1, we will get the following output:

```
Minimum of 10 and 20 = 10
Minimum of 10.000000 and 5.000000 = 5.000000
Minimum of a and A = A
```

Note that the compiler has generated the appropriate code for each of the function calls. The *fixed* keyword used in one of the cout statements is called *manipulator*. The manipulators are discussed in Chapter 1.

Overriding function template

In the above template for a `min` function, the implementation code was identical for all the data types discussed so far. The same template may be used for finding a minimum of two `double` numbers or two `long` numbers. However, let us consider that you wish to find the minimum of two constant character strings. Here, we will compare the two strings character by character and the moment we find that a character at any given position is different than the character at the same position in the second string, we will return the string containing the minimum of the two characters to the caller. For example, if we compare two strings, `MarkForValue` and `MarkForPrice`, the minimum of these two strings would be `MarkForPrice`. The first seven characters in the two strings are identical and the eighth character (`P`) is less than the corresponding character (`V`) for the first string. Obviously, the implementation of such a function would be significantly different from the implementation used in the template. So how do we override the function definition provided by the template? We write the new implementation as follows:

```
char* min (char *a, char *b)
{
    char *p1 = a;
    char *p2 = b;
    while (*p1 != '\0' || *p2 != '\0')
    {
        if (*p1 > *p2)
            return b;
        else if (*p1 < *p2)
            return a;
        else
            p1++; p2++;
    }
    return a;
}
```

To call the above overridden function, we use the following code:

```
char a[] = "MarkForValue";
char b[] = "MarkForPrice";
cout << "Minimum of '" << a << "' and '" << b << "' : " <<
        min (a, b) << endl;
```

The program code in Listing 12.2 illustrates how to override a default implementation code provided by a function template.

Listing 12.2:   Overriding default templates

```
#include "stdafx.h"
#include <iostream>

using namespace std;
```

```
template <class T>
T min (T a, T b)
{
    return (a < b) ? a:b;
};

void main()
{
    int i=10, j=20;
    cout << "Minimum of " << i << " and " << j << " : " << min (i, j)<< endl;
    float f1=10.0, f2=5.0;
    cout << "Minimum of " << fixed << f1 << " and "<< f2 << " : "<< min (f1, f2) << endl;
    char c1='a', c2='A';
    cout << "Minimum of " << c1 << " and " << c2 << " : " << min (c1, c2) << endl;
    char a[] = "MarkForValue";
    char b[] = "MarkForPrice";
    cout << "Minimum of '" << a << "' and '" << b << "' : " << min (a, b) << endl;
}

char* min (char *a, char *b)
{
    char *p1 = a;
    char *p2 = b;
    while (*p1 != '\0' || *p2 != '\0')
    {
        if (*p1 > *p2)
            return b;
        else if (*p1 < *p2)
            return a;
        else
            p1++; p2++;
    }
    return a;
}
```

The program output is shown below:

```
Minimum of 10 and 20 : 10
Minimum of 10.000000 and 5.000000 : 5.000000
Minimum of a and A : A
Minimum of 'MarkForValue' and 'MarkForPrice' : MarkForPrice
```

If we study the above output, we will notice that in the first three cases, the compiler uses the function implementation based on the template. For the last call that takes two char pointers as input, the compiler uses the overridden method implementation.

What happens here is that the compiler first checks the parameters in a method call, looks for any overridden method implementation and if none is found uses the template to generate the method code.

Discussion: We looked at the need for templates, how to define function templates and how to create functions based on these templates. While discussing the need for templates, we explained that the same functionality can be achieved using function overloading feature of C++. However, we mentioned that function overloading results in increase in code size. Does a template solve this problem? Once a template is created, the compiler generates the implementation code for each of the data types that our program needs. It implies that the compiler will generate several overloaded functions giving us no benefit of saving on the byte size. Though templates do not result in byte code size saving as compared to function overloading, they do help in keeping our source program concise and more readable. Since we would be maintaining a single implementation code by way of template, it also eases code maintenance. For bug fixing, instead of modifying several overloaded functions, we need to modify only a single implementation code in the form of a template.

Templates with multiple argument types

So far, we have considered a template that takes parameters of a single data type. What if we want to create a function that takes more than one parameter, each parameter being of a different type? Suppose we wish to write a template for a function that computes the exponential of a given number. We write the function prototype as follows:

```
int exp (int a, int b);
```

This function computes 'a raised to b' and returns the result to the caller. We may like to make the first parameter as `float` or `double` instead of `int`. Accordingly, the result return type will also change. Notice that we do not take care of arithmetic overflow here and assume that the returned value will fit the specified data type. Thus, the new prototypes may look like:

```
float exp (float a, int b);
double exp (double a, int b);
```

We can now develop a template for the above function prototypes. The template requires parameters of two different data types. We define the template as follows:

```
template <class T, class X>
T exp (T a, X b)
{
    T c = 1;
    for (int i=0; i<b; i++)
        c *= a;

    return c;
};
```

The template now declares two `class` variables, viz. T and X.

```
template <class T, class X>
```

The function name is `exp`. It takes two parameters, one of type T and the other of type X. The function returns a value of type T.

```
T exp (T a, X b)
```

In the function body, we create a variable of type T and assign an initial value of 1 to it.

```
T c = 1;
```

The `for` loop does a repetitive multiplication. The `return` statement returns the value of data type T to the caller.

When we make a call to function `exp` in our program, the compiler will replace T and X with the data types used in the method call. For example, the method call may look like:

```
int a = 2, b = 5;
int c = exp (a, b);
```

In this case, both T and X will be treated as of type `int` while generating the implementation code. However, if our call looks like the following, T will be of type `float` and X will be of type `int`.

```
float a = 2.5;
int b = 5;
float c = exp (a, b);
```

The full program that defines and uses the above template is given in Listing 12.3.

Listing 12.3: Multiple argument templates

```cpp
#include "stdafx.h"
#include <iostream>

using namespace std;

template <class T, class X>
T exp (T a, X b)
{
    T c = 1;
    for (int i=0; i<b; i++)
        c *= a;

    return c;
};

void main()
{
    int i=2;
    int e1=5;
    cout << i << " raised to " << e1 << " = " << exp (i, e1) << endl;
    float f1=2.5;
    int e2=3;
    cout << f1 << " raised to " << e2 << " = " << exp (f1, e2)
        << endl;
    double d=1.5;
    int e3=5;
    cout << d << " raised to " << e3 << " = " << exp (d, e3) << endl;
}
```

The program output is shown below:

```
2 raised to 5 = 32
2.5 raised to 3 = 15.625
1.5 raised to 5 = 7.59375
```

As can be seen from the output, the compiler generates the different code for each of the method calls depending on the data types of parameters used in the method call.

Class Templates

So far we have seen the use of function templates. Just the way function templates help us in writing generic functions, is there a way to write generic classes? C++ allows us to create generic classes using class templates. In this section, we will learn about class templates.

Suppose we need to write a class for well-known data structures such as map, stack, queue, etc. Such data structures can typically operate on any data type. For example, if we create a stack class or a queue class, it may be used for storing an integer, float, double, char, etc. We will develop a template for a stack class and use it to define stacks that can store different data types.

Before we discuss the development of a stack template, we will look at the general syntax for creating class templates.

Syntax:
The syntax for class template is as follows:

```
template <class T>
class Name
{
private:
    T a;
Public:
    T Method1();
    void Method2 (T data);
}
```

Here, we begin the definition of the template with the `template` keyword. This is followed by angular brackets that specify the generic data type `T` that the class is going to operate upon.

```
template <class T>
```

On the next line, we use the `class` keyword and the desired name for the template. Our program will use this name to create classes based on the template defined here.

```
class Name
```

The class definition follows its name. In the class definition, we use the generic data type specified on the template line. In the above definition, we declare a variable `a` of generic data type `T`.

```
T a;
```

We also write two methods, `Method1` and `Method2`. The first method returns a generic data type `T` and the second method accepts a parameter of type `T`.

```
T Method1();
void Method2 (T data);
```

The compiler replaces all the occurrences of generic data types with the real data types specified in the source program, during compilation.

Creating classes based on template

To create a class based on a template, we use the following syntax:

```
Name <datatype> MyClass;
```

Here, `Name` denotes the template name, `datatype` denotes the real data type that is used for replacing all occurrences of generic data type within the class definition while `MyClass` is the name for the real class to be generated.

To illustrate the use of class templates, we will now discuss the development of stack template and its use in the program code.

Class template for stack data structure

A stack typically defines two operations, push and pop. We *push* a data on the stack and later we may *pop* the stored data item from the stack. The stack follows Last In First Out (LIFO) strategy. The item that is pushed last is popped first. The number of items that can be pushed on the stack is determined by the stack size. The stack may store any data type, but not a mixture of data types. This requirement makes us think of a generic definition for the stack class that may be easily adapted to the desired data type during program development.

We begin our definition of stack template as follows:

```
template <class T>
class stack
{
    ...
}
```

The complete program listing for the stack template is given in the program example in this section.

Our stack class takes one generic parameter defined by `T`. In the body of the stack class, we create a private variable of type `T` as follows:

```
T stk [SIZE];
```

The `stk` variable declared above is of type array. The array size is determined by the pre-defined constant `SIZE`. Each element of the array is of type `T`. This generic parameter `T` will be replaced with some real data type during compilation. Thus, the `stk` array may store `int` or `float` or `double` or any other data type as defined by `T` during template specialization.

When we create a real class based on a class template, it is called specialization of the class template.

We also declare another `int` variable called `SP` in the class for tracking the stack pointer position.

```
int SP;
```

We now write the `push` method for our class. The declaration is as follows:

```
void push (T data)
```

The `push` method receives a parameter of generic data type `T`. This is replaced by the real data type at the time of compilation. The push operation pushes the received data on the stack and increments the stack pointer. If the stack pointer crosses the maximum stack size, we print a 'stack full' message to the user.

Next, we write the `pop` method.

```
T pop()
```

The `pop` method does not receive any parameter and returns a generic data type `T` to the caller. Once again, this generic data type will be replaced with the real data type at the time of compilation. The `pop` method checks the current stack pointer position. If it points to the bottom of the stack, we print an 'empty stack' message to the caller; otherwise, we retrieve the data item from the top of the stack and return it to the caller.

We now write a `main` function to test our stack template. We create a stack for storing `int` values with the following declaration:

```
stack <int> IntStack;
```

The compiler replaces the generic data type `T` by `int` data type during compilation process. The `IntStack` represents an object of `stack` class. To push an `int` data item on the stack, we use the following statement:

```
IntStack.push(5);
```

This pushes integer 5 on the stack. To retrieve data from the top of the stack, we call its `pop` method.

```
cout << "Popping: " << IntStack.pop() << endl;
```

We can easily declare a stack that stores characters instead of integers with the following declaration:

```
stack <char> CharStack;
```

Here, we have used `char` data type in place of `int` data type for the generic parameter `T`. The push and pop operations would be identical to the earlier case, except that we now operate on `char` data type instead of `int` data type.

The complete program demonstrating the declaration and specialization of `stack` template is given in Listing 12.4.

Listing 12.4:   Class template

```
#include "stdafx.h"
#include <iostream>

using namespace std;
```

```cpp
const int SIZE = 5;
template <class T>
class stack
{
    private:
    T stk [SIZE];
    int SP;

public:
    stack ()
    {
        SP = -1;
    },

    void push (T data)
    {
        SP++;
        if (SP == SIZE)
        {
            SP--;
            cout << "stack full" << endl;
            return;
        }
        stk[SP] = data;
    }

    T pop()
    {
        if (SP == -1)
        {
            cout << "empty stack" << endl;
        }
        else
        {
            T data = stk[SP--];
            return data;
        }
    }
};

void main()
{
    cout << "Demonstrating int stack" << endl;
    stack <int> IntStack;
    cout << "Pushing data 5 on stack" << endl;
    IntStack.push(5);
    cout << "Pushing data 10 on stack" << endl;
    IntStack.push(10);
```

```
    cout << "Popping: " << IntStack.pop() << endl;
    cout << "Popping: " << IntStack.pop() << endl;

    cout << endl << "Demonstrating char stack" << endl;
    stack <char> CharStack;
    cout << "Pushing data 'a' on stack" << endl;
    CharStack.push('a');
    cout << "Pushing data 'b' on stack" << endl;
    CharStack.push('b');
    cout << "Pushing data 'c' on stack" << endl;
    CharStack.push('c');

    cout << "Popping: " << CharStack.pop() << endl;
    cout << "Popping: " << CharStack.pop() << endl;
    cout << "Popping: " << CharStack.pop() << endl;

    cout << endl;
}
```

The program first declares a stack for storing int values, pushes two integers, immediately pops them and prints their values on the console. Note the order in which the data elements are popped—Last in First Out (LIFO). The program later declares another class instance called CharStack to store characters. It pushes three char items on the newly created stack, pops them and prints their values on the console. The program output is shown below:

```
Demonstrating int stack
Pushing data 5 on stack
Pushing data 10 on stack
Popping: 10
Popping: 5

Demonstrating char stack
Pushing data 'a' on stack
Pushing data 'b' on stack
Pushing data 'c' on stack
Popping: c
Popping: b
Popping: a
```

Likewise, we could create stack classes for storing float or double types of data.

USER-DEFINED DATA TYPES AS PARAMETERS

So far we have used pre-defined data types as parameters to the template. In this section, we will learn how to pass user-defined objects as parameters to the template. To create a user-defined data type, we create a class for the new data type. The objects of this class may be passed as parameters to the template.

We will modify the program from the earlier section to create a stack for storing user-defined objects. We will create a class for representing complex numbers and store the objects of this class on the stack.

The definition of `Complex` class is shown below:

```
class Complex
{
    int real;
    int imag;
public:
    Complex ()
    {
        real = 0;
        imag = 0;
    }
    Complex (int r, int im)
    {
        real = r;
        imag = im;
    }
    void dump()
    {
        cout << "real: " << real << " , imag: " << imag << endl;
    }
};
```

The `Complex` class declares two private members for representing the real and imaginary portions of a complex number. The no-argument class constructor initializes both these members to zero and the two-argument constructor initializes the data members to the respective parameters. The `dump` method dumps the contents of the complex number on the console.

We now create a stack for storing the complex numbers as follows:

```
stack <Complex> ComplexStack;
```

The `ComplexStack` is an instance of `stack` class and is capable of storing user-defined data type, that is, complex numbers. Note that the generic parameter is now replaced by the `Complex` class type. Thus, the compiler will replace all occurrences of generic parameter `T` in the template with the class `Complex`.

Once the `stack` object is created, we use our usual `push` and `pop` methods to operate on the stack. Before we push a complex data on the stack, we need to construct an object of `Complex` class. This is done using the following statements:

```
Complex c1(10,5);
Complex c2(20,4);
```

We push these data items on the stack by calling push method of stack class.

```
ComplexStack.push(c1);
ComplexStack.push(c2);
```

We retrieve the top element from the stack by calling its pop method. The pop method returns an object of the Complex class. We assign this to another Complex variable:

```
Complex c3 = ComplexStack.pop();
```

We now dump the contents of the retrieved data item on the user console for verification.

```
c3.dump();
```

The next data item from the stack is popped using similar syntax.

```
c3 = ComplexStack.pop();
c3.dump();
```

The complete program that uses the stack template to store and retrieve Complex data type is given in Listing 12.5.

Listing 12.5: Using user-defined data types in class template

```
#include "stdafx.h"
#include <iostream>

using namespace std;

const int SIZE = 5;
template <class T>
class stack
{
    private:
        T stk [SIZE];
        int SP;

    public:
        stack ()
        {
            SP = -1;
        }

        void push (T data)
        {
            SP++;
            if (SP == SIZE)
            {
                SP--;
```

```
                    cout << "stack full" << endl;
                    return;
                }
                stk[SP] = data;
            }

        T pop()
        {
            if (SP == -1)
            {
                cout << "empty stack" << endl;
            }
            else
            {
                T data = stk[SP–];
                return data;
            }
        }
};

class Complex
{
    int real;
    int imag;
public:
    Complex ()
    {
        real = 0;
        imag = 0;
    }
    Complex (int r, int im)
    {
        real = r;
        imag = im;
    }
    int GetReal()
    {
        return real;
    }
    int GetImag()
    {
        return imag;
    }
    void dump()
```

```
        {
            cout << "real: " << real << " , imag: " << imag << endl;
        }
};

void main()
{
    cout << "Demonstrating int stack" << endl;
    stack <int> IntStack;
    cout << "Pushing data 5 on stack" << endl;
    IntStack.push(5);
    cout << "Pushing data 10 on stack" << endl;
    IntStack.push(10);

    cout << "Popping: " << IntStack.pop() << endl;
    cout << "Popping: " << IntStack.pop() << endl;

    cout << endl << "Demonstrating char stack" << endl;
    stack <char> CharStack;
    cout << "Pushing data 'a' on stack" << endl;
    CharStack.push('a');
    cout << "Pushing data 'b' on stack" << endl;
    CharStack.push('b');
    cout << "Pushing data 'c' on stack" << endl;
    CharStack.push('c');

    cout << "Popping: " << CharStack.pop() << endl;
    cout << "Popping: " << CharStack.pop() << endl;
    cout << "Popping: " << CharStack.pop() << endl;

    cout << endl;
    stack <Complex> ComplexStack;
    cout << "Creating two complex numbers" << endl;
    Complex c1(10,5);
    Complex c2(20,4);

    cout << "Pushing Complex C1: (" << c1.GetReal() << ", "<< c1.GetImag() << ")" << endl;
    ComplexStack.push(c1);
    cout << "Pushing Complex C2: (" << c2.GetReal() << ", " << c2.GetImag() << ")" << endl;
    ComplexStack.push(c2);

    cout << "Popping complex numbers from stack" << endl;
    Complex c3 = ComplexStack.pop();
    c3.dump();
    c3 = ComplexStack.pop();
    c3.dump();
}
```

The program output is shown below:

```
Demonstrating int stack
Pushing data 5 on stack
Pushing data 10 on stack
Popping: 10
Popping: 5

Demonstrating char stack
Pushing data 'a' on stack
Pushing data 'b' on stack
Pushing data 'c' on stack
Popping: c
Popping: b
Popping: a

Creating two complex numbers
Pushing Complex C1: (10, 5)
Pushing Complex C2: (20, 4)
Popping complex numbers from stack
real: 20 , imag: 4
real: 10 , imag: 5
```

Note that the compiler uses the same template for stack class to generate different instances—classes that are used for storing and retrieving int, char and Complex data types on the stack data structure.

SUMMARY

In this chapter, we studied an important feature of the C++ language, templates. Template feature is not the part of the original specification for C++ language. It was introduced much later in the language and implemented by most of the vendors in their current implementations of C++ compilers.

The template is a footprint on which your functions and class definitions are based on. A function template defines a footprint that operates on a generic data type. The compiler replaces this generic data type with a real data type specified in the source program during a call to the function. Depending on the data type specified, the compiler will generate an overloaded function for each function call that uses a different data type. The benefit in using the template lies in the fact that it helps in creating concise code avoiding definition of several overloaded functions and in the software maintenance, as we need to debug and maintain only one implementation irrespective of the data type used in the function.

When we write functions based on a given template, we have no control on the function implementation as the compiler generates the implementation code for we. There could be situations where we may like to override the default implementation for a specific data type. C++ allows us to override template implementation by our own implementation for the desired data type. The compiler first looks for an overridden implementation, and if none is found, generates the function code based on the template.

C++ template feature allows us to create templates for functions that take more than one type of data. In the function declaration for such templates, we simply use more than one generic data type. All the occurrences of such multiple data types in the implementation code will be replaced by the respective real data types specified in the function call by the compiler.

C++ allows us to create class templates for creating classes that use different data types in different contexts. Typically, the class templates are useful for defining standard data structures such as stacks, queues, etc. A class template may be used for creating classes that operate on user-defined data types.

EXERCISES

1. What do you understand by templates?
2. Explain different types of templates and why are they used.
3. Write the syntax for a function template that takes arguments of a single data type.
4. Write a function template that takes two different data types of arguments.
5. Write the syntax for class template.
6. Write a class template to depict a Queue. Make necessary assumptions.
7. Modify the Queue template to use user-defined objects as its parameters.
8. Write a function template for the Multiply function, that multiples int, float and double value types.
9. Write a function template called Fibonacci to calculate and display data in different types such as int and long.
10. Write the template implementation of a List which allows accessing and retrieving of any type of data.
11. Write the template implementation of an HashMap which allows accessing and retrieving of values in key-value format
12. State whether the following statements are true or false.
    (a) A function template defines a footprint for a function that operates on a generic data type.
    (b) Depending on the data type specified, the compiler generates an overloaded function for each function call that uses a different data type.
    (c) The benefit in using the template lies in the fact that it helps in creating concise code avoiding definition of several overloaded functions.
    (d) C++ template feature allows us to create templates for functions that take only one type of data.
    (e) C++ allows us to create class templates for creating classes that use different data types in different contexts.
    (f) A class template can only be used for creating classes that operate on primitive data types.
    (g) C++ allows overriding function templates for any desired data type.
    (h) Template classes and functions make development easier and manageable by eliminating code duplication.
    (i) Multiple parameters are not supported while defining class and function templates.
    (j) Template arguments can take default values.

13

C++ I/O

The C language provides a rich functionality for input/output operations. C++ being a superset of C language supports the existing I/O functionality as defined in C language specifications. However, C language is not object-oriented. To support object-orientation in I/O implementation, C++ defines several classes that provide I/O operations. In this chapter, we will learn how to perform I/O operations using the pre-defined C++ classes. We will learn the following:

- What is a stream?
- Pre-defined streams in C++
- Formatting the program output using pre-defined stream classes
- Understanding use of manipulators in formatting the output
- Performing file I/O operations
- Files operating on built-in and user-defined data types
- Handling exceptions during I/O operations
- Character versus binary mode of file operations
- Random access files.

THE C++ I/O SYSTEMS

The C++ I/O system evolved over many years and thus has two subsystems, the older system that defines several classes for I/O operations and the new system that uses the template approach for defining several classes (*Templates were discussed in Chapter 12*). As the new system is essentially a superset of the old system, we will discuss here only the new system based on the templates.

The entire C++ I/O system is based on the use of *streams*. Streams are discussed in the following section.

STREAMS

A *stream* is a logical device that either produces or consumes the data. It is a medium through which a read/write operation is performed. The medium may be a source of data or a consumer of data.

Streams are of two types:

- Input stream
- Output stream

The *input stream* helps in reading data from a medium and the *output stream* helps in writing data to a medium.

The entire new I/O system of C++ is based on a template hierarchy. At the root, we have `ios` class. The three of the most important derived classes from `ios` class that are of our interest are listed below:

- `istream`—input stream
- `ostream`—output stream
- `iostream`—input/output stream

Figure 13.1 shows the class hierarchy of stream classes.

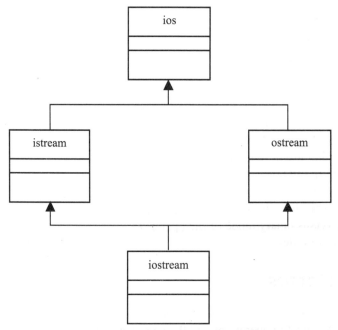

Figure 13.1 Stream class hierarchy.

We have two types of specializations based on templates—one for supporting 8-bit characters and other for supporting 16-bit wide characters.

We may use either 8-bit or 16-bit representations in your program to create a stream. Once a stream object is constructed, it must be linked to some media, such as disk file, console, printer, etc.

C++ provides a few pre-defined streams.

Pre-defined Streams

The C++ runtime provides four pre-defined streams:

- `cin`—standard input
- `cout`—standard output
- `cerr`—standard error output
- `clog`—buffered version of cerr

These streams are created whenever the C++ runtime is loaded in the system. These four streams are attached to pre-defined devices. The `cin` stream, which is an input stream, gets connected to the keyboard while the rest of the streams, which are of type output, get connected to the console by default. We have already used `cin` and `cout` streams in our programs in earlier chapters.

We will now discuss the functionality provided by the stream classes by taking some examples. The best way to learn the class functionality is to use them in your applications. With this approach, we will discuss various applications that use the several I/O classes provided in C++ standard library.

Formatting Output

Let us suppose that we wish to print the following invoice on the printer or on the user console:

```
P(IV) Computer  +10000.00
Less Discount    -500.00
Tax +100.00

Total:       +9600.00
```

We will use several formatting features provided in the `cout` stream to achieve the above result. If we examine the above output carefully, we will notice that the output uses two columns, in the first column we print the description and in the second column, a numeric value. The first column text is left aligned while the second column text is right aligned. The floating-point numbers printed in the second column are printed to two-decimal precision after the decimal point. The positive numbers are printed with the positive sign.

The full program listing that produces the above output is given at the end of this section.

We now discuss how to achieve the above output. To format the output, `cout` provides a function called `setf` that takes a single parameter as input. The parameter defines the desired formatting. The `setf` function is inherited from the base class `base_ios`. There are several other useful functions defined in this base class. We will discuss some of these as we proceed through the various examples in the chapter.

To achieve the left alignment for the column output, we use the following statement:

```
cout.setf (ios::left);
```

The parameter that is passed to the `setf` function is `ios::left`. Here `left` is a predefined constant in `ios` class. We use the scope resolution operator to specify that `left` belongs to `ios` class.

We set the column width by calling the inherited `width` method.

```
cout.width (30);
```

Finally, we output the desired text as follows:

```
cout << "P(IV) Computer";
```

Now, we do the second column printing. The text in the second column is right-aligned. We use the `ios::right` formatting constant for the second column.

```
cout.setf (ios::right);
```

We set the column width to 10.

```
cout.width(10);
```

The second column prints the numeric data. The number is printed to two-digit precision after the decimal point. We achieve this using the following method calls:

```
cout.setf (ios::fixed);
cout.precision(2);
```

To show the leading positive sign, we call `setf` function with `ios::showpos` as parameter:

```
cout.setf (ios::showpos);
```

Finally, we output the desired string in the second column:

```
cout << 10000.00 << endl;
```

After the second column is printed, we reset the right-alignment by calling `unsetf` method:

```
cout.unsetf(ios::right);
```

We repeat the above code for the rest of the lines to achieve the desired output. The complete program is given in Listing 13.1.

Listing 13.1:   Formatting output to console

```
#include "stdafx.h"
#include <iostream>
using namespace std;

int main()
{
    cout.setf (ios::fixed);
    cout.precision(2);
    cout.setf (ios::showpos);
```

```
cout.setf (ios::left);
cout.width (30);
cout << "P(IV) Computer";

cout.setf (ios::right);
cout.width(10);
cout << 10000.00 << endl;

cout.unsetf(ios::right);
cout.setf (ios::left);
cout.width (30);
cout << "Less Discount";

cout.setf (ios::right);
cout.width(10);
cout << -500.00 << endl;

cout.unsetf(ios::right);
cout.setf (ios::left);
cout.width (30);
cout << "Tax";

cout.setf (ios::right);
cout.width(10);
cout << 100.00 << endl;

cout.unsetf(ios::right);
cout.setf (ios::left);
cout.width (40);
char Separator[41];
for (int i=0; i< 40; i++)
Separator [i] = '-';
Separator [40] = '\0';
cout << Separator << endl;

cout.unsetf(ios::right);
cout.setf (ios::left);
cout.width (30);
cout << "Total: ";

cout.setf (ios::right);
cout.width(10);
cout << 9600.00 << endl;

return 0;
}
```

The program output is as follows:

```
P(IV) Computer +10000.00
Less Discount   -500.00
Tax +100.00
```
————————————————————
```
Total:      +9600.00
```

Having seen how to use some of the member functions of ios class for formatting the output, we will discuss other formatting tags provided in the ios class.

The `ios` Class Formatting Flags

The ios class provides several formatting flags. We have already discussed some flags such as fixed, showpos, left and right, in the previous section. In this section, we will discuss some more commonly used flags. The reader is referred to the C++ documentation for the complete list of flags.

The *boolalpha* flag

This flag is used to convert a bool variable to strings such as true or false. We set this flag on a given stream using the setf method.

```
stream.setf (ios::boolalpha);
```

Once the flag is set, the 0 is represented as false and 1 is represented as true. This is illustrated in the following program given in Listing 13.2.

Listing 13.2:   Entering boolean data by specifying formatting flag

```
#include "stdafx.h"
#include <iostream>
using namespace std;

int main()
{
    bool b;
    cout.setf (ios::boolalpha);
    cin.setf (ios::boolalpha);
    cout << "Enter a boolean: ";
    cin >> b;
    cout << "You Entered " << b << endl;
    return 0;
}
```

The program sets the boolalpha flag on both standard input (cin) and standard output (cout) streams. The user may now input the boolean as either false or true. The program output for the two different inputs is shown below:

```
Enter a boolean: true
You Entered true

Enter a boolean: false
You Entered false
```

The *scientific* flag

Once set, this flag causes the floating-point numbers to be printed in exponential format. The following code snippet illustrates the use of this flag:

```
cout.setf (ios::scientific);
cout << "Scientific format: " << 100.00 << endl;
```

The output produced by the above code would be as follows:

```
Scientific format: 1.000000e+002
```

MANIPULATORS

In the previous sections, we saw the use of some of the formatting flags for formatting the stream data. The alternate way for formatting stream data is to use *manipulators*. These are special functions that are included in an I/O expression to format the data. C++ defines several manipulators that provide functionality equivalent to the formatting functions of ios class. We will discuss the use of some of the manipulators in this section.

The endl Manipulator

We have been using endl in several of our programs in the earlier chapters. The endl manipulator, as we know, causes a newline character (' \n ') to be output. It also flushes the output stream. We use this manipulator as follows:

```
cout << "C++ endl manipulator" << endl;
```

This causes a new line to be printed after the specified message is printed on the console. For a console output, this advances the cursor to the beginning of the new line.

The hex/oct/dec/showbase Manipulators

We may like to display a given number in any of the base formats such as hexadecimal, octal or decimal. The hexadecimal numbers in C++ start with a leading 0x and octal numbers start with a leading 0. The showbase manipulator prefixes the given number with these characters while displaying the number in the respective base formats. The hex manipulator converts the given number to hexadecimal before outputting it. Similarly, the oct and dec manipulators convert the given number to octal and decimal formats before outputting. The program in Listing 13.3 illustrates the use of these manipulators.

Listing 13.3: **Use of manipulators**

```cpp
#include "stdafx.h"
#include <iostream>
using namespace std;

int main()
{
    int i = 256;
    cout << "Octal: " << showbase << oct << i << endl;
    cout << "Hex: " << showbase << hex << i << endl;
    cout << "Decimal: " << showbase << dec << i << endl;
    return 0;
}
```

The program first displays the given integer i in octal notation.

```cpp
cout << "Octal: " << showbase << oct << i << endl;
```

The showbase manipulator ensures that the leading 0 is added to the displayed number. The displayed number is the octal equivalent of the specified decimal number, i.e. 256.

The next program statement displays the number in hexadecimal format.

```cpp
cout << "Hex: " << showbase << hex << i << endl;
```

The showbase again ensures that the leading 0x is added to the displayed number. The hex manipulator converts the number to hexadecimal format before it is displayed.

Finally, the number is printed in decimal format.

```cpp
cout << "Decimal: " << showbase << dec << i << endl;
```

For decimal format, there is no leading character. The program output is shown below:

```
Octal: 0400
Hex: 0x100
Decimal: 256
```

The uppercase Manipulator

The uppercase manipulator prints the leading format characters for hexadecimal numbers in upper case. The following program statement illustrates the use of uppercase manipulator:

```cpp
cout << "Hex: " << showbase << uppercase << hex << i << endl;
```

The output produced by this statement is shown below:

```
Hex: 0X100
```

Floating Point Number Manipulators

The following program statement illustrates how to format a floating point number while displaying it on the console.

```cpp
cout << setfill('*') << setw(10) << fixed << setprecision(2)
     << 10000.00 << endl;
```

Here, we print the floating point number 10000.00 on the user console.

The setfill fills the leading spaces with the character specified in its parameter list. In the current statement, the leading character that is used is asterisk ('*'). The setw sets the output width to the value specified in its parameter. The fixed manipulator turns on the fixed flag discussed in the previous section and setprecision sets the number of decimal digits to display after the decimal point. The output produced by the above statement is shown below:

```
**10000.00
```

Note that for the manipulators in this example, we will need to add the following header to your source program:

```
#include <iomanip>
```

FILE I/O

In the previous sections, we have seen the use of pre-defined streams. In addition to this, C++ provides several classes for creating user-defined streams. The streams connected to the physical disk files play an important role in data storage management. Like for the earlier case, there are three types of streams, input stream, output stream and input/output stream. The derived classes for these three types of streams are as follows:

- **ifstream**—derives from the istream class and is used for reading data from a file.
- **ofstream**—derives from ostream class and is used for writing data to a file.
- **fstream**—derives from iostream class and is used to perform both read and write operations on a file.

The class hierarchy for these classes is shown in Figure 13.2.

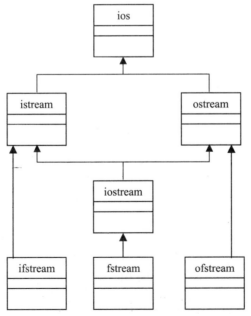

Figure 13.2 Hierarchy of file classes derived from stream.

We will now consider various operations supported by these classes.

Opening Files

When you open a physical file for reading/writing, you are essentially connecting this to a stream object. The following two ways may open the file:

- Pass the filename to the `stream` constructor
- Call the `open` member function of the `stream` class.

Using constructor

In this case, we pass the name of the physical file to the constructor of the stream class. For example, if we wish to open a file called 'autoexec.bat' for reading, we may use the following syntax:

```
ifstream infile ("autoexec.bat");
```

Similarly, if we wish to open a file for writing, we will use the following syntax:

```
ofstream outfile ("MyFile.dat");
```

Note that the above method call destroys the original file contents if one such exists; if the file does not exist it creates a new file using the specified name.

Using `open` method

In this case, we first construct the stream object. We call the `open` method on the stream object to connect the physical file to the created stream object. For example, to open the 'autoexec.bat' file for reading, we would use the following syntax:

```
ifstream is;
is.open ("autoexec.bat");
```

To open a file for writing, we use the following code:

```
ofstream os;
os.open ("MyFile.dat");
```

The above method call destroys the original contents of the specified file, if one such exists. To open a file for writing without destroying its contents, we need to use an overloaded `open` method as shown below:

```
os.open ("MyFile.dat", ios:app);
```

The second parameter in the above method call specifies that the file should be opened for append operation. In this case, the new data will be written to the end of the file.

Reading and Writing Files

After a file is opened for reading/writing, data may be read from or written to it using the indirection operators (>> and <<). To read data from the file, we use the overloaded << operator and to write data to a file, we use the overloaded operator >>. Note that both these operators are overloaded in the stream class.

Reading and writing standard data types

First, we will learn how to read/write standard data types to a physical file. Let us consider that we wish to write three integer data items to a file. We need to create a file for writing. We use the stream constructor to create the file and connect it to a newly created stream object.

```
ofstream writer("MyFile.txt");
```

The name of the file is `MyFile.txt`. If the file with this name does not exist, a new file will be created. If the file with the given name exists, it is open for writing and the existing file contents are destroyed.

We use the << operator to write to the file:

```
writer << 12 << " " << 18 <<" "<< 24;
```

The above statement writes three data items to the file: 12, 18 and 24. Each data item is separated by a space. This is required so that later when we read from the file, the three data items can be separated.

After writing the desired data, we close the file by calling the `close` method of the stream class.

```
writer.close();
```

We will now open the file for reading by calling the constructor for the `ifstream` class.

```
ifstream reader("MyFile.txt");
```

We now read the first data item from the file by using the overloaded >> operator.

```
int num1;
reader>>num1;
```

This reads the first data item from the file, namely, 12. Likewise, we can read the rest of the data items from the file. At the end, we close the file by calling the `close` method.

The full program listing for writing/reading standard data type is given in Listing 13.4.

Listing 13.4:   Reading, writing standard data types

```
#include "stdafx.h"
#include <iostream>
#include <fstream>
using namespace std;

void main()
{
    cout << "Opening/Creating MyFile.txt for writing" << endl;
    ofstream writer("MyFile.txt");
    cout << "Writing three data items 12, 18, 24 ..." << endl;
    writer<<12<< " " << 18 <<" "<<24;
    cout << "Closing output file" << endl;
    writer.close();
    cout << endl;
```

```
cout << "Opening MyFile.txt for reading" << endl;
ifstream reader("MyFile.txt");
int num1, num2, num3;
cout << "Reading three data items ..." << endl;
reader>>num1;
reader>>num2;
reader>>num3;

cout<< "Data Item 1: " <<num1<<endl;
cout<< "Data Item 2: " <<num2<<endl;
cout<< "Data Item 3: " <<num3<<endl;
cout << "Closing file" << endl;
reader.close();
}
```

When we run the above program, we will see the following output:

```
Opening/Creating MyFile.txt for writing
Writing three data items 12, 18, 24 ...
Closing output file

Opening MyFile.txt for reading
Reading three data items ...
Data Item 1: 12
Data Item 2: 18
Data Item 3: 24
Closing file
```

Handling errors during file open operation

A file open operation may fail due to unforeseen results. This causes an abnormal program termination. We can test for the success of file open before proceeding with the operations on the file. A call to the constructor in the above program returns a null object, in case of error. We test for the null object for any errors. The following code snippet shows how to test for the success of file opening:

```
ofstream writer("MyFile.txt");
if (!writer)
    cout << "Could not open file for writing" << endl;
```

Likewise, when we open the file for reading, check for the null value of the returned stream object as shown below:

```
if (!reader)
    cout << "Could not open file for reading" << endl;
```

Reading/writing strings

The indirection operator used in the previous program reads a data item from the file until it encounters a space or a newline character. As the strings would usually contain spaces, the indirection operator cannot be used for reading such character strings. The ifstream class provides several methods for reading strings from a file, one such method being getline. The getline method reads the character string until it encounters a newline or end-of-file character, whichever comes first.

We will write a program that writes three strings to a file and later set up a loop to read back these strings from the created file.

We open the file for writing by calling the ofstream constructor:

```
ofstream writer("MyFile.txt");
```

After testing for file open errors, we write a test string to the file.

```
writer<<"Test String 1" << endl;
```

Note that we have also written a newline character at the end of the string. Likewise, we will write two more test strings to the file. We close the file by calling the close method.

Next, we open the created file for reading.

```
ifstream reader("MyFile.txt");
```

We read the strings from the input stream by setting up a for loop as follows:

```
char str[50];
for (int i=0; i<3; i++)
{
    reader.getline(str, 50);
    cout<< str << endl;
}
```

The getline method takes two parameters, the first parameter is a pointer to the buffer where the read data is stored. The second parameter indicates the number of characters to read. The method reads from the file until it encounters a delimiter, i.e. a newline character or EOF or the number of characters specified in the second parameter—whichever comes first. After reading the string from the file, the program prints it on the user console.

The complete program listing for reading/writing strings to a file is given in Listing 13.5.

Listing 13.5:   Reading, writing strings

```
#include "stdafx.h"

#include <iostream>
#include <fstream>
using namespace std;

void main()
{
    cout << "Opening/Creating Myfile.txt for writing" << endl;
    ofstream writer("MyFile.txt");
```

```
    if (!writer)
    cout << "Could not open file for writing" << endl;
    cout << "Writing three test strings ..." << endl;
    writer<<"Test String 1" << endl;
    writer<<"Test String 2" << endl;
    writer<<"Test String 3" << endl;
    cout << "Closing file" << endl;
    writer.close();
    cout << endl;

    cout << "Opening Myfile.txt for reading" << endl;
    ifstream reader("MyFile.txt");
    if (!reader)
    cout << "Could not open file for reading" << endl;
    char str[50];
    cout << "Reading three strings ..." << endl;
    for (int i=0; i<3; i++)
    {
        reader.getline(str, 50);
        cout<< str << endl;
    }
    cout << "Closing file" << endl;
    reader.close();
}
```

The program output is shown below:

```
Opening/Creating Myfile.txt for writing
Writing three test strings ...
Closing file

Opening Myfile.txt for reading
Reading three strings ...
Test String 1
Test String 2
Test String 3
Closing file
```

Reading/writing user-defined types

So far we have considered writing basic data types and strings to a physical file. In practice, we define several structures or classes in our program that encapsulate the logically related data. For example, consider an employee structure. The employee structure contains various data fields such as name, age, gender, salary, etc. We will usually create a class for representing employee object in your application. Our application may contain several such employee objects. We may like to store the state of these objects to a persistent storage like a disk file.

In this section, we will create an `Employee` class, create few objects of this type and learn how to store/retrieve these objects to a physical data file.

The full program listing is given later in this section.

We create an `Employee` class having two `private` data members.

```
class Employee
{
    int EmpID;
    float Salary;
```

The `EmpID` stores the unique identifier for the employee and `Salary` field stores the employee's current salary. We will use only two data members here to keep our program simple. In real life, the employee class would contain several more fields.

We define two constructors for the `Employee` class:

```
Employee (int id, float salary)
{
    // implementation
}
Employee ()
{
    // implementation
}
```

The first constructor receives two parameters and uses them to initialize the two data members. The second constructor is a no-argument constructor that initializes the data members to default values.

We write `Dump` method for the `Employee` class that dumps the contents of the two data members on the console:

```
void Dump ()
{
    cout << "Employee ID: " << EmpID << " "
        << " Salary: " << Salary << endl;
}
```

In the `main` method, we construct a couple of `Employee` objects for storage:

```
Employee emp1 (1, 10000);
...
```

We open a file in output mode for storing the employee data:

```
ofstream os ("Payroll.dat",
ios::out | ios:: binary);
```

The file `Payroll.dat` is opened as an output file and is opened in binary mode. (*The character versus binary mode of opening a file is discussed later in the section 'Character versus Binary Mode'*.) All our earlier examples opened files in character mode.

We write data to the `payroll.dat` file as follows:

```
os.write((char *)&emp1, sizeof(Employee));
```

The `write` method of `stream` class takes two parameters. The first parameter specifies the data to be written and the second parameter specifies the number of bytes to write. Note that we use the typecast on the first parameter as the `write` method expects a pointer to the character array containing data. The number of bytes to write is decided by determining the size of the `Employee` structure/class.

Likewise, we will store the remaining employee's data to the disk file and finally close the file using `close` method.

To read the data from the stored file, we need to first open the file for reading. We do so by creating an object of `ifstream` class as follows:

```
ifstream is ("Payroll.dat",
ios::in | ios:: binary);
```

The first parameter to the `ifstream` constructor specifies the name of the physical file and the second parameter specifies the file mode. The mode used in the above statement indicates that the file is opened for reading (`ios::in` parameter) and is opened in binary mode as indicated by `ios::binary` flag. The two flags are logically ORed.

After opening the file, we read from it by calling the `read` method on the stream.

```
Employee emp;
is.read((char *)&emp, sizeof (Employee));
```

The first parameter to the read method is a pointer to the buffer in which the read data will be stored. The second parameter indicates the number of bytes to read.

We can examine the contents of the read object by calling the `Dump` method of our `Employee` class.

```
emp.Dump();
```

The complete program listing that illustrates how to read/write user defined objects to a physical file is given in Listing 13.6.

Listing 13.6:   Reading, writing user-defined types

```
#include "stdafx.h"
#include <iostream>
#include <fstream>
using namespace std;

class Employee
{
    int EmpID;
    float Salary;
```

```cpp
public:
    Employee (int id, float salary)
    {
        EmpID = id;
        Salary = salary;
    }
    Employee ()
    {
        EmpID = 0;
        Salary = 0;
    }
    void Dump ()
    {
        cout << "Employee ID = " << EmpID << " " << " Salary = "
        << Salary << endl;
    }
};

int main(int argc, char* argv[])
{
    cout << "Creating three employee objects ..." << endl;
    Employee emp1 (1, 10000);
    Employee emp2 (2, 20000);
    Employee emp3 (3, 8000);

    cout << "Creating/Opening payroll.dat file for writing" << endl;
    ofstream os ("Payroll.dat", ios::out | ios::binary);
    if (!os)
    {
        cout << "Could not open output file" << endl;
        exit(0);
    }
    cout << "Writing three employee objects ..." << endl;
    os.write((char *)&emp1, sizeof(Employee));
    os.write((char *)&emp2, sizeof(Employee));
    os.write((char *)&emp3, sizeof(Employee));
    cout << "Closing file" << endl;
    os.close();
    cout << endl;

    cout << "Opening payroll.dat file for reading" << endl;
    ifstream is ("Payroll.dat", ios::in | ios:: binary);
    if (!is)
    {
        cout << "Could not open input file" << endl;
        exit(0);
    }
```

```
    Employee emp;
    cout << "Reading three employee objects ..." << endl;
    for (int i=0; i<3; i++)
    {
        is.read((char *)&emp, sizeof (Employee));
        emp.Dump();
    }
    cout << "Closing file" << endl;
    is.close();
    return 0;
}
```

The program output is shown below:

```
        Creating three employee objects ...
        Creating/Opening payroll.dat file for writing
        Writing three employee objects ...
        Closing file

        Opening payroll.dat file for reading
        Reading three employee objects ...
        Employee ID = 1 Salary = 10000
        Employee ID = 2 Salary = 20000
        Employee ID = 3 Salary = 8000
        Closing file
```

Character versus Binary Mode

In the previous sections, we learned how to read/write character data files. While discussing how to read/write user-defined types to a file, we used binary mode for storing/retrieving objects of user-defined data types. We will elaborate more on these two types of file access in this section.

We access the file in character mode if we are reading/writing strings. The several built-in functions interpret the character strings appropriately while performing the file I/O. The C++ library provides two types of classes for dealing with character strings—one set operates on an 8-bit character while the other operates on a 16-bit character set. We may use any of the two options depending on whether your data consists of ASCII (one byte) or UNICODE (two bytes).

If we wish to deal with the raw data, i.e. the data at the byte level, we open the file in binary mode. In binary mode, the data is read/written at the byte level, for example, a newline character will be interpreted as two characters—carriage return (CR) and line feed (LF).

In this section, we will develop a file dump utility. We will develop two versions of the program. The first version will operate on character-oriented files and open the file using character mode. The second program will operate on binary files, i.e. files containing even non-printable data. We will use the binary mode for opening such files.

The `type/cat` Utility

We must have used the `type` utility provided on Windows or the `cat` utility provided on Unix/Linux that dumps the file contents on the user console. We will develop a small program here that does a job similar to *type/cat* utility. We will consider only the character-oriented files here.

We use the command line arguments to accept the file name from the user. The program prints the contents of the specified file on the user console.

We open the file specified on the command line by constructing an object of `ifstream` class:

```
ifstream is (argv[1]);
```

On opening the file successfully, we use the following loop to read the contents of the file line by line and print each read line on the console:

```
char ch[256];
while (!is.eof())
{
    is.getline(ch, 255);
    cout << ch << endl;
}
```

The loop uses `eof` method to test if the file is fully read. The `getline` method reads the file contents line-by-line. The first parameter to the `getline` method accepts the buffer address in which the contents are read. The second parameter specifies the number of characters to read. We specify 255 as the value for this second parameter with the assumption that no line will contain more than 255 characters. The `getline` method reads the file contents until it encounters a `newline` character or it has read up to the number of characters specified in the second parameter, whichever comes first. The program prints the read line on the user console by redirecting the data to `cout`. The full program for the `type` utility is given in Listing 13.7.

Listing 13.7: Program to dump text file contents

```
#include "stdafx.h"
#include <iostream>
#include <fstream>
using namespace std;

int main(int argc, char* argv[])
{
    if (argc != 2)
    {
        cout << "Usage:type filename" << endl;
        exit(0);
    }
    ifstream is (argv[1]);
    if (!is) {
        cout << "Could not open input file" << endl;
        exit(0);
    }
```

```
char ch[256];
while (!is.eof())
{
    is.getline(ch, 255);
    cout << ch << endl;
}
cout << endl;
return 0;
}
```

Assuming that the above program is stored under the name *type.cpp*, use the following command line to test the program:

```
type filename
```

Here, filename specifies any character file, the contents of which are to be dumped on the console.

Now, we will develop a file dump utility that dumps the contents of a binary file on the user console.

File dump Utility

To dump the file contents in hexadecimal, we open the file in binary mode and read its contents byte by byte. We open the file by creating an object of `ifstream` class:

```
ifstream in (argv[1], ios::in | ios::binary);
```

The second parameter in the above call to the constructor specifies that the file be opened in binary mode. We read the file contents by setting up a loop that checks for the end of file condition:

```
while (!in.eof())
{
    // read each byte and print on console
}
```

To read the file contents, we use the `get` method:

```
char ch;
in.get(ch);
```

The `get` method reads a single byte and copies it in the character variable specified in its parameter list. We print the character on the user console by using `cout` stream after providing some formatting on the character printed.

```
cout << setw(2) << hex << (int) ch << " ";
```

The character is printed in hex notation by using `hex` manipulator.

To print each hex character in upper case and to provide a leading zero, we provide general formatting before the `while` loop.

```
cout.setf (ios::uppercase);
cout.fill ('0');
```

The `while` loop advances the cursor to the next line after every 16 bytes. The complete program listing for the file dump utility is given in Listing 13.8.

Listing 13.8:   Program to dump binary file contents

```
#include "stdafx.h"
#include <iostream>
#include <fstream>
#include <iomanip>
using namespace std;

int main(int argc, char* argv[])
{
    if (argc != 2)
    {
        cout << "Usage: cat filename" << endl;
        exit(0);
    }
    ifstream in (argv[1], ios::in | ios:: binary);
    if (!in) {
        cout << "Could not open input file" << endl;
        exit(0);
    }

    cout.setf (ios::uppercase);
    cout.fill ('0');

    char ch;
    char count = 0;
    while (!in.eof())
    {
        in.get(ch);
        cout << setw(2) << hex << (int) ch << "";
        count++;
        if (count == 16)
        {
            cout << endl;
            count = 0;
        }
    }
    cout << endl;
    return 0;
}
```

A typical program output is shown below:

75	74	2E	66	69	6C	6C	20	28	27	30	27	29	3B	0D	0A
0D	0A	09	63	68	61	72	20	63	5B	31	36	5D	3B	0D	0A
09	63	68	61	72	20	63	68	3B	0D	0A	09	63	68	61	72
20	63	6F	75	6E	74	20	3D	20	30	3B	0D	0A	09	77	68
69	6C	65	20	28	21	69	6E	2E	65	6F	66	28	29	29	20
0D	0A	09	7B	0D	0A	09	09	69	6E	2E	67	65	74	28	63
68	29	3B	0D	0A	09	09	63	6F	75	74	20	3C	3C	20	73
65	74	77	28	32	29	20	3C	3C	20	68	65	78	20	3C	3C
20	28	69	6E	74	29	20	63	68	20	3C	3C	20	22	20	22
3B	0D	0A	09	09	63	6F	75	6E	74	2B	2B	3B	0D	0A	09
09	69	66	20	28	63	6F	75	6E	74	20	3D	3D	20	31	36
29	0D	0A	09	09	7B	0D	0A	09	09	09	63	6F	75	74	20
3C	3C	20	65	6E	64	6C	3B	0D	0A	09	09	09	63	6F	75
6E	74	20	3D	20	30	3B	0D	0A	09	09	7D	0D	0A	09	7D
0D	0A	09	63	6F	75	74	20	3C	3C	20	65	6E	64	6C	3B
0D	0A	09	72	65	74	75	72	6E	20	30	3B	0D	0A	7D	0D
0A	0A														

Firstly, we will develop a file copy utility that copies the contents of one file to another one byte at a time. Both input and output files will be opened in binary mode.

File copy Utility

The file copy utility accepts two command line parameters. The first parameter specifies the source file name and the second parameter specifies the destination file name. The contents of the source file are copied to the destination file.

We open the file specified by the command line parameter 1 for reading:

```
ifstream in (argv[1], ios::in | ios::binary);
```

We specify the binary mode while opening the file. The file specified by the second command line parameter is opened for writing:

```
ofstream out (argv[2], ios::out | ios::binary);
```

We now set up a loop for reading the contents of the input file and copying it to the output file.

```
char ch;
while (true)
{
    in.get(ch);
    if (in.eof())
        break;
    out.put (ch);
}
```

The get method reads a character from the input file into the character variable ch. If the character read is end-of-file character, we terminate the loop; otherwise we copy the character to the output file by calling the put method.

The complete program listing for the file copy utility is given in Listing 13.9.

Listing 13.9:   The file copy program

```cpp
// cp.cpp - copies source file to destination
#include "stdafx.h"
#include <iostream>
#include <fstream>
#include <iomanip>
using namespace std;

int main(int argc, char* argv[])
{
    if (argc != 3)
    {
        cout << "Usage: copy source destination" << endl;
        exit(0);
    }
    ifstream in (argv[1], ios::in | ios:: binary);
    if (!in) {
        cout << "Could not open input file" << endl;
        exit(0);
    }

    ofstream out (argv[2], ios::out | ios:: binary);
    if (!out) {
        cout << "Could not open output file for writing" << endl;
        exit(0);
    }

    char ch;
    while (true)
    {
        in.get(ch);
        if (in.eof())
            break;
        out.put (ch);
    }
    return 0;
}
```

To run the above program, use the following command line:

```
C:\>cp sourcefile destinationfile
```

RANDOM ACCESS FILES

So far, we have studied the sequential access to files. All the programs discussed in the previous sections accessed the file contents sequentially from start to end. In all such cases, the file pointer used for accessing the data advanced to the next byte following the number of bytes read after each read operation on the file. Every subsequent read operation takes place from the current file pointer position.

There are many situations where we will like to access the contents of a given file at random. In our earlier example of storing the employee salary records, we may come across a need to locate and print the salary of a certain employee given his/her ID. In such a case, we will like to read only the desired record rather than going through all the records sequentially from the start until we reach the desired record.

Sometimes, we may like to run through the list of records back and forth and print each one individually. In such cases, we need a random access on the records.

In this section, we will rework our program of employee records maintenance to access a record with a known position in the file, modify the employee salary for the retrieved record and re-write the modified record at the same old position.

We start with the program developed in the earlier section. We add one more method to our `Employee` class that will allow us to modify the `salary` field.

```
void SetSalary (float salary)
{
    Salary = salary;
}
```

In the `main` program, we will create three `Employee` objects, create a file with the name `payroll.dat` and write the three records to it. We close the file and reopen it for reading. We will read the three records sequentially and dump them on the user console. This part of the program is the same as the one developed earlier in the section *'Reading/writing user-defined types'*.

Now, we will study the random access to the created data file. We will modify the second record such that the salary for the second employee is changed from its initial value of 20000 to 12000. To access the second record, we use the `seekg` method of the stream class.

```
stream.seekg(1*sizeof (Employee), ios::beg);
```

The `seekg` method takes two parameters. The first parameter specifies the starting byte position of the desired record. We compute the start position of the second record by multiplying the record number minus 1 with the size of each record. Note that for the first record, the start byte position in the file is zero. Thus, for the second record, the starting byte position is (2–1) multiplied by record size and so on. Thus, in general, the start byte position for the *n*th record is (*n*–1) multiplied by the size of each record.

The second parameter to the `seekg` method specifies the position from which the above offset is calculated. In the above statement, we use `ios::beg` flag indicating that the position indicated by the first parameter is offset with respect to the beginning of the file. The other two valid parameter values for the second parameter are `ios::end` and `ios::cur`. The `ios::end` specifies that the offset is calculated with respect to the end of the file and `ios::cur` specifies that the offset is calculated with respect to the current file pointer position.

After seeking the file pointer to the desired location, we read the record by calling the `read` method.

```
stream.read((char *)&emp, sizeof (Employee));
```

The `read` method copies the read record in the buffer specified by the first parameter. The second parameter specifies the number of bytes to read, that is, the record size.

Once the record is ready in temporary buffer emp, we modify its `salary` field by calling the `SetSalary` method.

```
emp.SetSalary(12000);
```

We now reset the record pointer position to the beginning of the second record one more time. This is required as the previous read operation sets the file pointer pointing to the third record.

```
stream.seekg(1*sizeof (Employee), ios::beg);
```

Then we use the `write` method to write the modified record at the current file pointer position.

```
stream.write((char *)&emp, sizeof(Employee));
```

The file now contains the modified record. This can be verified by closing the file, reopening it for reading and dumping its contents on the screen.

The full program is given in Listing 13.10.

Listing 13.10:   File random access

```
#include "stdafx.h"
#include <iostream>
#include <fstream>
using namespace std;

class Employee
{
    int EmpID;
    float Salary;
public:
    Employee (int id, float salary)
    {
        EmpID = id;
        Salary = salary;
    }
    Employee ()
    {
        EmpID = 0;
        Salary = 0;
    }
    void SetSalary (float salary)
    {
        Salary = salary;
    }
```

```cpp
        void Dump ()
        {
            cout << "Employee ID: " << EmpID << " " << " Salary: "
            << Salary << endl;
        }
};

int main(int argc, char* argv[])
{
    Employee emp1 (1, 10000);
    Employee emp2 (2, 20000);
    Employee emp3 (3, 8000);

    cout << "Creating payroll data" << endl;
    ofstream os ("Payroll.dat", ios::out | ios::binary);
    if (!os)
    {
        cout << "Could not open output file" << endl;
        exit(0);
    }
    os.write((char *)&emp1, sizeof(Employee));
    os.write((char *)&emp2, sizeof(Employee));
    os.write((char *)&emp3, sizeof(Employee));
    os.close();

    fstream stream ("Payroll.dat", ios::in | ios ::out | ios::binary);
    if (!stream)
    {
        cout << "Could not open input file" << endl;
        exit(0);
    }

    cout << "The current data" << endl;
    Employee emp;
    for (int i=0; i<3; i++)
    {
        stream.read((char *)&emp, sizeof (Employee));
        emp.Dump();
    }
    cout << endl;

    cout << "Retrieving second record" << endl;
    stream.seekg(1*sizeof (Employee), ios:: beg);
    stream.read((char *)&emp, sizeof (Employee));
    cout << "Modifying salary for second employee" << endl << endl;
```

```
emp.SetSalary(12000);
stream.seekg(1*sizeof (Employee), ios:: beg);
stream.write((char *)&emp, sizeof (Employee));

cout << "Modified data" << endl;
stream.seekg (0, ios::beg);
for (i=0; i<3; i++)
{
    stream.read((char *)&emp, sizeof (Employee));
    emp.Dump();
}
stream.close();

return 0;
}
```

The program output is shown below. From the output, one can easily see that the file now contains the modified record:

```
Creating payroll data
The current data
Employee ID: 1 Salary: 10000
Employee ID: 2 Salary: 20000
Employee ID: 3 Salary: 8000

Retrieving second record
Modifying salary for second employee

Modified data
Employee ID: 1 Salary: 10000
Employee ID: 2 Salary: 12000
Employee ID: 3 Salary: 8000
```

Thus, we were able to access a random record in a binary file, read it, modify it and rewrite it to the same location.

In the next section, we will learn the use of another function called `seekp` that allows us to locate any randomly decided position in the file for update.

The `seekp` Function

Consider that we have to write a program to dump the numbers from 0 to 99 in a binary file. Each number is written as a two-character string. Between every two numbers we would add a space character. After creating the file, if we dump its contents using a `type` or a `cat` command, we will see all the numbers lined up one after another with no line breaks except for the default line break provided by the operating system. Such an output is shown below:

00	01	02	03	04	05	06	07	08	09	10	11	12	13	14	15	16	17
18	19	20	21	22	23	24	25	26									
27	28	29	30	31	32	33	34	35	36	37	38	39	40	41	42	43	44
45	46	47	48	49	50	51	52	5									
3	54	55	56	57	58	59	60	61	62	63	64	65	66	67	68	69	70
71	72	73	74	75	76	77	78	79									
80	81	82	83	84	85	86	87	88	89	90	91	92	93	94	95	96	97
98	99																

The output is definitely unformatted and we would like to format this properly while presenting it on the user console. If we provide a line break after printing a set of 10 numbers, the output would be better looking as shown below:

00	01	02	03	04	05	06	07	08	09
10	11	12	13	14	15	16	17	18	19
20	21	22	23	24	25	26	27	28	29
30	31	32	33	34	35	36	37	38	39
40	41	42	43	44	45	46	47	48	49
50	51	52	53	54	55	56	57	58	59
60	61	62	63	64	65	66	67	68	69
70	71	72	73	74	75	76	77	78	79
80	81	82	83	84	85	86	87	88	89
90	91	92	93	94	95	96	97	98	99

To achieve the above output while dumping the file contents using `type` or `cat` utility, we will have to replace the space character after every 10th number with a newline character. We use `seekp` method to achieve this.

We will now discuss the development of such a program.

We will first create the data file for our use in this application. We open a file for writing in binary mode:

```
ofstream os ("TextFile.txt", ios::binary);
```

We write numbers 0 to 99 to the file using the following loop:

```
for (int i=0; i< 100; i++)
{
    os << setw(2) << setfill('0') << i << " ";
}
```

The width allocated for each number is two characters. In the case of single digit numbers, we provide a leading zero. Each number has a trailing space character. After writing the numbers, we close the file. The file now contains the desired data. If we dump the contents of this file on the console, the output would be unformatted as shown in the previous program. So, we now proceed with adding a newline character after every 10th number.

We now open the file for both reading and writing. The file is opened in binary mode:

```
fstream stream ("TextFile.txt",
ios::in | ios:: out | ios::binary);
```

We set up a loop for 9 iterations. Note that we have to add totally 9 newline characters in the file—each added after the tenth number.

```
for (i=1; i< 10; i++)
{
    ...
}
```

Within the `for` loop, we seek the file pointer to the desired location by using `seekp` method.

```
stream.seekp(30*i-1, ios::beg);
```

The first parameter specifies the byte offset. For each number stored in the file, a three-character space is used (two characters for the number and one trailing space). Thus, for 10 numbers 30 characters are used. This is multiplied by the loop count. We want to replace the space character at this position with a newline character. The exact position of the last space would be one less than 30 multiplied by the loop count (`30*loopcount-1`).

The second parameter to the `seekp` function specifies the start position in the file from which the above offset is computed. We specify `ios::beg` here.

After seeking the file pointer to the desired location, we simply write the newline character at the selected position:

```
stream.put('\n');
```

Once the above modifications are done, we close the file. To dump the file contents on the console, you may use the `type` or `cat` command. In our program, we dump the file contents on the console by reopening the file, reading the characters one at a time and outputting the read character on the console.

```
while (!isf.eof())
    cout << (char) isf.get();
```

We will see the desired formatted output on the console when we run the application.
The full program is given in Listing 13.11.

Listing 13.11:   Formatting output

```
#include "stdafx.h"
#include <iostream>
#include <fstream>
#include <iomanip>
using namespace std;

int main(int argc, char* argv[])
```

```
{
    char str[50];
    ofstream os ("TextFile.txt", ios::binary);

    for (int i=0; i< 100; i++)
    {
        os << setw(2) << setfill('0') << i <<"";
    }
    os.close();

    ifstream is ("TextFile.txt", ios::binary);
    while (!is.eof())
        cout << (char)is.get();
    is.close();

    cout << endl << endl;

    fstream stream ("TextFile.txt", ios::in | ios::out | ios::binary);

    for (i=1; i< 10; i++)
    {
        stream.seekp(30*i-1, ios::beg);
        stream.put('\n');
    }
    stream.close();

    cout << "dumping new file contents" << endl;

    ifstream isf ("TextFile.txt");
    while (!isf.eof())
        cout << (char) isf.get();
    isf.close();

    cout << endl << endl;
}
```

SUMMARY

For any programming language, file I/O is an important feature. The file I/O operations allow us to read/write data through our program code to an external data store, such as disk file.

C++ provides an exhaustive library of classes for performing file I/O. These classes are based on the concepts of streams. A stream is a logical device that either produces or consumes the data. C++ library defines some standard streams which are opened for the user at the load time. These are cin, cout, cerr and clog.

A stream may be of input or output type. An input stream is used for reading data while an output stream is used for writing data. The cin is an input stream connected to the keyboard for reading the user input, while cout is an output stream connected to the console for displaying the user output.

The data that is output may be formatted as desired using the formatting flags provided in the `ios` class. Alternatively, we may use manipulators, which are the functions embedded in `cout` statement for formatting the data.

The streams may be connected to physical disk files for reading/writing data to disk. The new set of file classes are based on templates. These classes support both 8-bit and 16-bit character sets. The data that is written to disk may consist of standard data types or user-defined data types.

A file may be opened for reading/writing in either the character mode or binary mode. The character mode of file operation is used if we are dealing with files containing character strings. Binary mode is used when we want to deal with the file data at byte level.

A file may be read sequentially or at random. This chapter discussed both the techniques of accessing files.

EXERCISES

1. Explain the difference between sequential access file and random access file.
2. Define different type of modes in which files can be opened.
3. What is the use of `scientific` flag defined in the `ios` class? Explain with an example.
4. What is the use of `boolalpha` flag defined in the `ios` class? Explain with an example.
5. Write a program to output few strings to a file.
6. Write a program to read from the file created in exercise 1 and dump its contents on the user console.
7. Write a program to count the number of lines in a text file.
8. Write a program to determine the number of occurrences of any specified character. The file name and the desired character are specified as command line arguments.
9. Write a program to write objects of a class `Student` to a file.
10. Write a program to read `Student` objects from the above generated file and dump each `object` on the console.
11. Using the data file generated in Exercise 6, write a program to seek information about a student from the file. The program accepts the student's roll no and displays the student's information.
12. Write a program to copy contents of one file to another.
13. Write a program to imitate the `TYPE` command. Accept the file name as the command line argument and display the file contents on the screen.
14. Write a program to accept details of five employees and store them to a file.
15. Write a program to search for a particular employee stored in the file created in Exercise 14.
16. Write a program to open an existing file and then append the data to it.
17. Write a program to accept a file at the command line and then print the file size in bytes.
18. Write a program to open a file and start reading from the line specified by the user.

19. State whether the following statements are true or false:

   (a) A stream is an abstraction that either produces or consumes information.
   (b) In C++ a file maybe anything from a disk file to a terminal or printer.
   (c) A `stream` that provides data to the program is called output stream.
   (d) For opening a file for reading, we create an `ifstream` object.
   (e) The `ifstream.open()` method creates a new file if the file does not exist.
   (f) The `ofstream.open()` method always creates a new file if one does not exist.
   (g) File streams should be closed after performing any file operations to reflect the changes.
   (h) The `put()` and `get()` functions are used for handling blocks of binary data.
   (i) C++ input/output system cannot handle user-defined data types.
   (j) When we write an object to a file, both data members and functions of an object are written to the disk file.
   (k) We can add data to an existing file.

14

Strings

As we have seen so far, C++ does not have a built-in string data type. We create strings in C++ using character arrays. The manipulations of these arrays is complex. Strings are so commonly required in our day-to-day programs, that a dedicated class on strings is desired. This is now provided in ANSI C++ standard. It provides a class called string that stores a sequence of characters and provides several functions to manipulate it. In this chapter we will study this string class and its various member functions. In particular, we will study the following:

- Instantiating string class
- Initalizing string objects with user input
- Using overloaded operators in string class
- Using several methods of string class

CREATING STRING OBJECTS

The `string` class provides several overloaded constructors for creating string objects. We may simply declare a variable of string type as follows:

```
string s1;
```

In this case, the compiler would create an uninitialized object of string type that is referred using the variable name `s1`. Later in the program, we may initialize this string using the following syntax:

```
s1 = "Hello";
```

We may use other constructors to create string objects. For example, the following program statement creates a new string object and assigns it to variable s2.

```
string s2 = string (s1);
```

In this case, we have created a string object using a copy constructor. The newly created string object would have the same state as s1. It means the contents of s1 would be copied into the new object. The new object is referred using the variable s2.

Another way of constructing a string object is to use a character array as an argument to the constructor. This is shown in the program statement below:

```
string s3 = string ("Hello");
```

In this case, the newly created string object would be initialized to the character string "Hello" and is referred by variable s3.

To output the contents of the string object on the user console, we will use cout as usual. The complete program listing that creates three string objects and outputs them on the user console is shown in Listing 14.1.

Listing 14.1:   Demonstration of string class

```
#include "stdafx.h"
#include <iostream>
#include <string>
using namespace std;

void main()
{
    string s1;
    s1 = "Hello";
    cout << "s1: " << s1 << endl;

    string s2 = string (s1);
    cout << "s2: " << s2 << endl;

    string s3 = string ("Hello");
    cout << "s3: " << s3 << endl;
}
```

Note that use must include "string" header to include the string class in our application. The program output is shown below.

```
s1: Hello
s2: Hello
s3: Hello
```

User Input Strings

Sometimes, our program may like to accept strings from the user on the command line. To initialize a string object from the user input value, we may use cin class as usual. This is shown in the code below:

```
cin >> s1;
```

The program will wait for the user input on the execution of the above statement. The user input string will be copied into the string type variable s1. However, if the user input string contains spaces, the program will ignore all the spaces and assign only the first word to s1 variable. To overcome this limitation, there is another function provided. It is called getline. This function allows the user to input string with embedded spaces. The use of this function is illustrated in the code fragment below:

```
getline (cin, s2);
```

The getline method takes two parameters, the first parameter is a stream from where the input is sought. The second parameter is the destination into which the contents are copied.

The full program listing that illustrates these two ways of accepting user input strings is shown in Listing 14.2.

Listing 14.2:   Accepting strings from user

```
#include "stdafx.h"
#include <iostream>
#include <string>
using namespace std;

void main()
{
    string s1;
    cout << "Enter a string: ";
    cin >> s1;
    cout << "You entered: " << s1 << endl;

    getchar();

    string s2;
    cout << "Enter a string that includes spaces: ";
    getline (cin, s2);
    cout << "You entered: " << s2 << endl;
}
```

Note, the use of getchar method call between the two user inputs. This is required for removing the CR/LF (carriage return/line feed) from the keyboard input buffer after the first user input. The user after entering the string would press an Enter key on the terminal. The character sequence of this Enter key remains in the keyboard buffer and must be removed from the buffer before accepting another string from the user.

The output of the program is shown below.

```
Enter a string: Hello
You entered: Hello
Enter a string that includes spaces: This is a test string
You entered: This is a test string
```

Now, we will develop few programs to under string manipulations using the built-in methods of the string class.

Concatenating Strings

We will now write a program to accept two strings from the user, concatenate those, and output the resultant string on the user console. The full program listing that does perform these operations is given in Listing 14.3.

Listing 14.3:   String concatenation

```
// Concatenation.cpp

#include "stdafx.h"
#include <iostream>
#include <string>

using namespace std;

int main()
{
    string first_name,middle_name,last_name,name;
    cout<<"Enter First Name: ";
    getline(cin,first_name);
    cout<<"Enter Middle Name: ";
    getline(cin,middle_name);
    cout<<"Enter Last Name: "; .
    getline(cin,last_name);
    name = first_name;
    name = name + " ";
    name = name + middle_name;
    name = name + " ";
    name = name + last_name;
    cout<<"Name = "<<name<<endl;
    return 0;
}
```

In this program, we accept the user's first, middle and last names using three `getline` statements. We now create the full name for the user by concatenating the three input names. The string concatenation is performed using the overloaded + operator defined in the string class. For example, the following statement combines the contents of name to the contents of `middle_name` and assigns its value to the name string.

```
    name = name + middle_name;
```

Likewise, the three strings are concatenated along with the appropriate spaces in between. The resultant string is output on the user console using `cout` class. The program output is shown below.

```
Enter First Name: Sameer
Enter Middle Name: Raj
Enter Last Name: Rana
Name = Sameer Raj Rana
```

Substring Replacement

We will now write program that searches the occurrence of a specified substring in a given string and replaces it with a new string. Consider that we have created a greeting message to our friend such as "This is hello from Sameer" and later we decide to change the word "hello" to "hi". Substring replacement program does the same. The full program listing is given in Listing 14.4.

Listing 14.4:   Replacing substrings in a given string

```
// Replace.cpp
//program to replace the word hello with hi
#include "stdafx.h"
#include <iostream>
#include <string>

using namespace std;

int main()
{
    string s;
    cout<<"Enter a sting"<<endl;
    getline(cin,s);
    int index = s.find("hello",0);
    if(index > s.length())
    {
        cout<<"The word hello was not found"<<endl;
        return 0;
    }
    s.replace(index,"hello".length(),"hi");
    cout<<"New string = "<<s<<endl;
    return 0;
}
```

The program accepts the greeting message from the user using the `getline` method. We use the find method of the string class to locate the substring "hello".

```
        int index = s.find("hello",0);
```

The find method takes two parameters, the first parameter is the substring to be searched and the second parameter is the index at which the search should begin. If the substring is found, the method returns the index at which the substring is located. If the match is not found, it returns a value greater than the length of the input string.

After finding the match, we use the replace method of the string class to replace the substring with the new desired substring.

```
        s.replace(index,"hello".length(),"hi");
```

The replace method takes three parameters. The first parameter specifies the index at which the replacement should begin. The second parameter specifies the number of characters to replace; this is the length of the substring to be replaced. Note the way we determine the length of the substring. We specify the constant string "hello" in the program statement. This creates a temporary string object. We call the length method on this temporary object to determine the string length. The last parameter specifies the replacement string.

After the replace method is successfully executed, the string s would contain the new string with the appropriate replacement. We print this string on the user console. The program output is shown below:

```
Enter greeting message: This is hello from Sameer
New string = This is hi from Sameer
```

String Sorting

We will now write a program to sort a given set of strings. Consider that our program asks the user to enter the names of students. After accepting all the names, our program should display these names in the sorted order on the user console. The program is shown in Listing 14.5.

Listing 14.5:   String sorting

```cpp
//String sorting.cpp
#include "stdafx.h"
#include <iostream>
#include <string>

using namespace std;

int main()
{
    int N;
    cout<<"Enter number of names: ";
    cin>>N;
    getchar();
    string *s = new string[N];
    cout<<"Enter "<<N<<" names"<<endl;
    for(int i=0;i<N;i++)
    {
        getline(cin,s[i]);
    }
    for(int i=0;i<N-1;i++)
    {
        for(int j=0;j<N-i-1;j++)
        {
            if(s[j] > s[j+1])
            {
                string temp = s[j];
                s[j] = s[j+1];
                s[j+1] = temp;
            }
        }
    }
}
```

```
    cout<<"Names in alphabetical order are:"<<endl;
    for(int i=0;i<N;i++)
    {
        cout<<s[i]<<endl;
    }
    return 0;
}
```

The program first asks the user to input the number of strings he would enter using the following code fragment:

```
    cout<<"Enter number of names: ";
    cin>>N;
```

We remove the CR/LF from the buffer by calling the getchar method.

```
    getchar();
```

Next, we declare an array of strings for storing the user input strings.

```
    string *s = new string[N];
```

The size of array is specified as N. The resultant array will be accessed using the variable name s. Next, the program accepts the string names from the user using the following loop:

```
    for(int i=0;i<N;i++)
    {
        getline(cin,s[i]);
    }
```

Each input string is stored in the string array s at appropriate index. At the end of the loop, we will have all the strings input by the array stored in the array s. Our next task is to sort this array alphabetically. This is done using the nested for loop in the following code fragment.

```
    for(int i=0;i<N-1;i++)
    {
        for(int j=0;j<N-i-1;j++)
        {
            if(s[j] > s[j+1])
            {
                string temp = s[j];
                s[j] = s[j+1];
                s[j+1] = temp;
            }
        }
    }
```

The if condition in the inner loop compares two strings specified by s[j] and s[j+1]. Note how the two strings are compared. We use the overloaded greater than ("> ") operator to compare the two strings. This operator is overloaded in the string class. If the first string is greater than the second string, we swap the positions of the two strings in the array by using a temp variable to hold the value of the first string in between the swap operation.

We perform this compare and swap operation in a loop from the first index to the last index in the array by varying the value of j loop variable from 0 to N-i-1. We could have used N-1 as the limit; however, this would increase the number of iterations. Note that since the greater string is already placed at the end of the array, our loop need not compare the current string with those already placed strings at the end of the array.

The outermost for loop iterates through all the string objects in the string array. When the outer for loop terminates, we will have sorted strings in the s array.

We finally print the sorted list on the user console using the following for loop:

```
for(int i=0;i<N;i++)
{
    cout<<s[i]<<endl;
}
```

The program output is shown below.

```
Enter number of names: 5
Enter 5 names
Sanjay
Sameer
Nishant
Medha
Ashwin
Names in alphabetical order are:
Ashwin
Medha
Nishant
Sameer
Sanjay
```

Word Extraction

Now we will write a program that extracts all the words in a sentence as they occur, and prints each word on a new line on the user console. The entire program is shown in Listing 14.6.

Listing 14.6: Extracting words from a given string

```
// Word Extraction.cpp

#include "stdafx.h"
#include <string>
#include <iostream>

using namespace std;
```

```
int main()
{
    string s;
    string words[30];
    cout<<"Enter a string: ";
    getline(cin,s);
    int start=0, end=0;
    int wordsIndex=0;
    while(end < s.length())
    {
        end = s.find(' ',start);
        if(end > s.length())
        {
            end = s.length();
        }
        words[wordsIndex++] = s.substr(start,end-start);
        start = end+1;
    }
    cout<<"The words present in the string are:"<<endl;
    for(int i=0;i<wordsIndex;i++)
    {
        cout<<words[i]<<endl;
    }
    return 0;
}
```

The program first declares an array of string data type of size 30.

```
    string words[30];
```

This array would hold the extracted words. Next, the program accepts the string from the user using the following code fragment:

```
    cout<<"Enter a string: ";
    getline(cin,s);
```

The program then sets up a `while` loop to extract all the words till the end of the given string.

```
    while(end < s.length())
```

We use the find method of the string class to locate the space character in the given string.

```
    end = s.find(' ',start);
```

The find method takes two parameters, the first parameter indicates the character to search and the second parameter specifies the index at which the search should begin. The function returns the index at which the character is found; otherwise returns a very high value. If this condition occurs, we set the value of the end variable to the length of the input string so that during the next iteration, the while condition gets satisfied and the loop terminates.

```
if(end > s.length())
{   end = s.length();
}
```

Note that we do not break the `while` loop by using the break statement in the `if` condition, because the last word in the string is not yet extracted and stored in our words array.

We now extract the word from the string and store it in words array by executing the following statement:

```
words[wordsIndex++] = s.substr(start,end-start);
```

The method `substr` extracts the word from the start index to `end-start` index. Note that end-start gives the length of the word under consideration. We now reset the start variable for searching the new word using the statement:

```
start = end+1;
```

When the `while` loop terminates, we will have all the extracted words in the words array. We print this array on the user console using the following `for` loop.

```
for(int i=0;i<wordsIndex;i++)
{
    cout<<words[i]<<endl;
}
```

A sample program output is shown below.

```
Enter a string: this is a test string.
The words present in the string are:
this
is
a
test
string.
```

SUMMARY

In this chapter we studied the use of an important class called string which is defined in ANSI C++ standard. Several times, in our programs, we use character strings. The use of string class facilitates the easy manipulation of these strings in your application. We studied how to instantiate, initialize and output the contents of the string object on the user console. We also studied various methods defined in the string class that eases the string manipulations. We studied the use of overloaded operators such as plus (+) for string concatenation and the logical greater than (>) operator for string comparison. We learned the use of various methods such as `length` for determining the length of the string, `find` for searching the specified substring in a given string, and the `substr` method to extract a substring from the given string.

EXERCISES

1. List any five functions supported by the string class along with syntactical examples showing the use of each function.

2. Why can the 'cin' operator not be used successfully for taking a string as input?

3. What are the problems faced while using getline() function after a 'cin' command, and how are they resolved?

4. In which header file is the string class contained?

5. Write a program using the string class to take a string as input and to extract and display all words starting with a specific letter which is taking as input from the user.

6. Write a program to take the names of N students as an input and then display them in alphabetical order of their surname. Take the name followed by the surname as input into a single string. Also take N as input from the user side.

7. What is the output of the following code snippet:

```
string s1("Hello");
s1.insert(5," ");
string s2("World");
s1.append(s2.substr(5,1));
s2.erase(2,2);
string s;
s = s1 + s2;
cout << s << endl;
```

8. State whether the following statements are true or false:
   (a) The name of the header file containing the string class is <String>.
   (b) The 'cin' statement can be used to input the value of a string object.
   (c) The append() function can be used to append a string in between a string.
   (d) The call length(s) is valid, where s is an object of the string class.
   (e) The 'cout' statement can be used to display the contents of a string object.
   (f) The string class has several overloaded constructors.

Appendix A

This appendix will walk us through the steps involved in editing, compiling and executing the Hello World program discussed in Chapter 2 using Microsoft Visual Studio 6.0.

1. Start Visual Studio 6.0. We may do so by selecting Visual Studio 6.0 from the **Start** menu. The following screen is displayed.

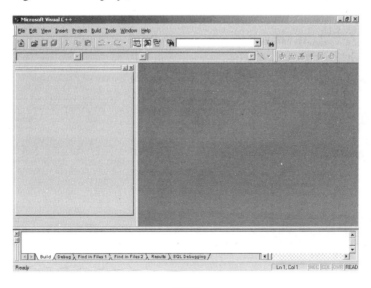

2. From the menu bar select **File | New** option.

   A dialog box for creating a new project is displayed. The new dialog box contains four tabs: **Files**, **Projects**, **Workspaces** and **Other Documents**.

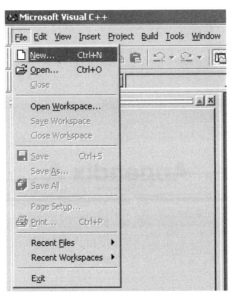

3. The **Files** tab lists the types of files that may be created by the wizard. This is typically used for creating and adding a new source file or a header file to our project.

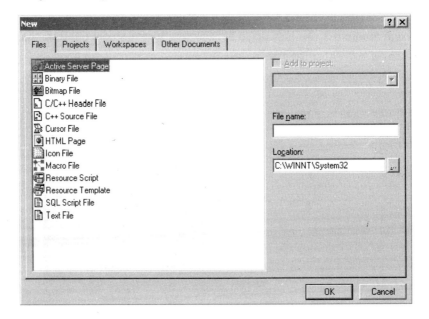

4. The **Projects** tab displays several project templates. We create different types of applications based on these project types.

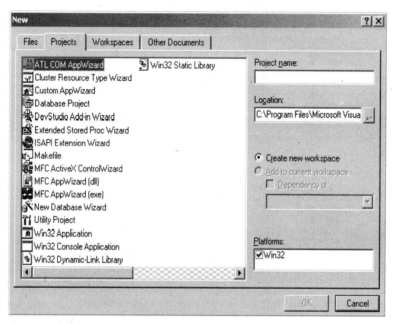

5. The **Workspaces** tab is used for creating our own workspace. We may define several projects in a workspace.

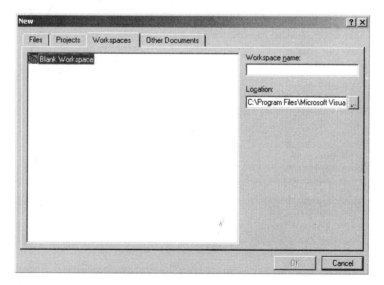

6. The **Other Documents** tab provides a list of different file types such as Image document, Word document etc.

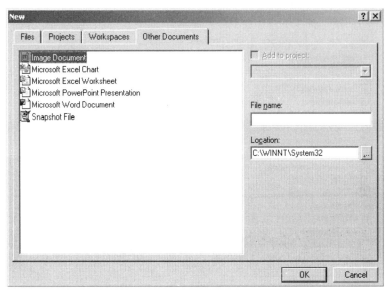

7. Go to the **Projects** tab and from the list of templates select **Win32 Console Application**. We will create a console application that runs under Windows. After selecting the project type, provide a **name** for it as **HelloWorld**.

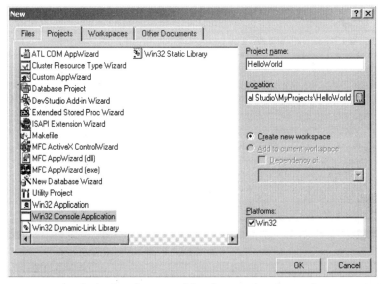

We may now enter the desired path on our drive for creating the project or accept the suggested path. We accept the defaults for the rest of the options. Our project will be created in a new workspace as the radio button for **Create new workspace** is enabled by default.
Click OK to move to the next step in wizard.

8. Select **A simple application** option and click **Finish.**

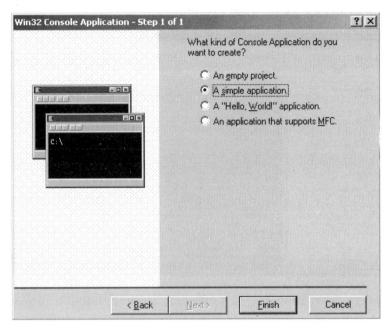

9. A **New Project Information** dialog box is displayed, showing all the selections made by us while defining the project.

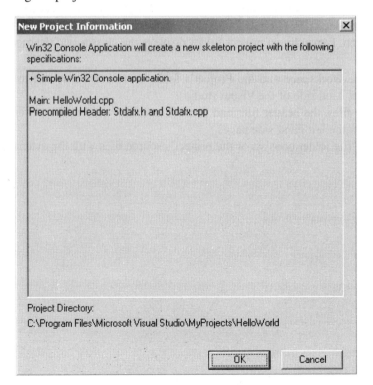

10. Click **OK** to continue.

11. The wizard creates a workspace and a project.

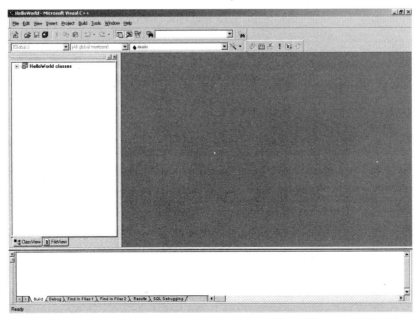

At the bottom of the left hand pane, we see two tabs: **Class View** and **File View**.

Selecting the ClassView tab displays the classes and their members for all projects in the current workspace. The Globals folder name shown in bold type represents the default project configuration. Expanding a project folder displays the classes and the members included in that project.

12. To view the Workspace and the Project's folder structure we switch to the **FileView** tab (Bottom left hand side of the Visual studio).

The source files, the header files and the resource files used in the current project are now displayed in the left hand side pane.

The source file folder consists of the project's source files with the extensions ".cpp".

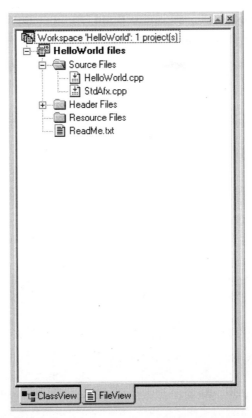

13. Double click on the *HelloWorld.cpp* file to view the code generated by the wizard.

```
HelloWorld.cpp
// HelloWorld.cpp : Defines the entry point for the console applic
//

#include "stdafx.h"

int main(int argc, char* argv[])
{
    return 0;
}
```

The wizard generates a `main` function that simply returns 0 to the operating system on termination. Edit this code to make the following changes.

```
#include "stdafx.h"
#include <iostream>
using namespace std;

int main()
{
    cout << "Hello World\n";
    return 0;
}
```

14. Now we build the project using the option **Build | Build HelloWorld.exe** menu option. The building process is displayed at the bottom of the studio in the **Build** tab.

```
------------------Configuration: HelloWorld - Win32 Debug----
Compiling...
StdAfx.cpp
Compiling...
HelloWorld.cpp
Linking...

HelloWorld.exe - 0 error(s), 0 warning(s)
```

Build / Debug \ Find in Files 1 \ Find in Files 2 \ Results \ SQL Debugging /

15. Once the project is successfully built, we execute the project using the option **Build | Execute HelloWorld.exe**. The code is executed and the output is displayed in the system console.

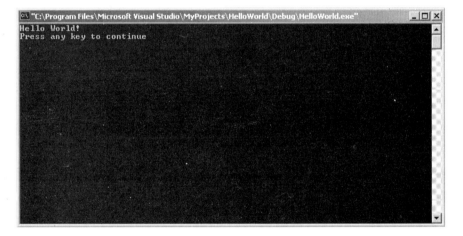

"C:\Program Files\Microsoft Visual Studio\MyProjects\HelloWorld\Debug\HelloWorld.exe"
Hello World!
Press any key to continue

Appendix B

This appendix will take us through the steps involved in editing, compiling and executing the Hello World program discussed in Chapter 2 using Turbo C++.

Use of Turbo C++ requires us to make few changes in the code presented in this book. The examples in this book are coded for Microsoft Visual C++ which is the later IDE. The modified Hello World program for Turbo C++ is shown below:

```
#include <iostream.h>
#include <conio.h>

void main()
{
    clrscr();
    cout << "Hello World" << endl;
    getch();
}
```

We can compare this program with the Hello World program presented in Chapter 2 for Visual C++ environment. The program from Chapter 2 is reproduced below for quick reference.

```
#include "stdafx.h"
#include <iostream>
using namespace std;
```

```
int main()
{
    cout << "Hello World\n";
    return 0;
}
```

Note the changes which we made in the original program. There are three major changes as listed below:

- Replace the header section as shown.
- Use `clrscr()` function call to clear the screen. This is optional.
- Uset `getch()` method to wait for the user input before quitting the application.

> **Note:** We would have to make the above changes in all our programs in this book to compile and run the code in Turbo C++ environment.

Now, as we have completed the changes in code, we describe the environment for editing, compiling, and running the program.

1. Start Turbo C++ by running **tc.exe** on the command line. The following screen is displayed.

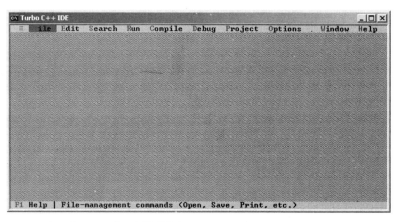

2. Open **new project** by opening **File/New menu** option.

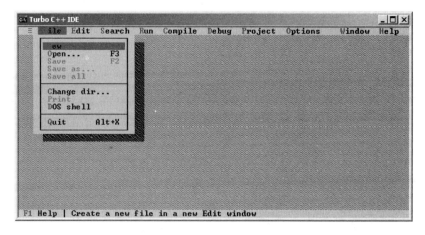

3. We will see a blank document called **NONAME00.CPP**. We will enter our program code in this document.

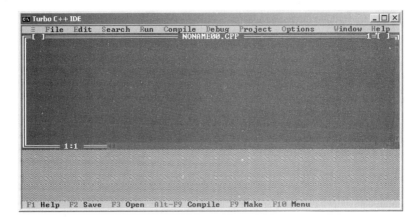

4. Enter the code as shown in the following screen shot:

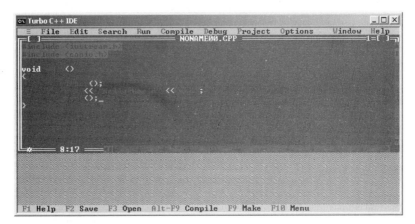

5. Now **save** the program by selecting **File/Save as...** menu option.

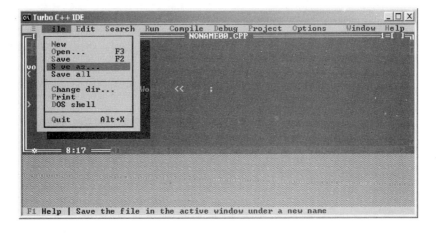

6. The IDE opens the **Save File As** dialog in which you will select the folder for storing the file and also enter the desired **name** for the file.

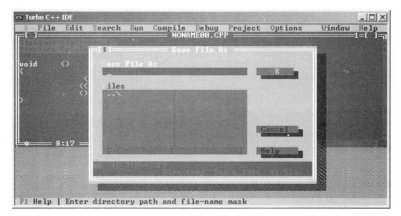

7. After selecting the desire location, enter the filename as "**hello.cpp**".

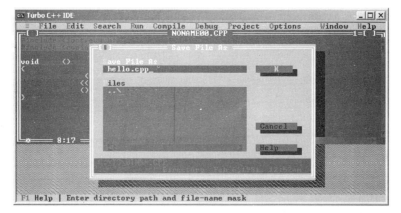

8. Note that the editor window now shows our file name "**hello.cpp**" at the center-top.

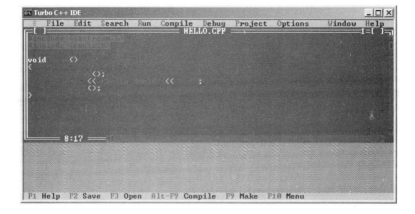

9. Now, compile the program by selection **Compile/Compile** menu option. Alternatively, we may use **Alt+F9** key combination to compile the code.

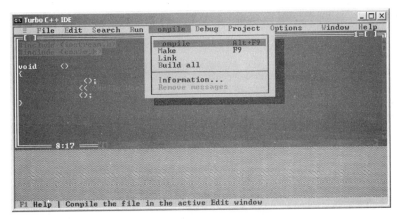

10. On successful compilation, we will see the screen similar to the one shown below:

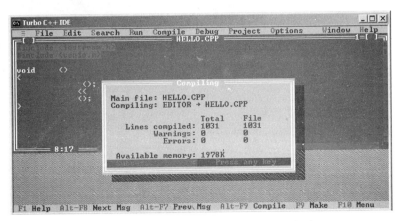

11. Now run the code using **Run/Run** menu option. Alternatively, we may run the code by pressing the **Ctrl+F9** key combination.

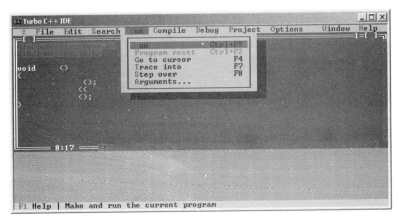

12. On successful run of the application, we will see an output in a separate window as shown below:

13. After we have finished using the IDE, we can close it by selecting **File/Quit** menu option or using **Alt+X** key combination.

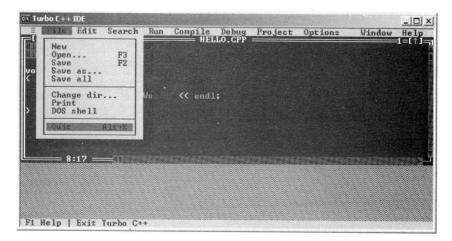

Index

Abstract class, 237
Access modifiers
    private, 93, 101, 207, 208, 209
    protected, 174–182, 211–214
    public, 93, 101, 209
Arrays, 48
    creation of character strings, 54
    n-dimensional, 70
    program to generate Fibonnaci numbers using arrays, 54
    program to illustrate use of single dimensional array, 52
    two-dimensional, 60–69

Bjourne stroustroup, 2

catch block, 242, 243 244
    multiple, 245

class(es), 4, 5, 90, 91
    generic, 274
    private and public declarations, 101
    static data members in, 105–107
    static member functions, 108–110
    using, 94
class constructors, 150, 151
    calling sequence, 189, 191, 201
    multiple, 153
    parameter passing, 205
    parameterized, 156
    superclass, 193
        passing parameters to, 194, 206
    with default arguments, 156
class declaration, 92
class definition, 93
class destructor, 162
    calling sequence, 189, 191, 203
class hierarchy, 6

Constants
    character, 16
    floating point, 17
    for, 38, 39
    integer, 17
    string, 16
Constructs
    continue, 40
    do-while, 35
    goto, 41
    while, 33
Copy constructor, 160

datatype, 26, 49
Data structures, 78
    accessing using pointers, 82
    creating an array, 82
    use of, 80
Data types, 18
Default constructor, 159
Double pointer, 76
    use of, 77

Early binding, 225
Encapsulation, 1, 4, 9, 91
Escape codes, 16, 17
Exception classes, 253–258
    descriptions, 260
    hierarchy, 259, 261
Exception handler, 242, 248
    multiple, 246
Exception handling, 243, 248
Exception passing, 251
Exceptional conditions, 241

File
    iostream, 11
    stdafx.h, 11
File classes, 293
File I/O, 293

Files, random access, 307–314
Function
    function name, 12
    main, 11, 13
Function prototype, 12

Header files, 12

Identifiers, 16
Inheritance, 1, 4, 5, 9, 168
    multiple level, 178, 198, 200
        class hierarchy, 215
        problems of, 214, 217
    syntax of, 183
    types of
        private, 184
        protected, 187
        public, 183
Inline functions, 99
ios class, 286
    formatting flags, 290
iostream, 286
istream, 286

Keywords, 18

Language constructs, C++, 9
Late binding, 225, 231
Literals, 16
Loop
    do-while, 35, 37
    for, 38
    infinite, 36, 39
    while, 34

main function, 2
main method, 152
Manipulators, 291–293

Member function(s), 97
    defining constant parameters, 119
    defining friend functions, 123
    passing parameters by reference, 116
    passing parameters by value, 114
    setting default values, 120
Methods, 7
Microsoft Visual Studio 6.0, 329

Namespace std, 11
Nested structures, 85

Object-oriented languages, 7
Object-oriented programming, 1, 2, 4, 9, 90
Objects
    creating, 96
    deleting, 97
Operator overloading, 132
    of addition operator, 132
    of array index operator, 140
    of assignment operators, 137
    of complex operators, 139
    of function call operator, 141
    of subtraction operator, 136
    of Typecast operator, 144
Operators
    arithmetic, 19
    bitshift, 22
    bitwise, 22
    cast, 24
    comma, 24
    decrement, 20
    dot, 80
    increment, 20
    logical, 22
    relational, 22
    scope resolution, 98
    sizeof, 25
    ternary, 24
    unary, 23
ostream, 286

Point class, 169

Pointer to a pointer, 76
Pointer variable
    address of, 75
    value of, 75
Pointers
    accessing variables, 72
    assignment, 71, 72
    declaration, 69, 70
    for calling overriden methods, 231, 232
Polymorphism, 1, 4, 6, 7, 9, 224
    compile time, 225
    dynamic, 225, 230
        merits/demerits of, 237
        method overriding, 230
    static, 225, 230
        function overloading, 225–229
        operator overloading, 230
Procedure-oriented programming, 2, 9
Program, Hello World, 10

Single inheritance, 170–173
Statements
    conditional, 26
        if, 26
        if-else, 28
        if-else-if, 29
        if-elseif-else, 29
    program, 26
    switch, 30
    variable declaration, 26
Streams
    hierarchy, 286
    input stream, 286
    output stream, 286
    predefined, 287
    user-defined, 293
string class, 317, 318
String concatenation, 320
String manipulations
    concatenating strings, 57
    palindromic strings, 59
    string reversal, 54
    string word count, 56
    string, word extraction, 324
String objects, 317, 318

String sorting, 322
Strings, reading/writing, 297
Substring replacement, 321

Templates, 265
    class templates, 266, 274–278
        using user-defined parameters, 280
    function templates, 266, 267
        multiple argument types, 272
throw statement, 242, 243, 251
Throwing exceptions, 250
try block, 242, 243, 245

try...catch block, 242
Turbo C++, 337

User-defined types
        reading/writing, 298
User input strings, 319

Virtual classes, 214
Virtual functions, 234–237
Virtual inheritance, 218
Void, 12